"Beryl Potter is an activist in the truest sense. Her rich, complicated life provides important insights into the strength and fortitude required to obtain the most basic disability rights."

Nancy Hansen, co-editor of *The Routledge History of Disability* and *Untold Stories: A Canadian Disability History Reader*

"Dustin Galer's organization of a vast array of rich material and his first-rate analysis conveys the life and times of controversial disability activist Beryl Potter with a familiarity and, at times, intimacy that will appeal to a wide audience. It's an easy read in the best sense—accessible, highly informative, and enticing to find out what happened next."

Geoffrey Reaume, Critical Disability Studies, York University

"At a time when the predominant image of people with disabilities was just starting to shift out of asylums, hospitals, and the dark places where they had been relegated for so long, Beryl Potter laid the foundation for the inclusion movement in Canada. *Beryl* is a story of a life in which dreams were shattered by a disabling accident but that was re-built through the experience of being seen and accepted. Beryl chose dignity over pity and agency over being tended to. There are lessons here for us all, from school kids to politicians, about what it means to be truly complete, and what it will take to make inclusion a reality. This is an inspirational story, told in just the right way."

Michael Gottheil, accessibility commissioner, Canadian Human Rights Commission

"Dustin Galer gives life to the story of Beryl Potter. His weaving of her early years to the troubles of life in England and then in Canada is engaging and readers will find the story captivating. Like many of us, Beryl came into advocacy because there was no choice. Her life demonstrated that her choices may not have been perfect but she owned them. Who could ask for more?"

Pat Danforth, current chair of the Victoria Disability Resource Centre and past executive member of the Council of Canadians with Disabilities

"Dustin Galer's writing draws us into a historical narrative that is an intellectual tale and a pleasure to read. This book is a fantastic addition to the collection of anyone with a passion for activism, social justice, and disability studies. It's also a great story."

Alexis Buettgen, adjunct faculty, Critical Disability Studies, York University; co-editor of Handbook of Disability: Critical Thought and Social Change in a Globalizing World

Beryl

Beryl Potter, ca. late 1980s.
Beryl Potter personal collection. Reproduced with permission.

Beryl

The Making of a
Disability Activist

Dustin Galer

Between the Lines
Toronto

Beryl: The Making of a Disability Activist
© 2023 Dustin Galer

First published in 2023 by
Between the Lines
401 Richmond Street West, Studio 281
Toronto, Ontario · M5V 3A8 · Canada
1-800-718-7201 · www.btlbooks.com

Library and Archives Canada Cataloguing in Publication
Title: Beryl : the making of a disability activist / Dustin Galer ; foreword by
    Judy Rebick.
Names: Galer, Dustin, 1983- author. | Rebick, Judy, writer of foreword.
Description: Includes bibliographical references and index.
Identifiers: Canadiana (print) 20230491952 | Canadiana (ebook) 2023049210X |
    ISBN 9781771136372 (softcover) | ISBN 9781771136389 (EPUB)
Subjects: LCSH: Potter, Beryl, -1998. | LCSH: People with disabilities—Civil
    rights—Canada. | LCSH: Human rights workers—Canada—Biography.
    | LCSH: Social reformers—Canada—Biography. | LCSH: People with
    disabilities—Canada—Biography. | LCGFT: Biographies.
Classification: LCC HV3024.C3 G35 2023 | DDC 305.9/08092—dc23

Cover and text design by DEEVE

Printed in Canada

We acknowledge for their financial support of our publishing activities: the Government of Canada; the Canada Council for the Arts; and the Government of Ontario through the Ontario Arts Council, the Ontario Book Publishers Tax Credit program, and Ontario Creates.

To my family

Contents

Foreword by Judy Rebick   *xi*

Prologue   *1*

1. Liverpool   *3*
2. Moonlight Flit   *11*
3. War, Marriage, and Motherhood   *17*
4. To Canada   *27*
5. Joining the (Paid) Workforce   *37*
6. An Ordinary Slip and Fall   *51*
7. Six Years of Pain   *61*
8. Addicted   *69*
9. Taxi   *73*
10. Life After   *79*
11. Nostalgia   *85*
12. A New Life   *97*
13. Ability Forum   *109*
14. Aware Bear   *115*
15. Leaning In   *123*
16. Transit Activism   *135*
17. Life Another Way   *145*
18. Rights   *155*
19. Equity   *169*
20. Access   *177*
21. Order of Ontario   *183*

22. Outside Looking In   *191*

23. Off the Record   *195*

24. Dennis   *203*

25. Power of the Story   *209*

26. An Ordinary Hero   *219*

27. Politics   *223*

28. Common Sense   *233*

29. Order of Canada   *241*

30. Final Stop   *247*

31. Remembrance   *255*

32. Aftermath   *257*

Epilogue   *261*

Author's Note   *271*

Acknowledgements   *275*

Notes   *277*

Index   *293*

Foreword
Beryl Potter: A True Hero

I met Beryl Potter during the 1980s. My paid job was at the Canadian Hearing Society. My boss there, Denis Morrice, the executive director, was invited to co-chair a new group that had formed called Disabled People for Employment Equity. It was a coalition between agencies serving people with disabilities and groups directly representing them. Denis asked me to take the position in his stead as he valued my work as an advocate. This was during the height of the pro-choice struggle, when I was becoming more and more of a public spokesperson for the movement.

I gladly took the position, not understanding at the time how much I would learn from the people I was working with. It was an extraordinary group of individuals, many of whom became well known in later years and almost all of whom were people with disabilities. I had already been working with Deaf people but had never worked with other people with disabilities.

Beryl was amazing. She was much older than the rest of us and seemed to me quite middle-of-the-road politically. At first, I just thought of her as a co-chair who would bring some credibility to the group because she had been working on other issues like transit through mainstream political channels. Others in the group like Gary Malkowski, who was the first politicized Deaf person I had worked with, and Angelo Nikias, a Blind man who had gotten the Canadian National Institute for the Blind (CNIB) to translate Marx's *Das Kapital* into braille, were pretty radical and identified with 1960s radical activists like me.

I didn't think of Beryl as an activist. That was the first thing I got wrong. As you will see in these pages, Beryl was a bold, brave, and imaginative activist who understood how to organize and how to take advantage of openings to make a powerful political point.

Beryl was a triple amputee. Even not knowing how much she had suffered through her various illnesses and surgeries, I admired her courage and determination to fight for people with disabilities. In the coalition, we discussed the importance of Judge Rosie Abella's report on employment equity. It was really the first time that the economic inequalities of people with disabilities had been officially recognized. What Abella called "target groups" for employment equity included women, visible minorities, Indigenous people, and people with disabilities. These groups had never worked together before. We realized that this was an opening to make sure that the government and the media understood how important strong measures for employment equality could be to people with disabilities.

To my knowledge, there had never been such a broad coalition of people with disabilities, and Beryl was key in bringing it together. I was able to contact NDP members of parliament to help us get access to government. Saskatchewan MP Lorne Nystrom let me know that we could directly confront then Prime Minister Brian Mulroney about the bill the Conservatives had drafted based on Abella's report. The bill had no teeth, and we didn't think it would work.

Mulroney always strode from the House to a room where he would meet with his caucus. Beryl, Angelo, Gary, and I flew to Ottawa to confront him. With Lorne's guidance, we gathered on the path of Mulroney's walk. He was an arrogant walker with big strides and a big smile on his face. His staff had, no doubt, told him there was a group of disabled tourists in the corridor that he should greet. Great photo op. When he was a few feet away he saw Beryl, whom he knew from a previous meeting, and then he saw me and knew he was trapped. Seeing the panic on his face was one of the highlights of my political career. He came to greet us, and Beryl grabbed his wrist. "Mr. Prime Minister," she said, not letting go. "Your employment equity bill has no teeth. It will do us no good." He offered a meeting with his senior policy advisor. That wasn't enough for Beryl. She wanted his promise then and there. I had to convince her to let go of him.

Later, as you will read, she disrupted Parliament, too, and through her determination and courage forced them to seat the many people using wheelchairs who we brought to what might have been the first demonstration on the Hill of people using wheelchairs, Deaf people, and Blind people some weeks later.

Beryl was an important influence in my life, as I am sure she was for many others. She taught me that intersectionality, a word we didn't even have back then, was essential for making sure that gains for one group applied to all groups. She showed everyone that people with disabilities could be a force to be reckoned with. She helped to build solidarity not only among people with disabilities but among all the groups mentioned in the Employment Equity Act.

When I ran for office in 1987, Beryl, along with Sam Savona, whom you will meet in these pages, organized a group of people with disabilities to canvass for my election. I'm pretty sure it was the first time people using wheelchairs, Deaf people, Blind people, and people with intellectual disabilities went door to door together, talking to voters about their issues and who to vote for. I still treasure a photo of Beryl and the others at my nomination meeting.

I know you will enjoy meeting this extraordinary hero of the disability justice movement in these pages and that she will inspire you as she inspired so many during her life.

Judy Rebick
Toronto, 2023

Prologue

Her electric wheelchair hummed as she zoomed up the ramp into her trusted minivan and hit the road, a long journey ahead. Before dawn on Saturday, April 14, 1986, disability activist Beryl Potter led demonstrators from across Canada in a convoy of accessible buses, cars, and vans, due east for the nation's capital. As members of parliament debated a federal bill that activists deemed would fail to make the labour market more equitable for disadvantaged groups, the demonstrators met the rising sun on one of the busiest freeways in North America, cramped and uncomfortable but hopeful their voices would make a difference. After the nearly five-hour drive from Toronto to Ottawa, many of the demonstrators, mostly disability activists and their allies, were already exhausted. The lack of accessible washrooms along the route hadn't helped.

Late in the morning, they began congregating in front of Parliament Hill under the clock of the nearly hundred-metre-high Peace Tower. It was a sunny but chilly day in early spring, a breeze unfurling their banners and rustling the black balloons many carried. With placards held high or strapped to their wheelchairs, they chanted slogans.

"What do we want?"

"Jobs!"

"When do we want them?"

"Now!"[1]

Trailed by photographers and news cameras, they marched past the Centennial Flame across the sprawling lawn until they met a set of stairs, one of many obstacles they confronted that day.

Outside the Parliament Buildings, Beryl wheeled up and addressed reporters. She was unlike the stereotype of an angry front-line activist, traditional but stylish, with pearls and a home sewn

1

black and white flowered dress. Not that long ago, she had a reputation for being a shy, retiring housewife, occupied with running her household, caring for her husband and three children, and balancing this with a full-time job.

Now, as she joined a crowd of one hundred and fifty demonstrators from across Canada, her voice rang out in strenuous opposition to the legislation and the continued exclusion of people with disabilities, and she declared that to prove her conviction she was willing to be arrested.

1.
Liverpool

The mystery of our lives, of course, is that they start long before we do, determined by people whose private history we rarely know.
—Rosemary Sullivan, *Shadow Maker: The Life of Gwendolyn MacEwen*

It started with a fever. The baby girl recently turned two years old when she began to shiver in her sleep, her fine brunette hair heavily matted, beads of sweat running down her forehead and across her flushed cheeks as constellations of red bumps formed mysterious patterns across her tiny body. Her endless wailing carried up and down the street, especially when out in her pram to take the fresh air. "Scarlet fever," the doctor told the mother. An antitoxin had been developed just a couple years earlier in 1924 in Chicago, but it was still common medical practice to inject a blood serum derived from horses into the abdomen of the infected. Mass production of penicillin would not happen for another twenty years, so there wasn't much for the little one to do but rest. Echoing scenes from the children's book *The Velveteen Rabbit*, the doctor had all her cherished playthings destroyed to rid the house of germs.

Weeks passed without improvement in the little girl's condition. She fidgeted endlessly, panting wheezily as her quickening heartbeat indicated she was getting worse. The infection progressed to acute rheumatic fever, though the doctor called it pharyngitis, a deadlier manifestation of the streptococcus bacteria. Her mother massaged wintergreen oil onto her inflamed joints, administering increasing doses of salicylates to counteract her skyrocketing fever. Known as Aspirin since its invention in 1899, salicylate tablets were commonly prescribed to relieve symptoms of rheumatic fever, but it was not always safe for children since toxicity levels were notoriously difficult to control in preverbal toddlers.[1]

Rheumatic fever was still a deadly affliction, and the medication did not seem to be helping. Exhausted, Amy watched over her sick baby day and night, her fatigue amplified by grief following the sudden death of her husband a few months earlier. At thirty years old, and mother to four older children, she could not bear another loss.

As the child muttered restlessly in her sleep, the night sky fell on the once joyful house. By the flicker of candlelight, Amy gathered the other children around the crib to say their goodbyes, their shadows darkening the walls in the cramped room. The younger children did not understand what was happening, but the oldest ones remembered similar events with friends and family in their working-class neighbourhood. The Spanish Flu pandemic of 1918 only eight years earlier had put the City of Liverpool on alert about the dangers of disease transmission. Some people had worn face masks to cover their nose and mouth.[2] But rheumatic fever was a more ancient affliction that claimed the lives of generations of children, their loss inscribed on many family trees. As the child became sicker, she was isolated to a separate room, the closed door muffling her hacking cough that echoed down the hallway and reverberated throughout the house. Amy knew it was not uncommon for babies to die like this.

One or two more worrisome nights passed, until it became clear this was not the end. Not long after the family had made their peace with the likely loss of their baby girl, her symptoms slowly began to recede, her dance with the deadly fever ending. Her breathing improved and the stiffness in her joints loosened with each passing day. Eventually, the child fully recovered, though her body would always remember this early brush with death.

Her name was Beryl Cicely Potter. She was born in Liverpool on June 15, 1924, into a large family with roots in the city spanning at least eight generations.[3] On the day of her birth, the *Liverpool Echo* projected the weather as "fair—then unsettled" with a "lighting-up time" of 10:34 p.m., instructing motorists, bicyclists, and drivers of horse-drawn carts when to flick on their lamps. The paper also advertised the latest Charlie Chaplin silent film, *A Woman in Paris*, showing at the Royal Cinema, a controversial drama featuring a spurned but unusually confident woman marked by tragedy who ultimately seizes her own destiny.

Beryl was the youngest and last child of Charles Ferdinand Potter. They lived in Wavertree, a suburban neighbourhood in east Liverpool where generations of the Potter family had lived since the eighteenth century. It was an area dominated by the railway. From the earliest sparks of industrialization, goods flowed into the port of Liverpool and on to global markets, with factories and trading facilities built along a spider's web of railway lines. Many people were drawn to the area by the availability of jobs and a large working class soon developed, children growing up surrounded by the soundtrack of rumbling locomotives and clattering boxcars. Liverpool was the British Empire's gateway to the world, a maritime mercantile city that played a key role in the mass movement of goods and people from Europe to America and around the globe. Its port and docklands bore witness to one of history's most profound economic success stories and greatest tragedies, with enormous profits reaped from the trafficking of goods and enslaved people from Africa, activities that financed the construction of elaborate civic, commercial, and cultural buildings in the city.[4]

Charles followed in his father's footsteps. Henry Potter had worked as a railway engineer,[5] one of the most respected positions in the industry, driving locomotives and smaller switcher engines that assembled and disassembled boxcars as they arrived in the city. By the time Charles was a teenager, Henry found him work as a shunter, a dangerous job that involved manually coupling and decoupling railcars.[6] The earliest recorded fatalities in the country occurred on the Liverpool and Manchester Railway at its opening in 1830, and the Wavertree Junction continued to be a notoriously dangerous place to work.[7]

A working-class but upwardly mobile family, Henry and Harriette Potter raised their four boys and three girls at 30 Spekefield Cottages near Edge Hill in east Liverpool. Built in the 1840s to accommodate the families of railway workmen, the planned neighbourhood offered relative serenity in an otherwise heavily industrial area. "There is no thoroughfare through its quiet precinct, and the rattle of carts and carriages is never heard," one contemporary observer wrote. "Each house has its pleasant garden in front, blooming with flowers laid out in multifarious variety as suits the taste of the occupants." It was the kind of home young Charles imagined raising his own family in some day, maybe something even grander with a bigger garden. But in 1890, Henry Potter died unexpectedly at age forty-four, transforming Charles's life in the process.[8]

At only eighteen years old, Charles became the family breadwinner. He was transferred to a safer job shunting passenger cars at the Lime Street Station in central Liverpool, perhaps to save the family from further potential devastation. The platforms hummed with busy travellers beneath a broad glass canopy, the clamour of whistling, hissing, and puffing steam engines announcing their arrival and departure. Not long after starting work at Lime Street, Charles became a transport police constable. He cut an athletic figure with thick dark hair, a steady gaze to his wide eyes, a slightly turned-up nose, strong jawline, and large hands. Pictured in his uniform, he sits proudly next to his Liverpool Police custodian helmet, its badge featuring the mythical liver bird encircled by a wreath capped by a crown signifying the monarch.[9]

In 1896, twenty-four-year-old Charles wed Mary Tipping, the daughter of a warehouseman who grew up in nearby Edge Hill. Their first daughter, Agnes, was born in 1899, followed in 1900 by a son,

Charles Ferdinand Potter, ca. 1890s.   Amy Catrina Potter (née Braun), ca. 1890s.

Beryl Potter personal collection. Reproduced with permission.

Bertram, who died within the year. By 1905, Charles was promoted to foreman and the family moved to 91 Earle Road, where they welcomed their second daughter, Teresa. Charles's life continued in twists and turns when tragedy struck late in 1910 as Mary died suddenly at age thirty-seven. For the next three years, Charles raised his two young daughters alone until he met Emma Amy Catrina Braun, known as Amy. Amy was born in 1893 into a German/Polish family that immigrated to England from America when she was two or three years old. Petite, with a slender neck, wild brunette hair, deep hazel eyes, and a youthful complexion, she held the reserved, mature expression of someone well beyond her years. Orphaned at a young age, Amy and her sister, Lily, moved first to a boarding house whose owners worked for Mr. Charles Morrison Riby, who ran one of the first cinemas in Liverpool, the Aigburth Assembly Picturedrome, later renamed the Rivoli Theatre. Charles and his wife, Annie, had no children of their own and became surrogate parents to the girls. Amy even assumed the surname Riby, a testament of affection to their adopted family.

Amy later moved to another boarding house at 1 Chestnut Grove and found work as a fruit confectioner, preparing jams and jellies for a local grocer. She lived just a six-minute walk from 1 Salisbury Terrace, a smart three-bedroom rowhouse where Charles now lived with his two girls. He was an attractive and industrious man, rising through the ranks, having recently become railway inspector. Charles was more than twice Amy's age and a widower, and it was perhaps an unlikely match. They may have met at the Picturedrome, or maybe he was a regular customer at the store where Amy worked long hours. One thing led to another, and on August 17, 1913, the couple wed at St. Mary's Church, an English Gothic-style Methodist church built in the early 1870s, the ceremony performed "according to the Rites and Ceremonies of the Established Church." Nine months later, the couple welcomed their first son, Eric Riby Potter. When Amy became pregnant with her second child in 1914, the family decided they needed a larger home. Fifteen-year-old Agnes and ten-year-old Teresa still lived with them, and the small rowhouse did not offer much extra space for the growing family. They found their new home just a few minutes away at "Rose Cottage," a charming two-storey Georgian house located at 35 High Street in Wavertree. Set more than thirty feet back from the road with a long, terraced garden surrounded by a sandstone boundary wall, the house miraculously survived the relentless construction of Victorian architecture that advanced the suburbs of Liverpool. It also fulfilled Charles's dream of providing his growing family a home worthy of the example set down by the ambitions of his late father.

It was all Charles and Amy could have asked for and more. Shortly after moving in, they welcomed their second son, Charles, on August 28, 1915. Marjorie came next in 1917, and by 1920, with the birth of Norman—Charles's sixth living child—they decided the family was quite full. But Amy was pregnant again in 1924 with their fifth (and final) child, Beryl.[10]

————————————

On Tuesday May 4, 1926, Britain was plunged into a general strike in support of coal workers facing a wage decrease coordinated by major mine owners. Railroad men, along with dock workers, power workers, and other unionized workers across the country walked off the job causing commuter chaos in London and bringing railway and port traffic in Liverpool and other large cities to a standstill. The *Manchester Guardian Bulletin* called it "the biggest industrial upheaval of our time." The stress of the strike weighed heavily on Charles, now chief inspector of railways, and sole breadwinner for his large family. As management, he faced the brunt of frustration and anger from workers on the job, and likely in his neighbourhood too.[11]

Two weeks earlier, on April 16, Charles underwent surgery for a duodenal ulcer that caused excruciating chronic pain in his stomach. He ate a bland diet and was only capable of digesting small meals. One contemporary treatment recommended milk be fed into the stomach through a nasal tube to neutralize stomach acids. The day of the strike, he was at work at the Lime Street main terminal when an agonizing cramping pain struck his abdomen. An ambulance rushed him to the Royal Infirmary just five minutes down the road on Daulby Street. Doctors immediately brought him into the operating room and performed an emergency surgery to relieve a "strangulation of the intestine," or hernia. He survived the surgery, but his prognosis was poor. Amy dashed to the hospital to be with her husband of twelve years in what would be his final moments. The following day, on May 5, 1926,

Charles died, aged fifty-three, nine years younger than the untimely death of his own father.[12]

Five days later, Charles's sister Edith filed his death certificate. Just two weeks after Beryl's second birthday, her father's probate paid out, leaving his widow £510.[13] It was a respectable sum, but not enough to support the family for long. Beryl would grow up without a biological father and his absence would haunt her during those critical early years of her development. But, now, as she battled rheumatic fever, her mother Amy faced financial ruin. Unable to support her family, Amy did what most widows in her situation did at the time.

Rose Cottage, 35 High Street, Wavertree, ca. 1915.
Beryl Potter personal collection. Reproduced with permission.

2.
Moonlight Flit

S hortly after Charles Potter died, thirty-two-year-old Amy met a wiry and persuasive twenty-eight-year-old patrolman named William Ralston Wallace. Maybe he was a trusted friend or co-worker of Charles and knew of Amy's unfortunate circumstances. William grew up the son of a cart driver in the poor part of the Toxteth neighbourhood, the second youngest of three boys and one girl. They married in the autumn of 1926, less than six months after Charles died. William moved in with Amy and her children at Rose Cottage, and in 1927, they welcomed their first child, Margaret (1927), followed by Joan (1929), Constance (1931), and Leslie (1932).[1]

"For a time, everything went smoothly," Beryl's older brother Norman remembered. Then everything changed when William lost his job. Apparently, the offence was reporting late to work.

"I had a flat tire," William allegedly complained to his boss.

"Yes, I saw you letting out the air," his sergeant reportedly jested.[2] It was a repeated offence that foreshadowed more problems to come.

Sometime into their married life, Amy learned that William liked to drink and gamble. He found work as a cinema fireman managed by his stepson Charles Jr. (Charlie). Early celluloid film reels were extremely flammable, easily igniting in storage or when set on hot projection equipment, so it was common practice for cinemas to employ an on-site fireman to handle such emergencies. While he was waiting to put out fires at the cinema, William carried a torch for a female co-worker that developed into an affair that produced a child. Charlie Potter fired his stepfather for the transgression, and thereafter, child support payments of two shillings and sixpence per week were deducted from the already strained Potter/Wallace family budget.

William later found work as a conductor on Liverpool's double-decker buses and trams. Pictured in front of a tramcar, William's thin, lanky frame barely propped up his crisp uniform and service cap as if the clothes were on display in a museum, the hulking mass of steel and glass hovering menacingly close behind. In another photo, he sombrely stands in front of the A621 double-decker at the bus depot, bespectacled with thick black frames perched on his gaunt pale face. William took pride in his appearance, his shoes always nicely polished and uniform neatly pressed. It was a livery he would inhabit until his retirement years later.[3]

Beryl's eldest brother, Eric, probably supported the family during his stepfather's job gaps, finding employment on the London, Midland and Scottish Railway (LMS) shunting passenger cars.[4] But financial hardship dogged the family, undermining the very stability Amy sought after the death of her husband. It soon became clear they could no longer afford to live at Rose Cottage, the birthplace and hearth of the Potter children, including their half-siblings Margaret and possibly Joan. Life at Rose Cottage began in a different time for the Potters with Charles's higher salary and fewer mouths to feed. The sandstone walled entrance and fenced garden could no longer insulate Amy and her children from the harsh realities of working-class life in the interwar period, the economy having tanked, plunging the country into financial chaos. William's low-paid job was unable to match the bills, the situation becoming increasingly dire.

William R. Wallace, ca. late 1930s.
Beryl Potter personal collection.
Reproduced with permission.

By 1929 and the birth of Joan, Beryl's second half sister from Amy's marriage with William, the family was already on the move. They fled one rental flat after another, often leaving in the dead of night to shirk landlords owed rent. Amy packed and repacked their few belongings into suitcases and snuck out under cover of darkness to evade angry confrontations with landlords and contemptuous glances of all the neighbours. Still, she felt their eyes lacerating her on more than one occasion as they fled, an infant strapped to her chest and several children in tow. Amy felt the shame in what they were doing, but it was a matter of survival as it was for many families like hers.

These "moonlight flits," as they were known in Britain at the time, were repeated at least eleven times over the next six years. Penny Lane, Barrington Road, Blantyre Road, Bagot Street, Upper Parliament Street, Grafton Street, Wellington Road, Smithdown Road, Cowper Road, Gidlow Avenue, Moscow Drive. Each neighbourhood was a rough facsimile of the next. The endless procession of temporary accommodation suggested they had become a family of travellers, their involuntary rootlessness the collateral damage of a deepening global financial depression. The deteriorating economy led to escalating unemployment, financial insecurity, and widespread homelessness that squeezed many similar households in Liverpool and beyond. Affordable housing was in short supply across the city during the Great Depression, and many families like the Potters had low expectations of stable housing.[5]

This nomadic rhythm was something Beryl came to know intimately in her childhood and adult life. With each move, teachers, classmates, and friends entered and exited her world, the suddenness of her departures making it difficult to maintain lasting relationships. It all might have seemed a great adventure to her at first, a new bedroom, a new street to play on, a chance to explore the unknown. But after the fifth, eighth, or tenth move when she was between five and eleven years old, it likely grew to be a stressful experience. She might have even felt homeless after such frequent decampments, an eternal transience that undermined any sense of belonging or security of place. It may also have contributed to a deep-rooted introversion that became a defining feature of her personality in adulthood.

Later in life, Beryl once remarked that she struggled with being overly self-conscious. "I just could not bear to go into a restaurant alone. I felt like everybody was looking at me. I had an inferiority complex, a very bad one." Whatever event or person sparked these feelings of inadequacy, it's possible their roots were laid down in childhood. Beryl was known to keep most of her inner turmoil to herself. She would describe her childhood as "normal and happy." Sundays were reserved for church, family outings, and visits to her step-grandparents, William and Martha, "where we enjoyed the best homemade bread in the world." Outwardly, she was every bit the well-adjusted young schoolgirl, apparently sociable and acquiescent, but also chronically shy. Like most girls growing up in the 1920s and 1930s, Beryl learned from a young age that girls and women were expected to be attractive, deferential, nurturing, and hardworking. A Christmas card from 1933 captures Beryl at age nine dressed in a brown wool jumper and collared blouse, her brunette hair cut in a practical but popular fashion with cropped bangs. Nearly adolescent, Beryl gazes out with large penetrating blue eyes, a tight-lipped smile projecting a coy but tender demeanour, and perhaps a streak of impishness.[6]

As Beryl grew into herself, she became known as congenial, someone who never complained about anything. She never talked about her childhood nor griped about her lot in life. For many members of the Greatest Generation (generally defined as those born between 1901 and 1927), being survivors of a great deal of hardship meant it was common to develop a forward-looking approach to life. And Beryl did not have to go far to find a model of quiet strength. Her mother, Amy, demonstrated what it meant to move on when faced with seemingly insurmountable challenges, epitomizing the stiff upper lip approach to life that Britons were widely known for. Whether it was dealing with unexpected deaths or poverty, Amy modelled the kind of quiet demeanour and practical attitude toward life that Beryl would absorb into her own character, and eventually use for her own salvation.

Beryl Potter, age nine, 1933.
Beryl Potter personal collection.
Reproduced with permission.

Beryl's brother Norman, on the other hand, responded to the family turmoil quite differently. He hit back with more of a quirky rebelliousness. It seemed he was always getting into trouble and running away. On several occasions, he would take Beryl on an adventure, without permission or notice. Once, when Beryl was around six years old, ten-year-old Norman took her for a train ride. Beryl always went along with her older brother. Four years her senior, Norman had ideas about where they would go, and it's not hard to imagine the impish little girl pictured a few years later in a 1933

Christmas card, looking forward to each new secret journey with her brother. On this occasion, however, they ended up an hour away in the seaside town of New Brighton by the River Mersey. Police spotted the children wandering around aimlessly and knew something was up. "Getting home, Willie taught me a lesson with the belt," Norman painfully recalled. "Eric and Charlie counted the welts."[7]

In 1936, the family moved one last time. It was a short walk from an apartment at 24 Moscow Drive up the road to 119 Moscow Drive in Stoneycroft, an affordable, comfortable neighbourhood.[8] A two-and-a-half storey brick Victorian row house with adequate space and decorative brickwork, the property featured an attractive bay window dressed in lace curtains, and a small private backyard surrounded by brick walls. A pair of cement posts and a low brick wall bordered the tiny front step, offset by the greenery of a few stumpy bushes.

Part of a Victorian-era boom in housing development, Moscow Drive was owned by evangelist Reginald Radcliffe, a preacher who travelled extensively throughout Europe and Russia. The Radcliffes developed their landholdings in Stoneycroft as working-class housing projects, naming the streets after points of interest in their travels such as Moscow Drive, Russian Avenue, and Kremlin Drive, resulting in peculiarly foreign-sounding street names in a decidedly British city.[9] It was a far cry from memories of life at Rose Cottage, where the busy shops and traffic along High Street were kept at a distance by the inner sanctum of its tranquil garden. Here, the homes along Moscow Drive sat virtually perched on the street. One could bound out the front door and reach the sidewalk in one long leap then look down long blocks of brick and stucco rowhouses that hugged the curves of the road. It was the kind of neighbourhood where one could spot a familiar face from a fair distance, fostering a sense of community, or at least a sense of close observation among its residents.

Within a year of moving in, again tragedy struck the family. In January 1937 Beryl's half sisters, Margaret (Peggy) and Constance (Connie), contracted diphtheria. Despite quickly declining rates of the infectious disease in the 1920s, this "plague of children," as it was sometimes frightfully described, persisted in low-income areas with low vaccination rates, crowded living conditions, and poor ventilation. Diphtheria was often mistaken for scarlet fever and can even emerge as a complication of the infection.[10] The children's symptoms, including weakness, sore throat, and fever would have struck Amy as eerily similar to Beryl's brush with death in infancy more than ten years earlier. On January 12, 1937, the sisters died within three hours of each other and were buried together six days later at Holy Trinity Cemetery in Wavertree. Trembling together with grief, thirteen-year-old Beryl held her mother, now forty-three years old, as they said goodbye to nine-year-old Peggy and six-year-old Connie.

Beryl was too young to have remembered her biological father's death, but the loss of two of her sisters hit her hard. By 1939, she had grown into a demure, melancholic girl in her mid-teens. A glamour shot captures her purity and innocence in a below-the-shoulder satin wrap, her hair pinned up exposing her collarbone and long neck. Her downcast eyes and anodyne expression may suggest she had become an introverted, soft spoken, likely depressed young woman, one who lived in the background with her own thoughts as company. She was not a teenager with a lot of friends or often out around the neighbourhood. She had survived enough turmoil already in her short life—a deadly illness, the loss of her father and two sisters, and at least twelve different homes. She retreated further inward, learning not to burden her family with any hardship, especially with the threat of a looming war coming to darken their doorstep.

3.
War, Marriage, and Motherhood

Beryl was fifteen years old when Britain declared war on Germany on September 3, 1939. During the First World War, Liverpool was beyond the reach of most German bombers and had eluded a failed attempt at a zeppelin bombing raid. Now, nowhere in England was considered safe, yet no one could have anticipated the horror and hardship that awaited them. Children were assembled in schools and issued name tags and gas masks in case the city was invaded by land, air, or sea—all of which were likely possibilities. Later that month, Operation Pied Piper evacuated 8,500 children to the countryside. By January 1940, there hadn't yet been any air raids, a period known as the "Phoney War," so nearly half of these children were returned to their homes. But by August, the long-anticipated attacks began and continued throughout the year. One raid during Christmas resulted in several direct hits on local air-raid shelters. There would be more bombing and more destruction to come.

In May 1941, the German *Luftwaffe* bombarded Liverpool in a blitz that lasted seven terrifying nights, killing nearly four thousand people and destroying half the port. During the May Blitz, the haunting echo of wailing sirens ushered residents into crowded bunkers and the Liverpool Central underground. Emerging from sleepless nights spent in shelters, bleary-eyed citizens collectively gasped in shock at scenes of total chaos and destruction. Widespread, uncontrolled fires raged throughout the city. Houses, docks, factories, and businesses were flattened. Railways and roads were severely disrupted, cutting off contact between families. During the war, Liverpool was the most heavily bombed area of England outside London, the principal target being the docks, which handled 90 per cent of all British imported Allied war material. There were approximately eighty air raids on Liverpool during the Second World War, resulting in fifteen thousand hits on the city. Despite the danger, over one thousand convoys still entered the city carrying vital supplies and soldiers for the war effort.

Beside those killed in direct bombing hits, there was a much larger population that survived near and remote misses. In his book *David and Goliath*, author Malcolm Gladwell explored the psychological effect of the Blitz on Londoners. Drawing on diaries, recorded memories, and various studies, he found that, contrary to popular belief, people were not irretrievably shaken and had no need of special asylums that were hastily erected to treat the expected psychological fallout of the relentless bombing. Unexpectedly, many people reportedly felt invulnerable when they survived the destruction that claimed so many others. Gladwell observed how the random outcomes of these bombing events resulted in a kind of psychological reinforcement on those who survived. "A near miss leaves you traumatized. A remote miss makes you think you are invincible."[1]

The situation in Liverpool was no different. Much of the bombardment of the city concentrated around the strategically important port and docklands, so suburban Stoneycroft to the northeast, where Beryl and her family lived, was spared much of the bombing activity. They were not entirely unaffected. The closest bomb fell just two hundred metres away from their home, with another fifteen bombs falling within a one-kilometre radius. The house at 119 Moscow Drive and the rest of the street remained remarkably intact. All those near and remote misses fortified Beryl's late teenage brain with a cocktail of fear, exhilaration, and sense of inviolability. What remained of her family at the start of the war was spared. She had survived against the odds. Life went on. It would not be the last time she would encounter such a potent brew of emotions.

Indeed, Beryl got on with the business of growing up and may have even developed a benign indifference to the bombings, as many did. She completed her grade twelve education at age seventeen and signed up with the Women's Voluntary Service as a nurse's assistant.

Her brother Eric married in 1940 to Catherine ("Kit") with Beryl as bridesmaid. Other happy events like these, including birthdays, anniversaries, and holidays punctuated the general malaise and occasional terror of wartime life in Britain. Beryl matured through it all, her stylish barrel curls framing the resolute countenance of a mature, intelligent young woman.

Beryl never talked about having any boyfriends when she was younger, and it's possible her reserved nature made it difficult for her to connect with suitors. At home, she busied herself looking after her two surviving younger half sisters, Joan and Leslie, while helping her mother with the cooking and cleaning. Whatever home economics education Beryl received growing up she got from her mother, instructing her on how to stretch a meagre income to serve the needs of their large family. Laundry day meant lots of scrubbing and rinsing in a big old wash basin set up in the backyard, everything hung to dry on the clothesline. Shopping at the local market was a relentless hunt to see how far a pound could stretch, a task made harder since they were still supporting the child produced from William's fling with the cinema worker.

If Beryl ever rebelled against the 1930s ideals of femininity, it would have been when she took up smoking at a young age. Like most young women of her generation, she likely picked up the habit in her mid-teens, those years of experimentation that lead so many into addictive behaviours that follow them into their adult lives. Magazines and film of the time glamorized smoking, and tobacco companies worked hard to establish cigarette smoking as a feminine practice to reverse its stigma in popular culture, a goal they eventually achieved. But it was still considered taboo for "proper" young girls to smoke. Whether it was social pressure from the girls at school or in her neighbourhood, Beryl eventually worked her way up to a pack a day, the red and black packaging of Peter Jackson cigarettes her eternal accessory.[2]

Before long, Beryl joined almost a million other British women working in munitions factories across the nation. Such work was voluntary until 1941, when the National Service Act conscripted British women aged twenty to thirty into factory work. The environs of Liverpool were ideally situated for such factories with good railway transportation access that allowed for the movement of essential workers and volatile explosives but located far enough from populated areas to minimize the risk of civilian casualties in the event of an accidental explosion or targeted bombing raid.

Beryl found work in the munitions factory at Kirkby, Lancashire, just nine kilometres from home. Kirkby was one of the largest Royal Ordnance munitions factories in the country with more than a thousand buildings crowded together in the otherwise sleepy rural area. Employment at the factory peaked at 23,000 mostly women workers who produced approximately 10 per cent of all British-made ammunition during the war. Thirty-seven kilometres of rail were laid to connect the factory site with Liverpool for secret trains that shuttled workers and munitions back and forth, making the officially unlisted (for security reasons) stop between the towns of Kirkby and Rainford. Extra-large platforms with spacious waiting shelters were specially constructed to handle the heavy influx of workers starting and ending their shifts together.

Punching in at Kirkby early in the morning, Beryl would have filed into the changerooms to dress into uniform clothes and shoes before entering the factory floor. After toiling alongside other women filling ammunition and producing shells and bullets for the vast war machine, she would have returned home late in the evening. The work was relatively well-paid but also tiring, fast paced, and dangerous, carrying a high risk of accidental explosion. Many workers lost fingers, hands, or eyesight. Some earned the nickname "canary girls" for the yellow stains on their skin and hair, a result of handling sulphurous chemicals all day long with minimal protection. In February 1944, an explosion at the plant left two women dead and several injured when a tray of fuses accidentally lit, blowing the roof off the building, and damaging the walls in the process. Just seven months later, another accident killed fourteen workers.

Such accidents underscored the danger and seriousness of the work, as well as the importance of women's contributions to the war effort. For Beryl, long days concentrating on performing precision routine tasks amid the clamour of factory equipment required extraordinary endurance. With enemy bombs threatening her hometown and daily reports of killed and injured British troops, the hazards she endured daily at work must have felt like a small contribution to the war effort compared to the sacrifices demanded of others, especially given the unprecedented propaganda campaign to blanket the British people with pro-war radio, film, and print advertisements.

Beryl's wartime experiences would also instill in her a strong sense of community service, though in later years, she would always gloss over any discussion of the war. It was common for young people of her generation who survived the violence and deprivation of war to want to forget about the hardships they endured with an eye toward moving on with their lives. In many cases, they sacrificed the best years of their youth for the greater good and carried their pain with them into their relationships with others. Beryl would learn firsthand what this meant when she met her future husband, Victor, who spent the war at sea.

––––––––––––

Liverpool played a central role in the long-running Battle of the Atlantic. During the war, 12.8 million tons of Allied and neutral shipping were destroyed, and 73,600 personnel from the Royal Navy were lost. The merchant navy paid a high toll with the loss of 30,000 mariners. Despite coastal patrols and aircraft support, merchant boats were under the constant menace of skulking German U-boats threatening to torpedo them at any moment.[3]

For merchant marines like Victor Bratton Carter, the drama of war played out in treacherous waters. Born in Belfast, Northern Ireland, into a house with five sisters, Victor was based in Liverpool and served in the merchant navy throughout the war where he saw action on multiple occasions. One of the most traumatic events occurred while he was walking down the street in Liverpool with a friend. He heard the familiar whistle of a German bomb in mid-flight. Before they could make it to safety, the bomb hit the ground nearby in a tremendous crash, the impact lighting a fuse that caused an overpowering explosion. Shrapnel flew like a spray of bullets in every direction as a shockwave from the ground-burst catapulted Victor away from the blast. His friend died on impact and, as Victor regained his senses, he lay in a debris field covered in his friend's remains. Victor was seriously injured but eventually recovered physically, though the event left a deep imprint on his mind, inflicting post-traumatic stress that remained a constant factor in his life.[4]

In November 1942, twenty-year-old Victor travelled as a crew member onboard the *Gypsum Empress*, a four-tonne British merchant steamship built in 1929 in Middlesbrough by the Furness Shipbuilding Company. The ship followed a well-travelled route from the coast of Guyana where ships were loaded with bauxite, then ferried back to the US via the Caribbean. An essential ingredient in the construction of airplanes, demand for bauxite soared during the Second World War, with the US alone producing some three hundred thousand planes by the end of the war. Two-thirds of all bauxite consumed during the war originated in British Guyana, requiring frequent cargo traffic in the region, a fact well-known by the German Navy. Given the spike in demand for bauxite after the US entered the war, the route was relatively routine by 1942, heightening the risk of attack by German U-boats.

The *Gypsum Empress* travelled with the TAG-18 (Trinidad, Aruba, Guantanamo) convoy, which included ships from the UK, Canada, Norway, US, and Panama. Thirty-seven merchant ships were escorted at different points by eight US Navy ships, including one destroyer and four submarine chasers. The *Gypsum Empress* was one of the smallest ships in the convoy, carrying 6,200 tonnes of bauxite ore with an international crew of forty men. Along with the captain, there were thirty-one crew members, four gunners, and four signalmen from Britain, Canada, America, Norway, Denmark, Holland, and France. Early in the morning on November 2, 1942, the convoy set out from the Port of Spain, Trinidad, joined by two destroyers as escorts and remote aircraft patrol. They tracked the coast of Venezuela before crossing the Caribbean Sea north past Cuba to Florida.

The convoy was shadowed by a single U-boat. *Kapitänleutnant* (lieutenant commander) Georg Lassen commanded U-160. An experienced commander, Lassen previously completed several highly successful tours on U-29, including the sinking of aircraft carrier *HMS Courageous*. On his first patrol as commander of U-160, he sank or damaged six ships worth 43,560 tons. The mission of U-boat warfare was not necessarily to kill as many enemy combatants as possible, but rather to disrupt shipping routes and sink a maximum amount of enemy cargo, the success of any operation measured in tonnage destroyed. Lassen rose quickly through the ranks, ultimately attaining *Korvettenkäpitan* (senior to the *Kapitänleutnant* position) and the coveted *U-Boot Kriegsabzeichen mit Brillanten* (U-Boat War Badge with Diamonds). U-160 was midway through its third patrol under Lassen, having left the captured French port of Lorient on the northwestern French coast on September 23, 1942, bound for Caribbean waters.

On its arrival, U-160 began shadowing the TAG-18 convoy. On November 3, at 2:02 a.m., U-160 torpedoed and sank the Canadian merchant steamer *Chr. J. Kampmann.* Four hours later, at 6:30 a.m., Lassen sank the motor tanker *Thorshavet.* Lassen followed the convoy's anticipated zigzag course typical for evasive manoeuvres. By 10:23 a.m. U-160 observed a watch vessel and another flank escort far offset from the *Gypsum Empress* and Norwegian tanker *Leda.* Lassen lined up to take his shot at both vessels and at 11:37 a.m. released three torpedoes.

Those few moments of suspense before the blast must have transported Victor back to that fateful walk with his friend, the eerie anticipation of an incoming bomb momentarily suspending time as the underwater executioner hurtled toward them. The *Gypsum Empress* was hit first as reported in U-160's patrol diary: "Hit center on ore freighter after 72 seconds. Heavy detonation observed in the center." The second and third shots hit the *Leda.* After waiting to hear "strong sinking sounds," U-160 dived to avoid detection by the escort ships and remained submerged for the next four and a half hours while the escorts released depth charges. By 4:00 p.m., Lassen rose to periscope depth, reporting "only one smoke feather is seen. Suspect that both ships are sunk." Amazingly, all forty crew onboard the *Gypsum Empress* survived. The *SS Yarmouth* transported the survivors, along with surviving crew from *SS Trafalgar*, to New Orleans, Louisiana, where they would eventually make their way home worse for wear.[5] The remains of the *Gypsum Empress* may have settled to rest in the shallow floor of the Caribbean Sea alongside hundreds of other ships, but the moment of its destruction, like the death of his friend earlier in the war, would live on in Victor's memory and reverberate throughout the remainder of his troubled life.

On May 8, 1945, with the surrender of Nazi Germany, Britons and Allies across the globe celebrated Victory in Europe or VE Day, marking the conclusion of nearly six years of combat and devastation in Europe. Victor returned to Liverpool, where he continued his service in the merchant navy. But postwar life was not easy for young

Victor. Like many others, he found a welcome escape at the local pub. Following the war, he began work for the Liverpool Transport Board as a checker. "Track walkers," as they were also known, were key to railway accident prevention, their shifts requiring them to travel the length of the rail system by foot or in special cars designed to inspect for flaws in the tracks, switches, and signals.

Beryl also found work in the railway after the war. Following the closure of the Kirkby munitions factory, she worked as a railway station master at a small station in Wavertree.[6] Station "Mistresses," as women working in the job were known, were responsible for keeping things at the station running smoothly, a mix between customer

Beryl, age 21, ca. 1945. Dressed in her station mistress uniform.
Beryl Potter personal collection. Reproduced with permission.

service and operations. At smaller stations, they would deliver departure and arrival announcements, help passengers navigate through the terminal safely and efficiently, and supervise porters responsible for luggage handling. Some station masters even had the notoriously unwelcome task of releasing baskets of homing pigeons for sport. Pigeon fanciers would send their trained racing birds by rail to a mutually agreed station for release, taking bets on which birds were expected to return first. Bird baskets covered in feathers and droppings would be hauled out of the train by hand and opened simultaneously, the station master then scurrying inside to send a wire to London confirming the release time. The time it took the birds to cover the distance home and rate of travel was then compared with other birds to determine the winning pigeon, the winners collecting bets and bragging rights.[7]

Did Beryl and Victor encounter one another at the station where she worked, Beryl covered in feathers and pigeon droppings? Their work would have given them an opportunity to cross paths. Perhaps Victor would stop in for a coffee at Beryl's station from time to time. Victor was fun-loving with an attractive Irish brogue, dimpled grin, and dark hair slicked back with Vaseline or Brylcreem. Beryl was demure and friendly with wide eyes and a kind smile. In her trim uniform of navy scarf, wool peacoat with shiny badge on her right lapel, she wore her hair in perfect curls beneath her hat. Thousands of couples across the United Kingdom, in a collective eagerness at the close of the war to get back to normal and start new families, rushed to the altar. Beryl and Victor were no different.

Sometime in early September 1945, Beryl became pregnant. Premarital conception was common in the UK in the 1940s, especially in the period immediately following the war. But it was still taboo, and most couples would have been pressured to marry as soon as possible. With reconstruction and building a stronger future for the country on the minds of everyone, childrearing was considered one of the top duties of British women during wartime and the postwar period as the population experienced a "baby boom."

Whether from a sense of duty or true love that generated a happy accident, on October 31, 1945, twenty-two-year-old Victor and twenty-one-year-old Beryl married. Marriage rates in the months and years following the war were among the highest ever seen in the

UK, eclipsed only by the start of the war when fear and uncertainty prompted many to marry. The ceremony took place at the local registry office at the West Derby Union Offices at Brougham Terrace. Built in 1902, the imposing three-storey Georgian brick and stone building led each couple through a double set of large oak doors ornamented with stone masonry arches. Mosaic tile floors and leaded stained-glass windows drew their eyes up toward the magnificent stained-glass domed skylight above the main staircase. Many postwar couples like Victor and Beryl married here when they were unable to afford an expensive church wedding, earning the building its nickname, "St. Brougham's." No wedding pictures survived from the event, and it was an intimate ceremony with Beryl's stepfather, William, beloved half sister Joan, and friend Ivy Bell lining up to sign the register.[8]

As Beryl and Victor celebrated their nuptials, the country was still sorting through the wreckage of the war, and reminders of ruin were everywhere. Moscow Drive had escaped the worst of the bombing, but you could read the weariness on people's faces. Never, even in the depths of the Great Depression, had so many people in the city become homeless. With a child on the way, Victor moved into his bride's family home at 119 Moscow Drive, where Beryl's mother Amy, along with William, Joan, her brother Norman and his wife, Evelyn (Eva), all lived. The Potters, Wallaces, and now the Carters were all under one roof. Beryl and Victor took a couple of rooms at the back of the house overlooking the garden and rear alley and settled down to start their lives together.

Despite the crowded living quarters, Beryl was jubilant. After a turbulent childhood and adolescence, she was ready to begin her life as a wife and mother. But starting over is never easy, as the saying goes. As soon as this new beginning dawned, the edges began to fray, and Beryl found herself on the move once again.

4.
To Canada

L ife in postwar Liverpool was gruelling. In the years following the war, mothers made meals from scraps, mended rags into clothing, and rationed fuel. The city suffered tremendously from wartime bombing with whole sections of central Liverpool flattened. Over eleven thousand homes were destroyed causing a chronic housing crisis and widespread homelessness. Many businesses closed permanently and there was a net loss of manufacturing resulting in mass unemployment. Austerity measures were introduced to control escalating deficits due to a spiralling economic crisis, resulting in a reduction of social programs and other municipal services when people needed them most. The local Co-operative Society became a lifeline, paying out quarterly dividends of one shilling and seven pence to help families keep food on the table.

Those who lived in the city through the postwar years described scenes of widespread destruction. This contrasted with the "strength, stubbornness, at times rebelliousness, and a dry, sarcastic and sometimes cutting sense of humour" characteristic of the people of Liverpool. Close-knit neighbourhoods banded together, encouraging each other with the mantra to "keep calm and carry on." Women took jobs outside the home in record numbers, balancing unpaid domestic duties and childrearing with paid work to supplement the family purse.

Life at 119 Moscow Drive echoed these broader conditions. Many newlyweds across Britain, such as Beryl and Victor, lived in crowded conditions with their families and took in boarders to help pay the rent. Finding and keeping work became extremely difficult. After they married, Victor lost his job at the Transport Board and bounced from one job to the next. When her new husband was between jobs, Beryl was the primary breadwinner with her employment at the train station, though this would not last for long. Many women like Beryl challenged gender barriers in the workplace during and after the war, working in factories, holding jobs previously reserved for men. But in the austere postwar period, traditional gendered lines of work were reasserted. Social expectations for women to return to the home were somewhat more flexible in working-class households where families relied on multiple members to earn an income, but the male identity as the family breadwinner remained largely intact in postwar Liverpool.[1]

On June 6, 1946, Beryl and Victor made their contribution to the global baby boom with their first child, Victor Jr. He was followed nearly two years later by another son, Dennis Gordon Carter (Dennis), on February 28, 1948. A year and a half later, in August 1949, Beryl became pregnant with twins. The pregnancy wasn't easy, nor was carrying two babies in her womb while caring for a toddler and an infant. She had a doublewide pram specially made in anticipation of the near Herculean task of leaving the house with four children under her wing. Near the end of her term, she became so heavily pregnant she could hardly lift her leg up on the sidewalk without assistance, and on May 22, 1950, she went into labour.

The first to arrive was a girl. But joy quickly turned to sorrow when an eerie silence replaced the expected squealing of a newborn. The baby was stillborn and had severe spina bifida. Minutes later, Beryl's labour resumed. Howling in grief, tears mixed with sweat streaming down her face, Beryl pushed through the pain and exhaustion. With a final excruciating push, her shrieks of pain were joined in chorus by the wail of an infant's healthy lungs. It was another girl. They named her Diane. One of the most popular girl's names of the 1950s, it stood for *divine* or *heavenly*, a fitting name given the conditions of her birth. But Beryl named her daughter after the American singer Dinah Shore whose top track of 1950, *My Heart Cries For You*, was playing on the radio during the delivery. For her middle name, Beryl chose Margaret, the name she had chosen for Diane's stillborn twin sister.

If the house was crowded before, it now was simply bursting at the seams. Squeezed together on a blanket for picture time in July 1951, five-year-old Victor Jr. and three-year-old Dennis lie on their stomachs offering different versions of a forced smile while one-year-old Diane sits behind them, her gleeful dimpled cheeks caught in mid-giggle.

Married with children, Beryl was expected to focus her energies on raising her children who would grow up knowing her mainly as a housewife. And she fit the conventional profile of a 1950s housewife perfectly. She loved to knit and sew, she was fastidious about cleanliness and order, and kept up with the current trends in clothing and hairstyles. One of her favourite pastimes was knitting. She would plant herself in a chair for hours knitting socks, sweaters, slippers, hats, and anything else to keep her hands busy. Beryl's mother, Amy, was still the matriarch of the busy house, leading the domestic chores as a general leads her army. When Diane grew a little older, she would help with the chores, fulfilling the expectations of the time that little girls needed to learn from a young age how to manage a household. With her brothers, Victor Jr. and Dennis, exempted from such "women's work," Diane would stand next to her mother, grandmother, and Aunt Eva, all the women of the house gathered together in the back garden, scrubbing, rinsing, and wringing the laundry before setting them on lines to air dry. Despite the laborious nature of the work, the shared activity bonded them in the brief interludes of wet English weather that otherwise prevented such communion outdoors. On Sundays when Victor was off work, he would sometimes take the family to the beach or other day trips in the car, a welcome reprieve from the daily grind.

The front of the house on Moscow Drive was sun drenched in southern exposure, but light failed to penetrate the back where the Carters lived. Diane remembers the place always being dark, the impossibly high brick walls encircling a tiny backyard, a canopy of criss-crossing laundry lines absorbing every drop of sunshine. "I remember the dark alleys behind the houses and running home as soon as the streetlamps went on." Wherever Diane went, so did her doll, its candy-striped dress, white sweater, and blond locks a miniature version of herself. Easter egg hunts were short affairs given the paucity of hiding places. Dressed in her knitted sweater and pleated skirt, Diane need only skip down a few steps to discover her prize, her blond curls bouncing in rhythm as she snatched her Easter basket waiting almost in plain sight next to the front gate, then squealed with delight before scampering back inside, reward in hand.

As his young family grew, Victor struggled endlessly to find and keep work. Nothing paid well in a slumping economy, and most available jobs were low paid without much security. He eventually found work in the suburb of Woolton at Bear Brand, one of the top producers of nylon stockings. In advertisements, its mascot teddy bear, complete with bowtie and top hat, curiously proclaimed, "Those amorous legs truly deserve those glamorous stockings." Victor worked as a hosiery knitter, an entry-level machinist position performing repetitive work. The factory floor clamoured with the noise of endlessly clacking knitting machines, circular metal jaws hungrily devouring limitless quantities of yarn that transformed into stockings. Located on the outskirts of Liverpool, not far from the Strawberry Field Girls' Orphanage soon to be immortalized in song by John Lennon, the massive factory complex presided over the local area with its tall, belching smokestack. In the postwar period, Bear Brand was one of the few large employers in Liverpool still hiring, but long-term prospects for low-skilled workers such as Victor remained bleak.

As Beryl's family grew, her older brother Norman and his wife Eva struggled to conceive a child. The couple desperately wanted a child of their own ever since they married in 1940 at age nineteen. They relished their close relationship with the Carter kids, and when it finally became clear they would never be able to have their own children, Norman made an unusual request of his sister. One day, he approached Beryl and asked if he could adopt his nephew Dennis and raise him as his own son. At the time, it was relatively common for other relatives to raise members of their extended family. It was not unheard of for siblings to discover they were in fact cousins, or the inverse. Birth control was somewhat rare in 1950s Liverpool and economic hardship often forced many working-class families into difficult decisions about how to structure their families. But for Beryl, this request appeared out of nowhere and caught her off guard.

Norman was always a bit peculiar. In his youth, he was dashingly handsome and fit. He retained his good looks well into mid-life, until the veil of his confident swagger dropped, revealing an eccentric, suspicious, and judgmental man with a stubborn and controlling temperament. Once, when he was served pasta, he turned his back to the dinner table because of a bigoted disdain for Italians. Years later, he would show up at his grand niece's wedding only to stand in the rear without speaking to anyone before leaving. At the end of his life, Norman stopped taking care of himself, his declining physical and mental health a growing concern to everyone around him. "Like it or not, you are my brother and I love you," Beryl once wrote to her brother, acknowledging their lifelong complicated relationship.[2]

Perhaps it was the affinity they all developed living in the same house together that motivated him to make such a request of his sister. Or maybe Norman saw Beryl and Victor struggling to make ends meet and wished to alleviate the burden of yet another mouth to feed. Since Beryl had three children and he had none, it made perfect sense to Norman that his sister would relinquish one of her sons to a couple who could bear none. Whatever logic he proposed to Beryl, she wasn't having any of it. She refused Norman's request, but in doing so, sowed the seeds of a resentment that lasted decades. By an ironic twist of fate, Norman would eventually have his wish, but never in the way he expected.

———

By the early 1950s, Beryl and Victor strained to see a future for their family in Liverpool. They could not stay at 119 Moscow Drive forever and the uncertainty of the labour and housing markets made it difficult for them to secure a place of their own. Things were not much better elsewhere as the country struggled to rebuild following the war, leading many other young couples like them to the same conclusion. It was time to look abroad for new opportunities. Compared to Liverpool, postwar Canada was full of promise. Beryl had never left the country of her birth, but Victor was practically a world traveller during his days in the merchant navy. He passed through Montreal on at least one occasion, and had a cousin living in Toronto, so Canada seemed like a good option for them.

In the postwar period, Canada was an industrial powerhouse seeking immigrants to fill jobs in manufacturing, construction, and other professional services. Commonwealth nations such as Canada, South Africa, Australia, and New Zealand were favoured destinations for British emigrants. They enjoyed special immigration privileges prior to the advent of the point system whereby applicants were scored according to language skills, education, age, and employment status among other categories. British citizens were automatically fast-tracked, and in 1951 a loan incentive program sweetened the deal by covering the passage and settlement fees of British immigrants at zero per cent interest. By contrast, the 1952 Immigration Act upheld racial discrimination against non-European and non-American immigrants, policies that were not overturned until 1962.

Canada was the most popular destination for post-war British immigrants, largely because of this booming economy and straight-forward immigration process, and regular queues formed outside Canadian immigration offices across the United Kingdom. In 1947, over seven thousand Britons left for Canada. That same year, the pre-mier of Ontario, George Drew, travelled to England to entice British immigrants to the province, handing out food parcels and coordin-ating media coverage of the first airborne immigrants to Toronto. At first, UK Prime Minister Winston Churchill was not pleased, branding British emigrants "rats leaving a sinking ship." But by 1952, after a visit to Canada, he reversed his position. "A magnificent future awaits [immigrants] in Canada," he proclaimed. It's unclear whether Churchill's endorsement had any direct effect on immi-gration rates, but the flood of people from Britain to Canada rose to a peak of seventy-five thousand in 1957, with over five hundred thousand British immigrants arriving in Canada altogether between 1945 and 1970.

Toronto was a top destination for many of these new arrivals. In the 1950s, the city was beginning to transform in many ways as it experienced a postwar boom in people, goods, and services. A new metropolitan government, led by its indefatigable chair Frederick Gardiner, built new buildings, highways, subways, parks, and roads. Countless acres of fertile farmland unravelled into sprawling new subdivisions. Skyscrapers sprouted up downtown, rapidly trans-forming the city's skyline. Construction reached a fever pitch with a burgeoning population of one million by 1951 that doubled by 1971. Author Rosemary Sullivan observed that 1950s Toronto was "still a Presbyterian construct, devoted to order and cleanliness, but that veneer had begun to crack as the city grew up and away from its col-onial roots."[3] The city was becoming more diverse, though most new arrivals were still from western and southern Europe due in large part to restrictive, and racist, immigration regulations.

On January 16, 1954, thirty-three-year-old Victor boarded the Cunard steamship *RMS Franconia* in Liverpool bound for New York. Constructed in 1922 and having served in the Second World War, the *Franconia* was in its last two years of service, delivering a generation of Europeans from Liverpool to Canada and the US. Boarding the ship must have felt a bit like stepping back in time for Victor. Dressed in his bomber jacket and waving goodbye to his family at the docks, the wind rustling his dark hair, perhaps he thought of the popular folk song "Leaving of Liverpool":

> So fare thee well my own true love,
> When I return united we will be,
> It's not the leaving of Liverpool that grieves me,
> But my darling when I think of thee.

Victor travelled north from New York to Toronto and stayed with a cousin while he searched for work. He sent back what money he earned, but it was not enough to cover the passenger and settlement fees they would eventually need to pay to sponsor the family's permanent immigration, regardless of whatever loan incentives the government was offering.

Months went by until Victor finally sent for Beryl and the children in late autumn. On November 5, they boarded the *RMS Empress of Australia*, bound for Montreal. The three- or four-day crossing was enough time for little Diane to make new friends. She bounced about the ship in her Mary Jane flats and peacoat, her blond curls and girlish giggle reminiscent of Shirley Temple fame. In the ship's manifest next to the box "Country of Intended Future Permanent Residence," they ticked "Canada." Beryl dreamt of a better life for her family, a typical 1950s utopia where Victor had steady work, their kids went to good schools, and she kept a clean, spacious home. These dreams held the promise of a happy and fulfilling future, one where she could forget about all the ways she may have felt her life had failed to measure up to these exacting standards.

But it was not to be. Beryl and the children stayed for seven months before leaving on June 17, 1955, back through the port of Montreal heading to Liverpool via Southampton aboard the smaller (and cheaper) *MS Seven Seas*. Frequently used by students and migrants for budget travel, the ship carried mostly visitors to the UK, except for the Carters, who this time marked "England" as their "Country of Intended Permanent Residence."[4] As Victor continued to struggle to secure a job, they were uncertain if they'd ever return to build a home in Canada.

As fate would have it, Victor finally found work as a bus driver with the Toronto Transit Commission or TTC in the autumn of 1955. The relatively well-paid job, unionized since 1899 by the Amalgamated Transit Union, meant he could finally afford to bring his family to live with him. Once again, Beryl and the children packed their bags and sailed to Canada onboard the *RMS Queen Elizabeth*, this time with their Uncle Norman and Aunt Eva, who decided to join them and make a new start for themselves. Eva was a gentle, mousy woman. She wore practical housedresses and curlers in her hair each night. Diane loves her aunt but has less fond memories of this transatlantic crossing because of her. "I spent the whole trip in the cabin with my aunt throwing up. My brothers were out having a good time on the *QE*, while I was stuck in the cabin with her!"

Arriving at Toronto's Union Station after a train ride from Montreal, they passed through the Great Hall, its lobby illuminated by impressive side arch windows and nearly ninety-foot-high ceilings buttressed by giant limestone columns. They descended underground to take the northbound subway train on the recently completed Yonge Street line, deboarding at St. Clair station and travelling west on the 512-streetcar, an unwieldy cylinder of red-painted steel, that carried them the last stretch of their long journey to their new home in the midtown suburb of Oakwood. Aptly named, the neighbourhood featured residential streets lined with majestic oak trees, their branches reaching skyward in a canopy that had just begun to shed its deep auburn and yellow foliage, carpeting the sidewalks and manicured lawns below in a kaleidoscope of colour. It was the epitome of 1950s suburban bliss. Along nearby St. Clair Avenue, a different canopy made of streetcar wires connected the buildings across the wide boulevard as a river of people trundled along in streetcars and sturdy Chrysler, Ford, and GM sedans.

Beryl was excited at this new opportunity to settle her family in a place where they could make memories and put down roots. Their apartment comprised the upper floor of a two-storey brick home at 124 Humewood Drive near Christie Street and St. Clair Avenue. It was small for a family of five and Beryl struggled constantly to keep the space clean to her exacting standards despite the mess that normally trails young children. A spacious porch and front lawn were a decided improvement from the cramped front step they left behind in Liverpool with plenty of space for the children to play. Norman and Eva moved in temporarily until they could find their own place, all of them living together in the same house just as they once did back in Liverpool, family ties bonding them in this new country.

———————

The Carters later moved to another nearly identical rented house just two blocks east, on Wychwood Avenue. By summertime, they already felt settled into the neighbourhood. Hot hazy days passed easily with the kids playing in the garden, their boundless energy often spilling into nearby Humewood Park, a small suburban greenspace bounded by 1930s-era brick homes, like one big communal backyard shared by all the neighbourhood kids. Not long afterward, they moved a few blocks west to another upstairs flat at 35 Holland Park Avenue, a larger apartment with more space to spread out. The landlady, Freda, was a friendly older woman who lived on the main floor. The house was a typical two-storey three-bedroom brick home in a quiet, leafy neighbourhood with a spacious backyard, good schools, transit, and nearby grocery stores. Freda quickly became a family friend, helping with laundry and even watching over the kids from time to time. The house had nearly everything a new working-class family could have hoped for in Canada and Beryl hoped it would be their final move, at least for a little while.

For now, they were a family at ease, living the suburban dream that captivated the imagination of so many in the 1950s. Beryl's joy registers in every photo that documents their early days in Canada, always immaculately dressed in a housedress or skirt with a blouse, cardigan, and pearls, her hair fixed just so, a pleasant smile permanently stamped on her face.[5] Life was good, or so it seemed, and she hoped it would last forever.

Left to right: Dennis, Diane, Beryl, and Victor Jr., spread out on the grass backyard of their Wychwood home, May 1955.
Beryl Potter personal collection. Reproduced with permission.

5.
Joining the (Paid) Workforce

With three school-age children and bills to pay, Beryl set out to find a job. In the passenger ship manifest on her trip to Canada, she indicated she was a housewife. But hers was a working-class household, one where middle-class gendered ideals of women's roles did not always reflect the financial realities of working families. In addition to the unpaid domestic work that she performed as a wife and mother, Beryl needed to bring in extra money to help supplement Victor's wages. She had previously worked as a nurse's assistant, a factory worker, and a train station mistress, so she was no stranger to working outside the home. But for the past ten years prior to their move to Canada, she was focused on raising three kids and helping her mother, Amy, then in her early sixties, with the household duties. Beryl loved looking after her children, but the family needed the money to survive. She also missed the social interaction outside the home. "I decided to find a job to help pay for a house and a car," she later wrote. "Everything was going well, we were happy in our nice new home, and enjoying what was to us a luxury—a beautiful car that took us on many happy outings into the country after church on Sundays."

In 1950s Canada, thousands of women found work in the retail industry thanks in part to the popularity of department stores such as Woolworth's, Eaton's, Kresge's, and Hudson's Bay Company. S. S. Kresge Company was founded in 1899 in Detroit and entered the Canadian market in 1929, opening nineteen stores across the country in its first year despite the stock market crash. By the 1930s, Kresge's was one of the most popular department stores in Canada and one of the largest employers of female retail workers in Toronto with two locations on Yonge Street, one at College and one at Richmond. Forerunner to the K-Mart brand, S. S. Kresge Co. popularized the "five-and-dime" variety discount store. Shoppers could enjoy the convenience and novelty of finding housewares, linens, clothing, school supplies, cosmetics, toys, and seasonal decor all under one roof.

Beryl got a full-time job at Kresge's flagship store at 1 Richmond Street at the southwest corner of Yonge and Richmond Streets in downtown Toronto. Behind the austere concrete walls and five-foot block lettering spelling out "S. S. Kresge Co." it was one of the busiest department stores in the downtown core. The store, spread out over five floors of retail space, featured a restaurant and lunch counter, bakery, and coffee shop. Past the bubble-gum machines and coin-operated riding horses was the bakery and lunch counter, tempting passing shoppers with freshly baked cakes and pies. Mothers with their children would stop by to sip soda from paper Dixie cups in metal holders at the lunch counter. Lively string music was piped throughout the building, creating a dreamy refuge from the hustle and bustle of regular life.

While Beryl worked the bakery and lunch counter, Eva looked after the children, and if she wasn't available, Freda the landlady, would see to them, the women of the house always expected to keep things running smoothly. Diane remembers these days with fondness for her Aunt Eva, less so of Uncle Norman. "I loved my Aunt Eva to death, but Norman, he was a mean son of a gun. He would not let her even go to the store to buy a loaf of bread if she ran out during the day. Poor lady. But Eva took good care of us while mum worked." Diane had a recurring nightmare of a wolf at her window poised for attack. It began when she was a little girl living in Liverpool and continued when she was in Canada, its source possibly linked to her uncle. "Norman would discipline us like he was our father. He once beat me on the bum with a belt and he would not let Eva come to console me. He'd lift us off the floor by our ears. He could be very mean." But Beryl had no choice but to rely on her family to look after her children when she was at work, grateful for their support, even if it meant leaving them with her peculiar brother.

At the lunch counter, Beryl indulged her love of cooking, baking, and the joy of interacting with children. There were times she might have been mistaken for being anti-social with her shy and soft-spoken manner, but interacting with customers was something she truly enjoyed. Diane recalls watching her mum at work. "There was something about the way she spoke and looked at people that made them feel like they had really been listened to. Even though she was shy, she liked to talk to people at work." She excelled at customer service, was a perfectionist, and rarely complained about anything, qualities that were highly valued in the retail environment where she worked. Her quiet charisma and solid work ethic endeared her to her employer, and within a year or so she was promoted to manager. During the 1950s, most staff in department stores such as Kresge's were female and managers were often male, but food preparation and service were usually considered women's work, creating a gendered enclave of limited upward mobility for women workers like Beryl.

Home was a different story. On some weekends, Victor would take the family two hours north to Innisfil Beach on Lake Simcoe near the town of Barrie to spend quality time together. Christmases and other family get-togethers were also typically happy occasions. On their parents' wedding anniversary, which was on Halloween, the kids would get dressed in their costumes and go trick-or-treating while Victor and Beryl enjoyed a romantic dinner to celebrate. These moments of happiness and togetherness were increasingly overshadowed by Victor's drinking. If he came home on Friday with his paycheque, the family knew it would be a good weekend. The children would watch from the window to see if he was walking or driving as a way of assessing his sobriety and preparing themselves for what was to come. If Victor appeared to stumble up the front steps, young Diane would run and hide in the closet. Sometimes, Victor would disappear for the entire weekend, showing up broke and hungover on Sunday night. One evening, he drunkenly drove his Buick onto the front lawn, the heavy radial tires screeching to a halt just before the vehicle plowed through the front porch.

It was usually better if Victor stayed away when he was drinking because he could also become violent. Once, he became upset with Diane for talking on the phone and stormed into the room, angrily ripping out the phone cord from the wall. He then charged around the house in a fit of rage, tearing out the rest of the phone lines. He never hit Diane or Dennis, but he would provoke his eldest son, Victor Jr., picking fights that would often become physical. "[Dad] was rough on [Victor Jr.]. He wanted him to be more like a sailor and he thought that meant he needed to toughen him up," Diane thinks. Victor Jr. always got the worst treatment when his father was drinking. "Once, my dad stormed into the room, pulled Victor Jr. off the top bunk and stuck his head in the oven. Why? Only he seemed to know because he always did crazy terrible things like that when he was drinking. If you did not laugh at one of his jokes, he would get mad. If you did laugh, he would still get mad. He was either very nice and sane when he was sober, or completely psychotic when he was drinking." Victor would sometimes direct his anger toward his wife. Once, he grabbed Beryl and pinned her against the bedroom wall, strangling her while Diane ran to call the police. By the time the police got there, he had calmed down and Beryl didn't want to press charges, but it was not the first time Victor's drinking was harmfully inflicted on his family, nor the last time police would visit their house for a domestic dispute.

This unpredictability created an ambient tension in the house, as if everyone were waiting for a bomb to explode in the middle of the living room. Like many women in abusive relationships, Beryl was convinced she could change her husband's ways. She had followed this man across the ocean to begin a fresh start and wasn't about to give up on him now. Separation and divorce were still relatively rare and little discussed in the 1950s and early 1960s, especially in suburban neighbourhoods like theirs, and it conflicted with the idealized vision of domestic life Beryl still held to firmly. Inside of her rocky marriage, Beryl believed the popular advice at the time, that it would be more traumatic for the children to break up the family than if she were to stay and make the best of it. Her desire for a clean and tidy house evolved into a compulsive need for order, as if the absence of dishes in the sink or dust on the counter helped to erase the growing dysfunction that undermined their happiness.

When Diane reflects on old television programs like *The Honeymooners, Leave It To Beaver,* or *Father Knows Best,* she sees a lot of the happy domestic life to which her mother aspired. "My mother lived a typical suburban life. When I watch a bit of those old shows, I think of mum and dad. The father walking in the door and asking, 'What's for dinner,' or the women always in housedresses even when they're cleaning. I don't ever remember seeing my mother in pants once in her life. She did her best to always have dinner on the table when she wasn't working. And she certainly kept everything neat and tidy."

"My mother was always a neat freak. I had one friend who used to drop bread crusts and crumbs on the floor and not pick them up. My mum got so mad at that she told me that friend could not come over for lunch anymore. Whenever I had a button come off a blouse or sweater, instead of finding a similar button, she would take every single other button off and sew them back on at perfect intervals. If I did not make my bed properly, she would take all the sheets off the bed and make me do it again with proper hospital corners and everything. Everything had to be done right and done her way. This was always part of her personality."

Beryl never had many friends she could confide in to confess her feelings. Other than the landlady Freda, who lived on the main floor and naturally would have been privy to the drama of the family upstairs, Diane can remember only one friend in her mother's life. Rose was the wife of Victor's drinking buddy, Jim, a Scotsman and fellow TTC bus driver who would occasionally come around the house. As couples, they would sometimes go out to dinner or to a club. Only once did Diane ever see her mother drink to the point of intoxication. "She was at her friend Rose's. The men had gone off for the weekend and we were all over at their house. It was the first time I ever saw her drink, besides the occasional Mint Julip, and certainly the only time I noticed she became a bit tipsy."

It was revealing that Beryl would only let her hair down when her husband was away. With Victor out of the picture, there was less to watch out for, fewer challenging behaviours to navigate, less need for her to be on duty to protect her children. Maybe it was Rose's influence that led Beryl to drink more than she normally would. Or maybe in Rose she found someone she could laugh with and blow off some steam. Was it Beryl's nature to be reserved, bottling up feelings with nowhere to go? Beryl's inner circle appears to have been small, whether by choice or accident. Her self-consciousness may have made her vulnerable to others' expectations. So when given the opportunity to escape that box, it makes perfect sense she would do so with a female friend, someone likely to understand the pressures she was under.

Beryl was always protective of her children, especially Dennis. From an early age, it was apparent Dennis was different from other children. At Briar Hill Junior Public School near Dufferin Street and Eglinton Avenue, he lagged behind his classmates in all subjects, so Beryl enrolled him in special education classes to help him along. His speech was a little different from the other kids, its cause unknown to the family at the time but likely to have been an auditory processing disorder common among people with intellectual disabilities. He endured bullying at school and was sometimes teased by his siblings or Victor when he was drinking.

Dennis never made any real friends and spent much of his time with his mother. "I don't ever remember him having friends, even as a young child," Diane remembers. "We'd play at the house as siblings, but I never remember him having a friend over. Mum always took care of him and worried about him all the time." Naturally, Dennis started emulating his mother's traits, picking up a compulsive need for cleanliness and order. To Diane, Dennis was just her quirky brother who sometimes had abnormal ways of doing things. It did not seem like much to tease him as siblings often do, rustling his hair when he came out of the shower having spent too much time combing it just right, or messing up the clothes he carefully set out on the bed. Dennis knew that he was different from his peers and the bullying he experienced made him defensive, particularly whenever he was made to feel "stupid."

Beryl was aware of her son's intellectual disabilities from a young age but decided not to have him formally diagnosed, hoping she could spare him from stigma and negative attention. "When she realized he was slower than other kids, she always defended the things he did or said, saying he did it without thinking," Diane recalls.[1] Beryl was probably acting out of instinct to protect her son, but she could also have been inspired by a contemporary movement of parents who subscribed to a belief about developmental disability that included refusing to institutionalize their children in residential hospitals and working to challenge negative stereotypes. Throughout the 1950s and 1960s, "Marching Mothers" of the Ontario March of Dimes became a ubiquitous presence in Canadian communities, raising awareness of the needs and abilities of children with disabilities.[2] Beryl may have met one of these women or learned about efforts to destigmatize children with intellectual disabilities, but by her own later admission, she never thought much about people with disabilities as a younger woman.

Beryl's education was interrupted at a young age by the war, and as an adult she did not read much beyond the occasional self-help book. Whether she personally interacted with or knew other parents of children like Dennis isn't clear. She may also have been in denial of her son's needs, dismissing his grades, speech difficulties, and comparisons with other kids as just another sign that he was wonderfully unique. Either way, she was convinced that Dennis was just as capable as anyone else and needed only her protection and encouragement, a response that nourished an inseparable mother-son bond. Beryl knew she could not shelter Dennis all the time, but believed that, together, they could find a way through.

Living in a suburban neighbourhood with one car for the family meant Beryl relied on public transportation to get to work. Some transit riders of the time likened the old streetcars to "cattle cars," rattly, noisy, bumpy, uncomfortable, hot in the summer and cold in the winter, impossibly slow, lumbering beasts stumbling down the centre of the road toward a far-off destination. A thirty-to-forty-minute commute today would have taken nearly twice that time in the early 1960s. Between the bumpy streetcar to Yonge Street and subway ride downtown to Kresge's, the long commute made it difficult for Beryl to be the kind of mother she wanted to be for her children.

It wasn't her fault. Economic realities meant that many children of working-class families returned to empty homes after school with both parents at work, especially during and after the Second World War. But to middle-class observers, this was seen as a moral problem that reflected negatively on mothers who were seen to be failing to provide adequate supervision of their children. Working mothers such as Beryl had little choice when trying to raise children while working outside the home, and the gendered nature of childrearing meant fathers escaped similar expectations to supervise children when they got home from school. With her work hours and long commute, Beryl could not always be present for parent-teacher meetings, school plays, bake-a-thons, or other typical school events that other students might have expected their parents to attend. Her job also seemed to give her something she could not get at home. "I don't think she would have wanted to stay home," Diane asserts. "She liked to work. She was always working."

Beryl also suffered from migraines that became increasingly debilitating. She would disappear for days at a time into the quiet of her bedroom, every creak of the floorboard or loud voice like nails dragging across a chalkboard. As her condition progressed in the late 1950s, she suffered acute nausea and vomiting. Diane remembers her mother often doubled over the toilet or a bucket, retching for hours. Sometimes she would not make it to the bathroom in time. "At home, she was in bed basically all the time. She used to throw up so much. I would sit out on the sidewalk and hold my hands over my ears. I would stay in bed and my knuckles would be white in the morning from holding the covers over my head so I could not hear her. I remember her smacking her head against the wall and floor because she just could not get rid of the migraines. It was terrible."

Treatment for migraines was still in its infancy in the 1950s. In 2008, the American Headache Society reported, "The combination of aspirin, caffeine, and butalbital (Fiorinal) became popular for the acute attack of headache. Hydergine (dihydroergotamine mesylate) was developed for migraine prophylaxis. Many other agents, including hormones and steroids, were recommended for acute and prophylactic therapy in the 1950s." Side effects of butalbital included nausea and vomiting, which helps to explain Beryl's daily struggle, even with the near-empty contents of her stomach. Diane remembers her mother surviving on nothing but coffee, the caffeine working to constrict blood vessels for some relief but providing little nourishment. With heavy caffeine intake, her body would have become dependent on the steady course of the stimulant and any decrease in consumption would have triggered withdrawal symptoms that could have lasted weeks, further adding to her misery.

Beryl's doctor started coming to the house to treat her when she could not make it to the clinic. During these years, the Carter house became a revolving door for doctors and nurses to treat her.

Diane remembers her mother's pale skin covered in circular brown stains from the antiseptic iodine patches that were applied before yet another stab with a hypodermic needle filled with temporary relief. For acute pain, Beryl would be put on a vial of morphine up to ten milligrams that would take twenty or thirty minutes to deplete. Given the short-acting nature of liquid morphine, the effects would last only up to four hours before the pain returned and she would need more, fuelling what was likely opioid dependency. "The doctor actually got looked into because he was coming too often to give her morphine," Diane recalls.

If the morphine helped with Beryl's pain, it also made it difficult for her to function normally. In the late 1950s and 1960s, doctors dispensed opioids more liberally than today, inadvertently creating substance abuse and dependency problems during a course of treatment. At the time, all manner of opioids, especially for pain relief, were marketed as safe with little evidence to the contrary. It wasn't until the late 1990s with the rise of the opioid epidemic when standards of care began to shift away from reliance on powerful opioid painkillers such as OxyContin for chronic conditions such as migraines. Isolated in her room—away from her children, her job, and household duties— she floated on a cloud that temporarily carried her to a place of her own drug-induced imagination. With cotton stuffed into her ears to muffle any noise, or doubled over the toilet when nausea overtook her, she retreated further within herself. She started taking more and more time off work as she tried to manage her illness, testing any patience her managers might have held for her. Keeping her job was a problem she would eventually need to face, but her throbbing head pushed out any other thoughts. Whatever pain relief the drugs offered, they also gave her strong hallucinations, lifting her out of her surroundings into sometimes terrifying worlds. Victor offered her little comfort, consumed with his own addiction, lacking the tools to bridge the expanding divide between them. "She got depressed and dad was of no comfort to her," Diane remembers. Human contact may have been what she was seeking, especially with her children, but whenever an inquisitive eye or ear approached her bedroom door, they were pulled away.

In 1962, after nearly a year of poor nutrition, unable to keep any food down, caffeine, over-the-counter drugs, and occasional morphine injections no longer providing relief, Beryl was finally hospitalized at Mount Sinai Hospital in downtown Toronto. She was fed intravenously and put on a morphine drip. The timing was particularly unfortunate for twelve-year-old Diane who needed her mother. "I got my first period," Diane says. "My dad had to phone his sister to come to the house, because I was home with my dad and two brothers." As her mother lay sick in hospital, Diane's Aunt Pam, who she did not know all that well, came to briefly explain what to do. When Diane visited her mother in hospital the next day, she told her what happened. Beryl felt awful she wasn't there to explain to her daughter what was happening to her body and to help her feel less alone, but it would be the first of many milestones in Diane's life that Beryl would miss through no fault of her own.[3]

During Beryl's illness, Victor Jr. did his best to earn some extra money for the family, taking up a paper route. He excelled and earned an award for his dedication. Beryl was so proud of her son that she wrote to the *Liverpool Echo Evening Express*. She had last written to the paper in 1944 at age twenty-one when she had become an occasional writer for the Children's Section. Now, she spoke to a columnist, boasting of her son's accomplishment to readers an ocean away.[4]

He's Top Newsboy in Toronto

Becoming a newspaper delivery boy in Toronto to earn a bit of extra money to buy comforts for his mother in hospital, 12-years-old Victor Carter, a Liverpool-born laddie, has just been named the leading newsboy in Toronto out of 1,300.

He gains an award and plaque from the Canadian Newspaper Circulation Managers' Association. The award is made on the basis of punctuality, appearance, popularity with the householders, and ability.

In his three years as a newsboy, Victor has never missed a delivery. His mother, Mrs. Beryl Carter, of 35 Holland Park Avenue, Toronto, sends me word that he is up at 5 a.m. to complete his round of 210 papers by 7 a.m. when he returns home for breakfast and school.

"He bought me a basket of fruit from his first week's wages," Mrs. Carter recalls. "That's when I was in hospital. Since then he has bought us gifts of books, dishes, a pop-up toaster and all kinds of things we have needed for the home. His average earnings are roughly 22 dollars (about £8) a week now."

Victor went to Lister Drive School in Liverpool and earned a scholarship there before the family moved to Canada.

His mother's parents, Mr. and Mrs. W.R. Wallace, lived at 119 Moscow Drive, Stoneycroft, Liverpool.[5]

Beryl eventually found a way to manage the migraines and nausea. When she returned from hospital, she realized it was essential to find work closer to home to avoid the commute downtown. One day, she popped into the bakery around the corner to buy a loaf of bread. Hunt's Bakery was a local favourite at the busy intersection of St. Clair and Oakwood Avenue. Situated across from Oakwood Collegiate high school and sandwiched between Calderone Shoes and Prime Restaurant, the tiny shop was a staple business in the local community for everything from fresh bread to delicious cakes and cookies, its canary yellow sign boldly asserting, "Hunt's Bakery: The Better Kind."

Spotting the "Help Wanted" sign in the window, Beryl asked for the manager. They needed a part-time bookkeeper and someone to oversee the front-end staff. It did not pay much, but it would afford Beryl more flexibility to juggle work and home life. She was also perfectly qualified, having worked and managed the bakery and lunch counter at Kresge's for around five or six years by that time. She got the job and quit Kresge's, relishing the quick streetcar ride or walk down Oakwood and flexible hours that allowed her to be at home to look after the kids when they got home from school.

Saturdays were one of the busiest days in the shop, mothers toting their children around on errands and customers popping in to pick up birthday cakes, cookies, and other delights. Beryl often brought twelve-year-old Diane and fourteen-year-old Dennis with her to work and paid them in misshapen pastries and candy, which, at that age, was enough to keep them coming back. Diane would help her mum behind the counter, learning basic accounting skills she would later build upon, or greeting people as they entered the shop. A few years later, Diane would find herself working at another Hunt's Bakery under altogether different circumstances.

In 1964, eighteen-year-old Victor Jr. signed up for the Navy. To others, it seemed he was following in his dad's footsteps, all those years

St. Clair Avenue at Oakwood, showing Hunt's Bakery left of streetcar, 1958.
Unknown photographer.

of "tough love" paying off. In reality, he was trying to escape. "Victor Jr joined the Navy to get away from his father's abuse," Beryl later wrote.[6] He moved to Halifax and worked on naval sonar equipment used in submarines. Even in Canadian waters, it was still a tense time to serve given Canada's commitments under the North Atlantic Treaty Organization. The October 1962 Cuban Missile Crisis was still within recent memory and the threat of Soviet invasion in North America by air or sea was not an unlikely scenario. If she was at all nervous about her eldest son setting sail, Beryl did not show it. Instead, she and Victor beamed with pride at their son's graduation ceremony in 1964 aboard his ship at the Toronto docks. On graduation day, Victor Jr. blended into the throng of young sailors in white crewnecks, navy trousers, and sailor's caps, Canadian flags fluttering above them in a patriotic scene. Victor Jr. was extremely intelligent and excelled in his career, eventually working for an aerospace company and a defence contractor. He married a Welsh woman named Marg, had three children with her in Halifax, and they moved to England. They later divorced and he moved back to Canada where he had another relationship with a woman named Wendy, though that did not last long. Back in Toronto, there was another marriage and another divorce as Victor Jr. searched in vain for happiness.

On December 29, 1964, the Carters drove to the Toronto International Airport to welcome family flying in from England to celebrate the holidays. It was still a time when people got dressed up to go to the airport, the heyday of PanAm luxury air travel before the advent of the budget airlines. Beryl and Diane looked quite glamorous, wearing a black fur coat and fur-trimmed coat respectively. Victor and Dennis were each in a suit and tie with dress shoes and fashionable overcoats, a picture-perfect family appearing as if on their way to church instead of the baggage claim department. That New Year's Eve, they hosted a celebration, the festive atmosphere furnished with tinseled garlands and Christmas lights. The *Lawrence Welk Show* flickered in the background as the Lennon Sisters crooned "What Are You Doing New Years Eve?"

Beryl and Victor had each other to hold that night, dressed to party, their heads adorned with paper hats, surrounded by their loving family. No one could have guessed it would be the last time they would ring in the New Year like this.

6.

An Ordinary
Slip and Fall

By 1965, Beryl was promoted to full-time assistant manager and payroll administrator at the bakery. The family needed the extra money. Victor lost his job as a TTC bus driver when his drinking began intersecting with his work in increasingly dangerous ways. Victor and his fellow bus driver and best friend, Jim, would regularly park their buses at the Fairbank Hotel and Gentlemen's Club, a strip club located at Vaughan Road and Oakwood Avenue, and go into the bar for the night. Around 1965, someone reported them to their supervisor and Victor was fired. After that, he began drinking more heavily and the family's home life entered a death spiral.

Beryl chose to see this as a temporary setback, still determined as ever to hold her family together. But she was growing more isolated than ever. Between working full-time hours, coming home to a house that needed cleaning, a family that needed feeding, kids that needed attention, and still plagued by migraines, living on coffee, and not having a husband she could trust, Beryl was severely stretched. During this time, family and close friends describe her as being introverted—but what did that mean? She was juggling a lot and holding it all close to herself. She can't have been sleeping well and exhaustion undoubtedly played a role in how she presented to others. She must have been completely overwhelmed. How does a person open space to let others into a life so finely balanced?

She began working longer hours at the bakery, picking up extra weekend shifts whenever she could. Having recently celebrated her fortieth birthday, and sitting behind the cash register, exhausted, she contemplated her life. She had been in Canada less than ten years, but what did she have to show for it? As the threads of her marriage unravelled, she despaired about the gap between the future of plenty she envisioned in Canada, compared to the reality of the life in which she now found herself.

Saturday September 11, 1965, began like most other days. Beryl rose before dawn, slipping out of her nightgown into a pleated skirt, blouse, cardigan sweater, and pearl necklace laid out by her bedside. She neatly pinned up her hair and stepped into a pair of low-heeled pumps to take the five-minute streetcar ride down Oakwood Avenue to Hunt's Bakery. It was a cloudy but seasonably warm morning, the scent of fresh-baked rolls wafting down the street to greet her as she turned the corner onto St. Clair Avenue, the telltale sign that the baker was already hard at work.

By mid-morning, the bakery was humming. Mothers darted in and out, rushing to complete the weekly shopping. Others lingered over the display cases, drooling children eagerly calling attention to the fresh sugar cookies, chocolate éclairs, and mini square cakes tempting them behind the glass. Beryl endlessly criss-crossed the store, greeting customers, chatting up the regulars, working the cash register, and stocking the shelves and display cases. The energy in the shop was frenetic as Beryl scurried back and forth. Crossing the yellow checkered tiled floor, as she had done countless times before, she stepped on a piece of discarded cellophane paper often used to wrap Hunt's famous candies. The thin transparent sheet was like a sheet of ice precariously located in the centre of a high traffic area. She slipped instantly, landing hard on her right knee.

"How, with all this, could I ever visualize the simple but devastating incident that took our happiness and changed the lives of our entire family," she later wrote. No one could have imagined an ordinary slip and fall such as this would represent the beginning of six long years of unimaginable pain and loss. Years later, Beryl would reflect on that fateful moment. The bustling shop, the sensation of falling, the cold tiled floor, the shock of impact, the embarrassment and recovery as she wobbled unsteadily to her feet.

She was stunned at first, but quickly collected herself and proceeded on with her work. She limped a little through the rest of her shift and noticed some swelling around her knee. She applied an ice pack for the rare in-between moments when she could sit down and paid little attention to the nagging sensation in her knee, partly because she had suffered leg pain in the past, including varicose veins and a kneecap that continually popped out of its socket.

"I continued to ignore it, then Vic brought the children to meet me and took us out to dinner," Beryl recalled. Later that evening as she dressed for bed, she realized her knee was noticeably swollen. "When I tried to get up the following morning, I was shocked to find my leg so badly swollen I could not even stand on it."

Within a day or so, Beryl consulted a doctor who referred her to the hospital. Unknown to her at the time, a blood clot had already formed behind her right kneecap. After a series of tests, she learned the clot developed into deep vein thrombosis. Unlike superficial thrombophlebitis—*thrombo* for clot, *phlebitis* for inflammation—which forms along veins near the surface of the skin, the clot in her leg formed in an arterial vein deep within her thigh muscles. She suffered from lifelong poor blood circulation, the legacy of permanent heart damage sustained during the rheumatic fever that nearly took her life as a child. She may also have had a genetic predisposition to deep vein thrombosis that was unknown to her or the doctors at the time.

A crescendo of excruciating pain marked each passing day, with one of the major veins that run up the back of the leg delivering oxygen-poor blood back to the heart blocked by the clot behind her knee. This meant her venous system was under extraordinary pressure to carry the same volume of blood and now relied on the network of superficial veins to do the same job. Throbbing and cramping sensations grew steadily unbearable as her swollen limb became red and warm to the touch. Beryl was injected with heparin, an anticoagulant, and put on a strict order of bed rest. The deep-seated clot presented a serious life-threatening risk of pulmonary embolism should it become dislodged and migrate to the lungs to block an artery. Deep vein thrombosis was not well understood in the mid-1960s, though reports began to surface that Richard Nixon suffered from deep vein thrombosis following an accident in 1960 that nearly resulted in the loss of his left leg.[1]

As Beryl's condition worsened, Diane, now fifteen, treated her mother's swollen leg at home. At first, compression stockings and dressings were changed once a day, then twice, and sometimes three times a day. Over the course of two years following her accident, Beryl's leg became so swollen and firm all the way to her feet that she could no longer stand upright. Diane watched in horror as her mother's leg transformed into a pillar that seemed detached from the rest of her body. "Her leg was so hard you could knock on it. It was thick all the way down to her foot, like a tree trunk."

Diane resembled her mother in more ways than one. They both had soft blue eyes, a button nose, thin eyebrows, and a broad smile. Usually soft-spoken, they were both excellent storytellers, drawing in listeners with their infectious energy and enthusiasm. They carried themselves similarly too, projecting a friendly, sanguine temperament and dynamic personality. When Diane and Dennis were children, Beryl would occasionally read to them, selecting some of the most popular volumes of the 1950s, such as *Goodnight Moon*, *Curious George*, *Pippi Longstocking*, *The Secret Garden*, or *The Lion, the Witch and the Wardrobe*. Diane admired this and would come to emulate her mother's love of family above all else.

Now, it was Diane's turn to look after her mother. As Beryl's condition worsened through the late 1960s, Diane's teenage life increasingly revolved around her mother's care. Along side treating her mother's leg, Diane did the housework, the cooking and cleaning. She had an after-school part-time job followed by homework then housework, so there was little time for Diane to connect with friends or be a typical teenager. "I felt a bit deprived, like I had no teenage life because I was being the mother. I was doing everything in the house, and I just felt kind of deprived. I just never had the time to go out with friends. Actually, I did not have any friends; from the time when I got married, I did not have any because I did not have time to associate with anybody because I was always going from school, coming home, doing housework, going to visit Mum in hospital, and what have you." When Diane was in Grade 10, she dropped out of school at Vaughan Road Collegiate so she could help her mother at home full-time.

Diane found a part-time job at another Hunt's Bakery at St. Clair and Bathurst Street across from St. Michael's College School, a private Catholic boys' school near the upscale neighbourhood of Forest Hill in midtown Toronto. Between caring for her mother, household duties, and now working part-time, Diane's role in the household far outstripped her age.

During these years, the family's financial situation became increasingly precarious. In the months following her accident, Beryl was completely off work. Since her accident occurred at her workplace, she was eligible for worker's compensation benefits, which helped keep the family afloat. But it was not nearly enough to get by, and the bills began to pile up. Victor's sister, Pamela, found Dennis work as a bellboy at the Sutton Place Hotel where her husband was the manager. A thirty-three-storey concrete building with traditional European charm, complete with marble flooring and enormous chandeliers in the lobby, the glamorous hotel was once the meeting place of international celebrities and dignitaries. Even with Dennis and Diane's paycheques, the Carters racked up more and more debt and started falling seriously behind on their finances.

Beryl was soon fitted and trained to use crutches. They were uncomfortable and cumbersome and accompanied by painful rehabilitation. She would hobble around the house as best she could and would try to contribute to the cooking and cleaning, but the pain always got the better of her. Watching her daughter work herself to exhaustion each day made Beryl feel helpless. She soon felt the ache of despair and fatigue of depression creep into her mind and body as months and years passed like this, her leg becoming more swollen by the day, the monotony of life punctuated by medical appointments and meetings with insurance companies or caseworkers from the Workers' Compensation Board. Most office visits were downtown, which meant taking a taxi or having someone drive her, navigating busy streets and sidewalks to get in and out as quickly as possible to minimize the pain and discomfort of the journey.

Victor was present on occasion in the weeks and months after Beryl's accident when the hope of successful medical intervention still seemed like a real possibility. In one photo, Beryl stands with crutches in a white hospital gown, Victor supporting her from behind, his head at her shoulder, hands clasped around hers in an intimate embrace.

Her head turned toward him, lips curled into a grin as she looked down at his mouth, open in a wide toothy smile for the camera. Maybe it happened to be a good day, one where the sun shone down, and the physical and emotional pain receded just enough to forget about things for a little while. Beryl saved the photo as a reminder, a snapshot of happier days in their rocky relationship. But in the two years that followed her initial accident, Beryl and Victor's marriage went from bad to worse. Victor was unprepared to support his wife's emotional needs during her ill-health and dealt with the loss through denial and escapism. He drank even more, an entrenched coping mechanism, disappearing on binges for longer and longer periods of time. Unable to cope with the daily reminder of Beryl's injury and escalating needs, he abandoned all responsibility for his wife and teenage son and daughter. With the burden shifted onto Diane, Victor became an increasingly minor presence in the home.

Beryl's condition eventually developed into a condition called *phlegmasia cerulea dolens* (painful blue inflammation) where the venous drainage becomes so impaired that it backed up into the arterial drainage. She had been subjected to a battery of medications and procedures as the doctors tried all manner of things to dissolve the clot and improve blood flow. Blood thinners, salicylates, anticoagulants such as heparin on an intravenous drip, pain management medications such as Demerol, and various surgical procedures. Nothing seemed to help, and her condition continued to deteriorate.

Photos of Beryl in the hospital during this time show a woman trying her best to put on a good face despite the pain that consumed her. Her leg was entombed in special compression stockings, a hospital gown having replaced the fashionable dresses that she would normally have worn. She would commiserate with staff in the hospital gift shop as she was pushed around in a wheelchair, her smile unable to distract from the dark circles around her eyes. When at home, she lay in bed propped up by pillows, a patterned pink nightgown with lace collar, hair neatly coiffed. She would pass the time knitting, a hobby that permitted the faintest semblance of normalcy during those long days as the sun's rays passed from one side of the bed to the other.

Eventually, Beryl's condition progressed to *phlegmasia alba dolens* (painful white swelling) and her leg turned a milky white due to lack of arterial flow, intense circulatory pressure preventing any forward profusion. The pain now emanated not from the obstruction of the blood clot but from the lack of oxygen in her circulatory system. The backed-up blood flow resulted in a cascading death of cells that would eventually lead to gangrene if left untreated. Amputation was the last resort, but it was quickly approaching as the doctors increasingly ran out of options. In 1967, the doctors informed Beryl that her leg needed to be amputated. Instead of shock, anger, or sadness, Beryl was relieved. "I was rejoicing when they told me, 'Okay, that's it. We're going to amputate.' I felt good because I thought I'm going to get rid of the pain."

In October 1967, she was prepped for an above-the-knee amputation at Mount Sinai Hospital. The procedure, which lasted several hours, involved dividing and clamping the muscles and blood vessels. A flexible wire saw, called a Gigli saw, was used to cut through the bone. The muscles were then sewn and shaped, forming a stump to cushion the bone. Nerves were divided and carefully placed to avoid causing pain, and the skin was closed over the muscles to complete the stump. Temporary drains were inserted into the stump to allow blood and fluid to drain from the area for a few days while dressings and compression stockings held the stump in place.

Following the surgery, as the fog of those waking moments slowly lifted, she began to piece things back together, her memories arriving in disordered flashes. The uncontrollable sensation of falling. Her daughter dutifully wrapping and unwrapping bandages. Assortments of doctors' offices, each a sterile copy of the one before with few personal features to distinguish them. The anesthesiologist, poised with a face mask and taut headband. Nervous anticipation as the world around her began to fall away. She remembered the pain most of all, agonizing, unceasing, throbbing pain that ripped through her body.

In the days that followed her amputation, Beryl recovered in an eighth-floor hospital room overlooking University Avenue. As the hours ticked by in her empty room, she fell into a contemplative mood. She would stare out the window and watch as pedestrians rushed up and down the sidewalks along the busy stretch of road. "Those people don't even realize they're running around on legs," she thought to herself. Even watching television failed to provide enough of a distraction as her eyes drifted downward, pairs of legs in conversation with one another in episode after episode of the soap operas she watched. Beryl no longer counted herself among "those people" who thought little of the miracle of their mobility, nor the stairs and doors that lay in their path.

On the day Beryl was due to return home from hospital following her amputation, it was not Victor who picked her up but Diane and Dennis. Carefully mounting the steps together, arm in arm, they met Victor at the door. He was getting ready to leave for a date with another woman. A mournful silence fell over them in the entryway, the air charged with anger and disappointment. Victor awkwardly manoeuvred around his wife, and as Diane helped her mother settle onto the sofa, he quietly slipped out, the click of the door signifying what should have been the end.

One day, not long after Beryl returned from hospital, Diane boarded the subway and, as she sat down, she looked up. There was her father sitting directly opposite her with a woman thirty years his junior. Blood drained from Victor's face as the shame washed over him before he and the young woman exited at the next stop. Diane returned home, packed her father's belongings in a paper bag and hung them on the door. When he arrived later, Diane met him outside. "Get the hell out and don't come back!" she shouted at him.

He slept elsewhere that night, but eventually made his way back home. Victor pleaded with Beryl, telling her he'd never do it again. And eventually, she let him back in. Throughout Beryl's recovery, Victor would repeatedly come home drunk after spending time with other women, each time Beryl admitting him back into their lives. Diane was disgusted with her father's behaviour, especially at a time when her mother needed him most. "He kept telling her, 'I love you. I'll never do it again. Blah blah blah.' He tried for a long time to get back with her."

––––––––––––

Psychological reactions to amputation vary greatly depending on a person's life and medical history, including whether an amputation was planned or happened unexpectedly due to trauma. For most, the primary reaction to amputation is defined by a sense of loss. Loss of function as individuals discover they can no longer perform tasks the same way, and a loss of self-image as they grapple with permanent changes to their body. About a third of amputees struggle with depression, decreased self-esteem, and social isolation, often tied to a loss of independence, employment, and relationships. A period of grieving typically follows a five-stage pattern that begins with denial and anger, then bargaining, depression, culminating in acceptance.

A Sunday morning marked the first time Beryl decided to leave the house following her amputation, venturing out to go to church. Dressed in her new turquoise winter coat, leaning on Diane for support, they shuffled to the bus stop on Oakwood Avenue. As they slowly approached, a woman and her child stood waiting at the stop. The child stared at Beryl then bent down to examine the anomaly beneath her coat. "Hey lady, where's your other leg?" It was an innocent question with no hint of malice. The moment might have passed without much thought as so many similar moments would come to pass whenever Beryl was out in public. But her amputation was still a new thing to her. She blushed and stammered out a reply, but her sensitivity got the better of her. Frazzled, embarrassed, and choking back tears, she turned and hobbled back home.

A few days later, Diane prepared dinner for the family, then left for an evening shift at Hunt's Bakery. Around seven o'clock, she had a terrible feeling something was wrong at home. She called and the phone rang and rang with no answer. "I'm sorry, but I have to go home right away," she told her boss. Diane hopped on the next bus and ran home as fast as she could. Flinging open the front door, she heard a loud thump. An empty bottle of painkillers went spinning across the room as Beryl slumped onto the tiled floor. "Mum!" Diane shrieked, rushing in to cradle her mother's head in her arms. Beryl was unconscious and her skin was cold, as if she had just emerged from an icy bath. No one else was home, so Diane dialled zero, breathlessly begging the telephone operator to be connected to ambulance dispatch.[2] Beryl was still breathing slowly, her pupils replaced by bottomless black pools that reflected Diane's worried expression back at her. Paramedics soon arrived and pumped Beryl's stomach with a slurry of activated charcoal to absorb whatever toxins had not already trickled into her bloodstream. By the time she arrived at hospital, her normal respiration rate of approximately sixteen breaths per minute had declined to around six breaths per minute.

Miraculously, Beryl survived the attempted suicide. Ironically, it was her body's dependency on the painkillers that ultimately prevented her from overdosing before help could arrive. Beryl later recounted the episode to an interviewer. "Some days I did not even bother getting dressed. I never answered the phone. Finally, I got so depressed one night that I grabbed the bottle of pills on my bedside table and decided to kill myself."

When she awoke in hospital the next day, she turned to her daughter. "I'm not a mother. I'm only half a person," she cried in a raspy whisper, her throat still raw from the exertions of the paramedics.

"You don't need legs to be a mother," Diane reassured her. "You know we all love you. You will always be our mum."[3]

7.
Six Years of Pain

After Beryl's injury in 1965, the Ontario Workers' Compensation Board enrolled her in an outpatient program at the Downsview Rehabilitation Hospital. Since Beryl's injury occurred in the workplace, she qualified for benefits so long as she completed her mandatory rehabilitation program. Injured worker advocate Steve Mantis remembers life at Downsview. He was forced to attend the hospital in 1978 when, as a twenty-eight-year-old carpenter from Thunder Bay, he lost his left arm in a winch accident.[1] "What I was really struck by when I first went to Downsview was the mixed messaging. On the one hand, it's rehabilitation and the other hand it's policing. I found people were being assessed as to whether they were really hurt or not. I remember we had a new doctor who was dedicated to the amputees. I introduced myself to her because I thought she's an important person to have a relationship with over time. She said to me, 'Boy, so glad to be here on the amputee ward. I know these people are really hurt.' I did not challenge her, but I thought, 'Wow, you're a doctor and you approach your patients with that attitude.'" Mantis said amputees were given special treatment at Downsview. "At mealtime, they'd have hundreds of people lined up down the hall. Amputees did not have to wait in the lineup. We'd go straight to the front and right to our table like we were special."

Built in 1958 at Keele and Wilson in North York, the hospital featured a sprawling campus of austere modernist buildings connected by long green linoleum corridors, the kind of sterile institutional environment that defined 1950s-era hospital environments. Acres of lawn surrounded the facility allowing for the performance of outdoor physical and occupational therapy exercises during the non-winter months. Two decommissioned railway boxcars stood seemingly abandoned in a back field, filled with boxes of varying size, shape, and weight. The boxcars had specially built staircases to allow entry and exit of a procession of injured workers who would continually load and unload the boxes onto the containers, as if preparing for the arrival of a train that would never come.

The cold institutional feeling of the place was enhanced when the entire site was enclosed by a tall steel fence and security gate controlling outside access to the campus, or possibly to keep would-be delinquents from escaping during program hours. Injured workers would dress in a uniform of jeans and blue T-shirts to distinguish them from staff who wore white shirts, an administrative innovation that created an environment not dissimilar from a psychiatric hospital or medium-security prison. A clinic section served those with relatively minor injuries and a separate hospital section was reserved for those with severe conditions, such as back injuries and amputations. Attendance was compulsory for anyone in the province of Ontario requiring rehabilitation and in receipt of workers' compensation benefits, meaning many injured workers had to travel hundreds of miles away from their homes and families to keep their benefits.

Life at Downsview was highly regimented, a full calendar of physio and occupational therapy constituting the day's work. Most patients had the same goal: to get in and out as quickly as possible. Many injured workers were focused on getting approval from the doctors that their course of rehabilitation was finished so they could return home to their lives and families. Beryl was no different. She progressed through her physical therapy program, carefully heeding the warning that amputation had not entirely removed the prospect of devastating blood clots that could reappear at any time. But she was determined to adapt and regain control over her life. The faster she progressed through the program, the sooner she could be fitted for a prosthetic leg and figure out how to craft a new life for herself.

Since Beryl lived locally, she wasn't required to reside on campus but was still expected to be on-site from 9:00 a.m. to 5:00 p.m. and actively participate in all assigned rehabilitation activities. Rules on the Downsview campus were strictly enforced and any deviation risked financial penalties and possible withdrawal of benefits. Punch cards were used to monitor patients' movement through the facilities and to ensure all activities were being attended. Often, injured workers who skipped an activity or failed to show up would have their benefit cheques docked a day or half a day as punishment. After hours, residents would leave their crowded dorms that slept six to ten people at a time and migrate to the recreation room to play games, watch sports, and socialize. People were constantly being assessed about their fitness to return to work, and surveillance of residents continued in these off hours. One particularly egregious expression of power and surveillance came in the form of a two-way mirror in the rec room that enabled staff to monitor all recreational activities, also serving as a reminder to patients they were constantly being watched.

As Beryl struggled through the pain of daily rehabilitation at Downsview, her marriage progressed in the opposite direction. Two years after her accident and the same year she lost her right leg, Beryl could no longer pretend her marriage to Victor was for the benefit of the children. His blatant philandering, drunken absences, and lack of support eroded her steadfast belief in the potential for his redemption. Diane says it took the combined intervention of herself, Dennis, and Victor Jr. to convince their mother to finally put an end to the relationship. "I remember being around sixteen or seventeen, my brother Victor had come home from the Navy. Denny, Victor, and me told her, 'That's enough. We're not putting up with this anymore. Nobody's happy.' We convinced her she needed to leave Dad for good. But he did not want to go, so we called the police."

Even with the police there, Victor refused to leave. Beryl decided that if Victor would not go, then she would leave, despite her fragile condition. Diane recalls the day they left. "I remember the policeman saying, 'Now, you're the ones that are walking out. We're supporting you, but you've decided to leave the home, right?'" At the time, there was no uniform divorce law in Canada, and Ontario hadn't updated its divorce legislation since 1930, meaning many women had few options when seeking a divorce. A husband could allege adultery whereas a wife must allege adultery plus other grounds. Divorce law in Canada wasn't overhauled at the federal level until the following year, when both spouses were put on more equal footing.[2] Experienced Toronto police officers responding to a domestic dispute in 1967 would have taken extra care to determine whether Beryl was voluntarily leaving the home, knowing this was an issue that might be resurrected later as a second grounds for defence in a possible divorce proceeding. If Beryl was being forced out of her home, she could ostensibly use this fact and Victor's infidelity as dual grounds for divorce. But if she was leaving voluntarily her consent to the officer's question could be used in defence of Victor to deny her spousal support, should she later sue him civilly. It's uncertain what arrangement they later worked out between themselves, but it does not appear to have involved the court system.

Beryl, Diane, and Dennis found a cheap apartment in a low-rise building at Dufferin and Eglinton, not far from a Methodist Episcopal Church. Unlike the quiet surrounds of Holland Park Avenue, traffic roared outside their windows, the noise seeping through and thundering against the outside wall to their three-bedroom flat. Beryl and Victor remained married until 1971, when their divorce was finalized so he could marry his new fiancée, Eva Cameron. Victor had deeply hurt his family, but Diane would still invite him to Christmas, New Year's, and other celebrations so long as he refrained from drinking. He was amicable with Beryl during these occasions, but years of neglect and betrayal could never fully repair the broken trust and disaffection.

A few weeks after Beryl moved into their new apartment, she made a connection with a fellow Downsview patient. He was a French Canadian man who walked with a cane and, since he wasn't from the area, he stayed on campus. Downsview patients housed at the hospital would take any opportunity to leave campus after hours to get away from the monotony and surveillance. Beryl lived only fifteen minutes away by car and, now separated from Victor, felt emboldened to invite friends to the apartment on weekends. It began slowly with this one companion, and Beryl enjoyed the distraction, company, and attention. But word got around, others tagged along, and soon it was out of Beryl's control. There would be drinking and partying, which Beryl did not like. But there was also enjoyment in the relaxed company and the attention from men, both much lacking in her recent years. There does not appear to have been sexual relationships with the men who followed her home, but female patients were in the minority at Downsview and therefore the subject of a lot of attention from the men. "At that point it was overwhelmingly men at Downsview," observes Steve Mantis. "So, when you got a lot of men and a few women, you can imagine, there's a lot of attention paid to the women by the guys."

Beryl had experienced years of Victor's physical and emotional abandonment and relished the opportunity to make new friends. But she was not practised at setting and enforcing boundaries in this unfamiliar social situation. The men were also escaping their own sense of isolation at Downsview, displaced far from their homes and looking for a place to party off-campus, away from the prying eyes of staff and doctors.

When strange men began lurking the hallways and peeking into the bedrooms at night, Diane, now in her late teens, decided she had had enough. Infuriated at the invasion of her privacy, she decided to move out, and her then boyfriend Dave helped her find an apartment. Beryl was defensive at first but then realized Diane was almost an adult and could make her own decisions about where she wanted to live, especially given the difficult situation in which they now found themselves. Dave worked for the Canadian National Institute for the Blind, better known as the CNIB. He got Diane a job there as a book-keeper, a moment of serendipity and a harbinger of things to come, considering her mother's ongoing journey through the healthcare system. While Beryl was still in and out of hospital, Diane found her mother and brother a cheaper apartment near Avenue and Davenport Roads, not far from her own place at Dufferin and Eglinton. Beryl and Dennis's new apartment was similarly located in a traffic corridor near a busy intersection on the first floor of a low-rise building, the constant rumble of cars and motorcycles not much better than the apartment they had just vacated. The turmoil contributed to Beryl's ongoing struggle with depression. "It was a very traumatic time for me. I just lay on the chesterfield making life miserable for myself and everybody else," she later admitted.[3]

Beryl apologized to Diane, realizing she had lost control over the situation with the men she brought home. Years later, Diane reflects on that time in her mother's life. She was surprised her mother would let someone like that man into their house given his drinking and the friends he brought with him to party. In retrospect, however, she could see her mother was grasping for something lacking in her life. "He obviously gave my mum something that my dad did not, especially companionship and caring. They probably had lunch together a few times and he gave her that comfort that she needed."

———————————

Diane did not let any of this slow her down. After years of caring for her mother, brother, and father, she was ready to move on with her life. At her new job at the CNIB, it wasn't long before her attention turned toward the handsome accounting supervisor with an attractive Latino accent. (Diane had, by this time, put some distance between herself and Dave.) This new young man's name was George Juda, a clean-cut, sweet young Venezuelan man with a great sense of humour and a kind smile, later decorated by a chevron moustache. Men and women often sat separately in the cafeteria, so Diane and George would make eyes at each other across the room, Diane giggling with her workmates. They would meet later to play shuffleboard in the lower floors, kindling their budding romance. George's family was of Catholic Polish and Lithuanian descent, originally hailing from Krakow, Poland. He was born in Roth, Germany, but by the time he was three months old they were on a boat to Venezuela where George grew up before immigrating to Canada in 1961 with his mother and grandmother, both named Maria. As a result, George did not speak much English at first, but that wasn't a problem for Diane. By 1968, they got an apartment together at Pape and Danforth in Toronto's Greektown. Meeting George marked the beginning of a transition in Diane's life as she asserted more independence from her mother and the accompanying care needs.

On November 22, 1968, Diane and George married. Beryl was in hospital and unable to attend the ceremony. Her medical ordeal continued to unfold as pain wracked her body. The newlyweds, still dressed from the wedding, went to Beryl's bedside at Mount Sinai Hospital. George, impeccable, was outfitted in a pinstripe tuxedo, blue tie, and white carnation, a symbol of purity and good luck. Diane was luminescent in a white embroidered bridal gown, her veil pinned back by a satin bow into a strawberry blond pixie cut, a corsage of white carnations brightening the otherwise sterile room. The gown was altered in the front to allow extra room for an increasingly conspicuous baby bump that seemed to grow by the day.[4] A wicker bassinet, handmade by CNIB workers, awaited their first child, born in 1969, whom they would name Michelle. Beryl lay in bed in a pink gown gazing adoringly at the couple, her tousled hair and clammy jaundiced skin an ever-present reminder of her poor health. There was unmistakable joy in the room, but also sadness, concern, and regret. There would be more missed life events when Beryl was in hospital recovering from yet another surgery, but in the simplicity of the hospital room, about as far as one could get from a celebratory environment, Diane shared with her mother the most important part of any wedding; love, pride, and hope for a better future.

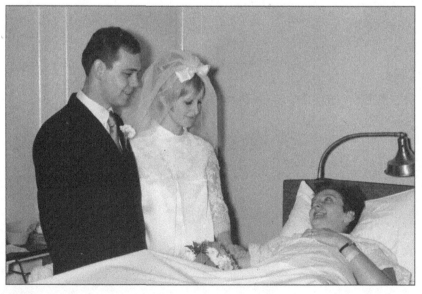

George, Diane, and Beryl, 1968. Beryl Potter personal collection. Reproduced with permission.

8.
Addicted

Beryl took a heavy prescription of the powerful opioid narcotic Demerol to cope with the ceaseless pain. She began taking the painkillers soon after her initial accident and the volume of pills tracked the escalating pain she experienced. She was already familiar with the pull of addictive cravings that accompanied her regular morphine treatments during her battle with migraines, so she was reluctant to take more painkillers, but she knew she could not survive without them either. Diane never witnessed her mother passed out on sedatives, but she could see that whatever pain the pills took away, they were also compromising her mother's mental health. Large daily doses of sedatives numbed more than Beryl's physical suffering. The brown-tinted glass bottles of tiny white pills offered her an emotional escape, temporarily transporting her to another place where the despair and uncertainty of her declining health was bathed in a drowsy fog.

Like morphine, Demerol is typically discouraged for long-term active use. Beryl developed a dependency on the drug within weeks after her first surgery, and soon she was unable to bear the pain without the drug's constant presence in her bloodstream.[1] She later talked about her struggle with addiction as a warning to others. "I became addicted to the painkiller Demerol. I'd ask for them and even demand them simply because I knew my doctor's signature would make them available to me. Doctors are far too easy with medication. The withdrawal from those drugs caused me more stress and discomfort than the actual amputations."[2]

Stuck in bed for days, months, years, Beryl watched endless hours of televised melodrama. "It was very depressing, and I was addicted to soap operas. You know, from ten in the morning to four in the afternoon, I was absorbed in that box." The flickering television screen with familiar characters that segued from one program to the next provided a reassuring structure to the day. She once confessed to a documentarian that she also began having terrible dreams. "Oh, I used to have really bad nightmares. One was, I had a picture of my granddaughter as a baby for my hospital room and she was standing in her crib, playing with a little toy. The next thing I could see was that she was playing with my hand and the blood was all over her face and she was laughing and swinging it around. The blood was flying. It was horrible." Another dream was more existential. "I had this man around my arm. We were walking downtown, and we were both blind. And we walked into a pool of water and were so warm. Oh, it was so beautiful. Then, all of a sudden, I could see, and my eyes were open, and it was blood that we were walking around in. And I wanted to lead him out. I kept saying, 'No, you've got to come out.' And he said, 'No, no. I like this,' while I was pulling him and trying to lead him out."

Beryl rarely complained about anything, even during the worst of her medical ordeal, but after her amputations, she would sometimes scream as a stabbing pain sparked in her legs or arm, as if tortured by an invisible enemy. "I have phantom pain," she later explained in an interview. Eventually she learned how to manage it. "By tapping the end of the stump, I can numb the nerve that's causing that pain and just keep tapping it until the pain disappears."[3]

Despite encouragement from friends and family, Beryl became convinced her life was effectively over. "It was during these six years of pain and despair that I came face to face with an indescribable fear; I was slowly losing my body, and because of my addiction, losing the respect of my family, and because my husband could not accept what happened to me, he turned to alcohol," wrote Beryl, convinced she was the cause of Victor's alcohol fuelled betrayal.[4] She internalized most of her feelings of inadequacy, quietly resenting herself for not being able to take better care of her kids, believing it was her fault. She no longer felt like an active participant in life, but a spectator, one whose medical problems had ruined her family beyond repair. She had prided herself on being a good wife and mother, but now it had fallen apart. Being assisted with bathing and dressing was distressing and undignified to her. Those physically assisting her would often accidentally touch a private part of her body. "It was embarrassing and very hard for her to rely on others like that," Diane remembers.[5]

Beryl was increasingly engaged in negative self-talk, constantly needling herself with endless despairing questions. "Is this my life now?" "How can I be a real mother to my children?" "How am I supposed to support myself?" "Will I ever walk again?" As the questions piled up in her mind, especially during long hospital stays, the trauma of intensive care began to take a serious toll on her mental health. Thoughts of ending her life again returned. The Demerol did not discourage these feelings. Opioid use disorders were not well understood in the 1960s, but subsequent studies demonstrate strong correlations between opioid use and suicidal ideation, including increased suicide attempts and planning, partly because people have access to a drug that can be used to kill them. At high enough doses, Demerol and other opioids suppress the hormones in the brain that control the involuntary drive to breathe, making them dangerous for either acute or chronic use.[6] Beryl likely knew the drugs were compromising her mental health but could not see another way to cope. She sunk further and further into despair. "I was depressed, unhappy, and hurting inside because of what I had done to my children's lives," she later wrote.[7]

Around 1968, Beryl's depression and clouded judgment led her to thoughts of planning another suicide attempt. Each time she went under the surgeon's knife, she began to pray for release from the torture. "What have I done to deserve this?" she wept to herself. One day, complaining of pain, she convinced Dennis to get her more painkillers from the pharmacy. She amassed a quantity of pills and took them all at once. She fell asleep, only to wake up later in a restless fever. The heavy doses of opioids and other drugs coursing through her body likely prevented another intentional overdose, now the second time she was spared from an attempt to end her life. It seemed she had power over nothing, even the decision to end her own pain. So, with no options, she resigned herself to the sadness and pain that enveloped her.

9.
Taxi

Sunnybrook Hospital was a former military hospital that only a few years earlier, in 1966, had transitioned to become a teaching hospital run by the University of Toronto. It featured the top prosthetics department in the city and Downsview amputee patients were typically sent there to access the prosthetics clinic. Approximately one month into her post-amputation rehab program, Beryl hailed a taxi to take her to Sunnybrook to be fitted for a new prosthetic leg. It was one of those appointments that filled many new amputees with a combination of exhilaration and dread as ill-fitting prosthetics could inflict new kinds of pain and pressure on tender stumps. It also typically marked the start of a new phase of recovery, another step toward independence, something Beryl desperately yearned for.

Staring out the backseat window, filled with nervous anticipation, suddenly a car slammed into her taxi. The short twenty-minute ride to the prosthetics clinic ended instead at the emergency department. "Talking of freaky accidents, it was the freakiest of them all," she later remembered.[1] Her body slammed into the door, her left leg caught behind the seat. Much like Beryl's initial fall, it was a relatively minor accident and would have been entirely forgettable, if not for her propensity to develop blood clots. Doctors said the incident was enough to cause a resurgence of thrombophlebitis, this time in her left leg. A familiar pattern of swelling and pain followed as a new blood clot cut off circulation in her remaining leg.

Six months after her first amputation in 1967, Beryl was prepped for another above-the-knee amputation. The surgery was successful but came with unexpected complications. During her immediate recovery, the application of a dirty bandage resulted in the development of an uncontrollable staphylococcus infection. "The problem was compounded by an orderly's mistake," Beryl explained, recounting the agonizing series of events that forced her back to the surgeon's table again and again. "He took off the dressing, and it fell on the floor. Without thinking, he picked it up and put it back on again. As a result, I ended up with a staph infection, had forty operations to my hip and spent a whole year lying on my side."[2]

One day when Diane was visiting her mother, she was horrified to discover live maggots wiggling and crawling all over the infected leg.[3] Shock quickly turned to fury as she interrogated the doctors and nurses about the level of care her mother was receiving. Over the next twelve months, Beryl fought a losing battle with the infection as it crept across her body, boils swelling and erupting like active volcanoes leaving open sores that scarred her skin. The bacteria slowly poisoned her blood, the risk of fatal septicemia resulting in multiple courses of antibiotics and at least forty operations. The fresh wound of the amputation continually fell apart as infection set in, requiring surgeons to scrape away more and more infected tissue and bone.

In 1969, orthopedic and vascular surgeons decided further amputation was required up to the hipbone on her left side. It was a highly dangerous and invasive surgical procedure that involved cutting through all the muscles around the femur head, disarticulating the femur and ligament from the hip joint leaving the pelvis intact. The surgery was, and remains, extremely rare, generally considered only as a last resort for uncontrolled infections, malignant bone tumours, or extensive trauma.[4] It also carried a high risk of mortality, especially for patients like Beryl with vascular diseases. Forced to negotiate an impossible bargain, her life hanging in the balance, Beryl had no other choice but to proceed and hope she would survive the hours long procedure.

Diane and Dennis marked time impatiently in the waiting room, hoping for an end to their mother's endless torture. Eventually, a surgeon emerged to announce the procedure was a success. But Beryl would pay a heavy price. Post-operative hip disarticulation patients generally have a relatively short window of time to become ambulatory, if ever. Energy expenditure for such patients to regain mobility increases up to 90 per cent, meaning it takes much more energy to move the body. Rehabilitation of a prosthetic hip socket fitted with prosthetic legs and feet required painful courses of physiotherapy. But given Beryl's circulatory issues and risk of a resurgence of deep vein thrombosis, she was instructed to remain bedridden to avoid risking the production of more deadly blood clots.[5] The lifesaving decision also deprived her of any chance of walking independently again.

Beryl stirred in her bed, groggy and slightly dazed. Willing her heavy eyelids to open, she squinted to reveal the familiar outlines of a hospital recovery room. She inhaled, drawing in the sharp nauseating scent of disinfectant that permeated the space. Looking toward her open door, an endless parade of strangers click-clacked up and down the hallway, reminding her of the sound that announced the arrival of her teachers in grade school. Murmured conversation accompanied the hurried passage of men clad in white coats and women in rustling white skirts and caps. Light streamed in from a window, its curtains impossibly out of reach, illuminating the walls and linoleum floors, both a sickly shade of green. She hated green walls, but at least this time she had a window.

Thin white curtains hung from the finicky ceiling track encircling her cold metal bed. She knew from past battles with similar contraptions that no amount of tugging would budge them, so she left them alone. Instead, she reached up, instinctively pushing the arm of the light fixture away from her head. An armchair sat in the corner facing her, its indented vinyl cushions revealing countless hours of use. A television sat perched on a metal frame across the room staring back at her, its blank screen reflecting a warped version of the sparsely furnished room. Noticing the remote control on her side table, she fumbled with the device to see if she had a television that worked. Next to her on the nightstand sat a rotary phone with a set of instructions in bafflingly tiny lettering that required close study. She had been in so many rooms like this before. Looking up again she noticed a glass IV-drip bottle suspended from a metal pole. She traced the intravenous line down her arm and remembered the pain started in her leg. Reaching down to soothe the lingering aching stabs reignited by her memory, her fingertips traced the edges of her right thigh until they touched the edges of heavy gauze. She reached for her left thigh, also wrapped in gauze. She recoiled slightly before continuing further until her fingers found empty space where her legs used to be, wondering how it was possible for pain to come from emptiness.

As the reality of her future as a wheelchair user dawned on her, Beryl had little time to grieve the loss of her legs. For months, she was forced to lie on her right side to allow the wound surrounding her transected left hip to heal. This, too, had horrendous consequences. In the late 1960s, effective deep vein thrombosis prevention was less developed than today's standards of care where evidence of it under a surgeon's direct supervision could be considered tantamount to medical malpractice. Beryl was likely put on a steady heparin IV drip, an anticoagulant meant to prevent clotting, and her stumps were wrapped in elastic compression and adhesive strapping. But the constant pressure of having to lie on her right side, coupled with this extended period of low mobility, left her with a seriously compromised cardiovascular system. Soon, blood clots began to form in her right arm, blooming into the terribly familiar painful swelling. The exhausting dance with death seemed endless, her body exposed to new threats on a near constant basis. "Will this ever stop?" she wondered.

In 1970, Beryl's right arm was amputated above the elbow. Since she was right-handed, it meant she would have to relearn how to do everything with her left hand, including manipulating an electric wheelchair when someone wasn't pushing her. Recuperating from the surgery that took her right arm, a dark cloud descended on her once again. Locked in the incessant battle with an invisible enemy, she became ever more mournful and depressed. There were more infections and more blood clots, the counter-offensive arsenal of antibiotics, blood thinners, and pain meds waging a losing battle with her declining health.

In 1971, a bit of plaque or a small blood clot travelled up to the artery of her right eye, constricting the blood vessels to her retina causing an "eye stroke," or retinal artery occlusion. The resulting scar tissue caused permanent blindness in her right eye. The eye was eventually replaced with a glass eye. "I was completely blind for three days, but fortunately, the sight came back in one eye," she later described.[6] In the context of her series of cardiovascular crises, Beryl's blindness was possibly another consequence of her childhood bout of rheumatic fever that left her with an irregular heartbeat, or arrhythmia. The smooth valves of her heart were hardened by the fever, the inflammation creating the conditions that allowed clots to form later in life.

Beryl may also have suffered from an underlying genetic or acquired hypercoagulable state that increased the likelihood of her to develop blood clots. When the body is severely inflamed, patients in her condition can develop disseminated intravascular coagulation in which blood clots form throughout the body blocking small blood vessels. If Beryl had a congenital condition, such as hemophilia or Von Willebrand disease, she probably would have known about it earlier in life. It was more likely, then, that the unique constellation of circumstances surrounding her initial fall—the untimely taxi accident, the staph infection, heart damage from the childhood fever, and long periods of immobility due to successive surgeries—each coalesced and contributed in their own way to the cascade of events during those long six years in and out of hospital.[7]

Beryl later alluded to another factor that contributed to her blindness. Apparently, she had an allergy to iodine. It's possible she discovered the allergy in the early 1960s when she was struggling with migraines, the doctors and nurses using antiseptic iodine patches to sanitize her skin for injection. In 1970 when she was battling infection following her hip disarticulation, the battery of antiseptic drugs doctors prescribed likely included iodine. It's possible doctors did not know about the risk of iodine toxicity to the retina,[8] or the risk was weighed against the potentially lethal spread of the infection. Whatever the contributing causes, it was later discovered Beryl's right ocular artery was damaged and she would remain permanently blind in that eye.

Confronted with roadblock after roadblock in her journey toward recovery, Beryl dug deep within herself, summoning a reserve of willpower that is often only available to those who have survived prior hardship. As her limbs and senses were claimed one by one, somehow, she found the energy to mentally adapt to her altered reality despite her deepening depression. "I was just getting rid of all my spare parts," was a line she often repeated, a darkly humorous narrative she invented to take back control over the reality of her uncontrollable deteriorating health.

Beryl decided she could figure out how to navigate the world from a wheelchair, but to her, blindness was an entirely different reality, and not one she was prepared to accept at first. How could vision ever be considered a spare part? In a fit of despair, she attempted to overdose on painkillers again, the third attempt on her own life. As with previous suicide attempts, her body's dependency on the opioids meant she simply blacked out and woke up the next morning with a serious headache, dry mouth, and fever. She later reflected on her feelings of hopelessness to an interviewer. "I just wanted to die. I just did not want to go on living anymore." Contemplating the possibility of life nearly without any limbs and compromised vision truly scared her.

Beryl struggled to reorient herself in the aftermath of multiple amputations, a mental and physical trauma that would be insurmountable to most people. Her ordeal forced her to constantly come up with a new vision of life after she got better, adjusting her expectations about the loss of function that accompanied each amputation, not to mention the radical change in her appearance and physiology. The unrelenting and successive nature of her medical journey must have felt like a never-ending onslaught, a constant attack that would have caused post-traumatic stress in the strongest of minds. With her life perpetually hanging in the balance, it was difficult to imagine what future awaited her should she survive all of this, and whether she'd even want what was offered. Later, she summed up her feelings about this time to an interviewer. "I thought, 'This can't happen to me, you know, it's not happening. I'm going bit by bit.'"[9]

10.
Life After

After a final suicide attempt in 1971, Beryl refused to take any more opioid painkillers. She could now see what it was doing to her mind, so she rode the sweaty, nauseous wave of withdrawal under hospital supervision for the next forty-eight hours, followed by three weeks of sleepless nights.[1] "When I finally came out of the hospital for good, I miraculously lost all desire for drugs," she later said.

When suicide failed to deliver the release she yearned for, she became introspective about the purpose of her survival. "The doctor told me I could not be rehabilitated. I was told I could only live at home if I had a full-time nurse-housekeeper. He said I would never be able to do anything for myself, or even sit up for any length of time." Considering the prognosis, she became introspective. "Why am I still alive?" she wondered. "What do I have to live for?"

Recovering from the operation that removed her eye at Sunnybrook, Beryl openly shared her quest for meaning with the hospital chaplain. Baptist Pastor Bob Rumball visited Beryl often over the six long years she spent in and out of hospital. He had a sturdy build, with a short crop of curly brown hair, broad nose, piercing blue eyes, and full lips that when parted in smile revealed a wide gap between his front teeth. Rumball was also a former Canadian Football League halfback for the Toronto Argonauts and champion of the d/Deaf and hard-of-hearing communities since 1956 when he established a church at 56 Wellesley Street in downtown Toronto to minister to the spiritual and social needs of the Deaf. He also served as chaplain at several downtown hospitals where he repeatedly encountered Beryl in recovery from her various surgeries. Five years her junior, Rumball was a plain-speaking and friendly conversationalist. They would chat about Beryl's life before her accident, her gritty roots in working-class Liverpool, her loneliness since leaving her husband, and the struggle of coping with her deteriorating health. Rumball's no-nonsense attitude and down-to-earth style endeared him to Beryl, and they quickly became friends.

Beryl confessed her desperation to Rumball, heavy gauze still shielding her right eye socket as tears streamed down her cheeks. He sat next to her on the bed, placing his heavy mitt of a hand on her shoulder. "You want to feel sorry for yourself? Okay, come with me," he winked, motioning toward the hallway. Positioning his burly frame next to her bedside like he was still a halfback bracing for a pass, he helped Beryl transfer to a wheelchair and pushed her down the hall. They entered a common area filled with other amputees and people with disabilities socializing and playing games together. "You see, there is life after disability. Even someone with one arm and one eye has something to give," he told her.

She would later describe it as her moment of revelation. After her talk with Rumball, while in hospital and in outpatient rehabilitation clinics, Beryl began actively getting to know others around her. Hearing their life stories, interests, goals, and challenges made her feel part of a new peer group. She experienced a metamorphosis in her attitude toward disability and a renewed perspective on her own future, crediting Pastor Rumball for lighting the flame that led her out of the gloom of suicidal depression. His example of disability advocacy also laid the foundation for what would become her new purpose and mission in life.

Beryl attended church occasionally before her accident, but she did not consider herself all that religious. After her seemingly miraculous survival, however, she embraced her spiritual side more freely, even consulting the Bible from time to time. "The big guy up there did this to me for a reason. He's got a plan," she wrote later in life. "God's gift to me is life, and it is what I do with this life that will be my gift to Him."[2] She expanded on her thoughts in a later interview. "God never gives us a cross heavier than we can bear. He's always been there. I've been very, very close to death. There'd even been nights when Dennis had been called into the hospital [to say goodbye]. But somebody's always there looking after me. Somebody's always there bringing me out of it. I can't help what I feel. I really feel that this was for a reason."[3]

Within months of her talk with Rumball and beginning to visit other amputees in the late 1960s, she started receiving invitations to speak at different churches about the role of God in her life. She obliged these requests, but then often carried on with a lecture about the inaccessibility of most churches and how they should do something about it, a message that likely received a mixed response by audiences expecting to hear a purely inspirational story.

––––––––––

Once Beryl discovered the spark that inspired her to carry on, Dennis became her cheerleader, showing up for her with daily doses of motivation and support. Back at home in their apartment, working to put her suicidal thoughts and depression behind her, she learned to adjust to a new domestic life. "Dennis fired the housekeeper and started to encourage me to do things for myself," she told one columnist. One night while Dennis was at work, Beryl decided to clean the apartment, later describing this as the beginning of her quest to take back her independence. "I was determined I was going to make it, so when Dennis went to work one night, I think it was sheer willpower that made me do it. I pulled all the furniture out into the middle of the room—I don't know how I got it there—and I vacuumed. But then I could not get it back, and I sat there, and I was crying and I phoned Dennis. It was about 3:00 in the morning. I said, 'Dennis, I can't get out of the living room. Come and help me!'"

"When I was unable to see, he helped me around. I was right-handed before my accident, and it was Dennis who brought me a pencil and made me write my name over and over. Later, he made me knit. I'd just sit for hours knitting away with one needle under my stump. I was having a problem finding comfortable clothes, so Dennis said, 'Make your own.' I scoffed at him at first but then he put a sewing machine in front of me and today I make all my own clothes. It's cheaper that way anyway." Before her accident, Beryl regularly knitted and sewed garments for Diane, making dresses and suits she would wear to work. Now, Beryl would design and create dresses that made it possible for her to dress herself and still look attractive. She adapted her sewing machine, raising the electric foot press to chest level so she could depress it with the stump of her right arm while guiding the fabric with her left hand. She eventually became so proficient that she began making clothes for other people.

Beryl shared her love of knitting and sewing with her two-year-old granddaughter, Michelle, teaching her how to sew, which inspired her creative side. Michelle was fascinated by the things her grandmother would create, receiving gifts of handmade clothes for her Barbie dolls and handmade knitted sweaters for her teddy bears. Years later, Michelle reflected on the creativity of her grandmother. "She knit me a pink and white rabbit that I still have. It still smells like her, but that's probably because she smoked so much!" In the family cottage hangs a framed needlepoint that Beryl stitched with her one arm that says, "God Bless Our Place."

As Beryl's condition stabilized, her days were now dominated by occupational and physical therapy to gain a level of physical independence while learning new adaptations along the way. With three fewer limbs and limited eyesight, she had to learn anew many of the simple tasks of daily living most people take for granted. Michelle witnessed Beryl's adaptations in action. "One time we came in and she was making her bed. It was kind of amazing. She would roll around on the mattress, hooking the fitted sheet over the side with her one hand then roll over to the next corner. It was kind of funny to watch and she would be laughing and making jokes. I thought of running over to help her but did not really need to because she obviously did it all the time herself."[4]

Beryl earned a bit of self-confidence with each new successful adaptation. "I learned to sit up. Even though doctors told me I'd never be able to sit for any length of time. I started by sitting up for an hour at a time and then for longer periods until I was eventually able to sit up for sixteen hours a day." She even gained bragging rights about her physical therapy. "These are the easiest push ups in the world," she joked as she demonstrated her one-handed push ups on her bed to a documentary crew. Diane remembers when her mother started wearing makeup again. Before she lost her right arm, she would have applied her makeup with her dominant right hand, so this was yet another thing she had to learn and it did not go as she planned the first few attempts. "She wanted to try and start wearing makeup, so we were there to help her. Well, the eyeliner pencil was going all over her face. She started laughing which got us all going. But she thought, 'I'm going to do it.' She was just so determined to do everything herself, so she just kept trying." Later, she would expertly apply her makeup with perfect ease, selecting her favourite tube of red lipstick, and patting on some blue Estée Lauder eyeshadow with her index finger.

As anyone who has undergone physical rehabilitation knows, it is the daily struggle and small accomplishments that form the building blocks of success. Even retrieving a glass of water was a struggle at first until Beryl figured out a system to fill the glass without spilling water everywhere, a feat celebrated by her son. "That first glass of water was like champagne," he told an interviewer.[5] In the months and years following her amputations as she learned how to adapt and navigate her new life after disability, Beryl achieved far more than the doctors could ever have expected. She had the love and support of her family, and Dennis stepped up in a big way. Beryl credited him as the one person largely responsible for her successful recovery and reintegration.

None of this would have been possible without Dennis's support. "If I asked him to pass me something he'd say 'What's wrong with you, get it yourself,'" Beryl told an interviewer. "I complained about not being able to buy a dress that was comfortable on my hip, so Dennis comes up with a great idea: make your own. I make all my own clothes now."[6] The final frontier for Beryl was the kitchen. She decided one day she would do something special for Dennis, as she explains to an interviewer. "He had never missed a day of visiting me in hospital and he'd done so much for me. I'd never given anything in return or stopped to think how much he had suffered. No one has asked him about his feelings. I decided that one way to say thank you was by cooking a meal. I practised for days." Peeling potatoes became her Mount Everest, each pass of the knife whittling large potatoes down to the size of peas. "A little imagination and it's surprising what can be done!" Eventually, she came up with the idea to fix a potato in place with the sharp end of a few nails as she removed and replaced it on the nails with one hand until it was fully peeled. "Finally, the meal was ready. The look of amazement on Dennis's face when he came home from work was all the encouragement I needed. There were tears in his eyes. He sort of laughed and cried, and he was angry for me doing it. The whole thing wrapped in, well, I guess it was pride."[7] New modified gadgets started populating the drawers in her kitchen, many of them homemade, including magnetized wands to access cans of food. Nothing was off limits now.

Reflecting on her six years in hospital, Beryl decided to affirm her commitment to a new life after disability. Echoing those first encouraging words from Pastor Bob Rumball, she told herself, "Hey Beryl, you're alive. Be thankful. It may not be much of a life, but my goodness, you can make something out of it."[8]

11.

Nostalgia

For forty years of her life, Beryl navigated the world as a relatively healthy, able-bodied person. She never struggled to find an accessible entrance or washroom. People did not stare at her as she went down the street. No one ever offered unsolicited prayers. She never had to field awkward questions from strangers about her body. She never felt the need to put at ease others who were uncomfortable in her presence. She never had to endure the patronizing tone of those who questioned her comprehension of what was being said to her. It was as if she now encountered the world for the first time, venturing out as a middle-aged triple amputee wheelchair user with a visual impairment. Previously unseen barriers lurked around every corner. Sidewalks without curb cuts, doors without automatic buttons, inaccessible washrooms, and a lack of elevators. Access to restaurants, cafés, grocery stores, offices, and other public amenities each came with their own set of complications that needed to be navigated. Most buses and subways were out of reach and paratransit services were virtually nonexistent in early 1970s Toronto. Then there were the social attitudes. Some people tried to be helpful, others would cross the street as if she were contagious. Those who did not know what to think would simply gawk, studying her as if she were an unusual art installation sprung to life.

Beyond adapting to life as a disabled person in an inaccessible world, a series of other important life events happened to Beryl during this time. On April 3, 1971, her mother, Amy, died at Rathbone Hospital in Liverpool. Amy was eighty years old and struggled with Parkinson's disease, her death resulting from complications from terminal bronchopneumonia and "gangrenous bedsores."[1] It had been almost two decades since Beryl had last seen her mother in person, but the time and distance did nothing to diminish her devastation, their loving mother-daughter bond still stretched tightly across the Atlantic. Beryl was particularly upset that she was unable to attend her mother's funeral because she was still in hospital recovering from eye surgery. Amy had done so much to provide for her daughter the kind of tools she was now using to survive, her example of resiliency fortifying Beryl with the resolve to rebuild her life.

In 1971, Beryl's divorce from Victor was also finalized. Prior to the introduction of the Divorce Act (1985), couples seeking a divorce due to marriage breakdown were required to live apart for at least three years. Around 1969, Victor fell in love with Eva Cameron, a sweet-natured, petite woman who worked as a registered nurse. The official conclusion of Victor and Beryl's marriage marked the end of a long and emotional chapter in Beryl's life. "We have found the kind of forgiveness in our hearts that we never knew existed. The children and I have been able to forgive and understand Vic," she later wrote in a speech. She would also describe him as a "very good friend,"[2]

Victor (rear left) at a family get together at the Juda house.
From left: Dennis, Michelle, Victor, Diane, Beryl, George, wife of a cousin, Victor Jr., 1985.
Beryl Potter personal collection. Reproduced with permission.

though they spent little time together and only then at occasional holidays when Victor was instructed to be on his best behaviour. In a videotaped interview many years later, she summarized the circumstances of her divorce, always putting the blame on her accident, her downcast expression revealed a deep disappointment from that dark chapter in her life.[3]

During this time, an official letter arrived in the mail sent by the Department of Citizenship and Immigration. Beneath the official letterhead in bold capital font was written "NOTICE TO APPEAR: TO TAKE THE OATH OF CITIZENSHIP" followed by a list of instructions. Beryl, Diane, and Dennis were living in Canada as permanent residents since the mid-1950s and enjoyed special treatment as British subjects under the Canadian Citizenship Act (1947). But they did not yet have the full democratic rights of naturalized Canadian citizens. In terse legal language, the letter instructed them to take the required oath or risk deportation to England. After making the necessary arrangements, the three of them attended a special citizenship ceremony in downtown Toronto. The large room was filled with chairs facing a dais where a justice of the peace sat, shrouded in a black robe, flanked by two Canadian flags. An officer of the Royal Canadian Mounted Police stood at attention, his red tunic and Stetson hat an unmistakable icon of the Canadian frontier that seemed at odds with the modern downtown Toronto setting. A large crest bearing the Arms of Canada was mounted on the wall with a crown representing the monarch, a portrait of her majesty looking down on the ceremony from a large picture stand.

As the swearing of the oath began, the justice of the peace instructed everyone to raise their right hand. Beryl exchanged an anxious sideways glance with Diane and Dennis. "But I don't have a right hand!" Beryl mouthed to Diane. Beryl lifted her left hand as they all recited in unison. "I swear (or affirm) that I will be faithful and bear true allegiance to Her Majesty Queen Elizabeth the Second, Queen of Canada, Her Heirs and Successors, and that I will faithfully observe the laws of Canada and fulfil my duties as a Canadian citizen." Afterward, they all sung the national anthem, O Canada, followed by the signing of the oaths.

Ironically, the ceremonial confirmation of her status as a Canadian citizen elicited pangs of nostalgia for Liverpool. It had been such a long time since Beryl had been back in England, and she began to reflect on all the ways her life had changed in wrenching twists and turns since arriving in Canada almost twenty years earlier. She decided she wanted to visit her hometown. In June 1971, against the strenuous advice of doctors since she was still recovering from a kidney infection and the eye surgery, she hatched a plan to visit family in England with Dennis. He was now twenty-one years old and left Liverpool as a small boy but still carried a hint of his Scouse accent—his pronunciation of "Liverpool" sounding more like *"Liva-pewl"*—though his sister Diane had shed her accent long ago.

As their airplane descended toward Speke Airport (now John Lennon Airport), Beryl traced the familiar outlines of her beloved city, piers jutting out from the docklands into the River Mersey as ships passed by, some pulled by tugboats along the Manchester canal just south of the airport. Wavertree was somewhere off to the east, motorways slicing through endless blocks of rowhouses like puzzle pieces scattered across a table. After touching down, Dennis and Beryl exited the arrival gates. "Joan!" Beryl screeched as she spotted her half sister, Joan's curled blond hair and confident expression the spitting image of their late mother. Driving north from the airport, they passed the old hosiery factory in Woolton where Victor once worked. They checked in at a local hotel where they encountered the first of many obstacles. In the early 1970s, wheelchair accessibility in Liverpool was virtually nonexistent. Most sidewalks, buildings, washrooms, buses, and trains were completely inaccessible and disability rights activists had only just begun to fight back against the status quo. In the hotel carpark, Beryl found herself trapped by a lack of any curb cuts. Her wheelchair did not fit in the hotel washroom and the use of public transport was almost impossible.

After settling in, they decided to visit Beryl's stepfather, William. Driving north on the Queens Drive motorway, Beryl spotted a white sign on a low stone wall that read "Moscow Drive," the final stop on her adolescent "moonlight flits." Some of the houses were a bit shabbier, but the neighbourhood seemed mostly frozen in time, save for the presence of newer models of cars parked along the road. The sturdy two-and-a-half storey Victorian row house at 119 Moscow Drive stood much as it always had in the centre of a long block of houses, two stone pillars and a small front gate welcoming them in. Pulling up to the house, Beryl was struck by the memory of her mother, her affectionate smile, deep-set eyes, and sturdy calloused hands, rough from decades of hard work raising nine children. They last stood together in this spot when Beryl, an able-bodied young wife and mother of three, departed for a new life in Canada.

The low curb from the roadway to the sidewalk and front steps meant Beryl had to be carried up inside the house as her stepfather William welcomed them. Now seventy-three years old and heavily bespectacled, his head atop his wiry frame carried a cap of wispy white hair. Beryl had an amicable relationship with her stepfather, who practically speaking was the only father she knew, but the absence of her mother leant a different feel to the reunion, perhaps a little awkward. The house was much as she had last seen it, full of memories, each turn stirring up flashbacks of her life as a younger woman: scrubbing and hanging endless loads of laundry with her mother in the backyard; hearty stews bubbling on the stovetop and the scent of pie baking in the oven; Christmas celebrations and special Sunday dinners; watching from the sun-drenched bay window as Diane collected her Easter basket. Unfortunately, the place also now proved quite inaccessible. She was barely able to move down the narrow corridors or navigate across rooms full of a lifetime worth of furniture, her wheelchair snagging on an obstacle each time she turned a corner. The upper storey where she had started her family with Victor was virtually impossible to visit without Herculean effort from Dennis and another sturdy helper.

Word somehow got around to the local newspaper about Beryl's story and her homecoming. A reporter from the *Liverpool Echo* interviewed Joan and Beryl about the family reunion, which produced a classic inspirational tale of triumph over misfortune that such newspapers often trafficked. "A woman of courage born and bred in Liverpool has returned to her native city. But she is no ordinary exile returning to her birthplace." The article recounted Beryl's accident story and medical nightmare, including the years of torment and successive amputations, eschewing any in-depth analysis of her situation. Joan attested to Beryl's astonishing resilience. "Despite everything she is still as cheerful as she was before her misfortunes." Beryl chimed in, telling a version of her story that emphasized her strength of character and accomplishments, as if nothing could slow her down or induce melancholy. "There's no point in being depressed by it. Life is too short. I do all my own housework. I can embroider, sew, and knit, and I dress and take care of myself completely. I bet doctors in the hospital that I would get on a double-decker bus in Liverpool, and I won the bet."[4]

Beryl visited her youngest half brother, Leslie, in Plymouth, the teenage brother she left behind now grown from a scrawny sixteen-year-old to a nearly forty-year-old man. Joan and Beryl visited Beryl's birthplace at Rose Cottage on High Street, home to all the Potter children before the death of her biological father, Charles, changed everything. The current residents allowed them in for tea and Joan snapped a picture of Beryl and Dennis on the front step. Perhaps Beryl glimpsed the room where she fought back that deadly fever, the first of many times her life hung in the balance. She hadn't lived at Rose Cottage since she was a five-year-old girl, but the memory of a life before poverty gripped their family was still etched somewhere inside her.

The sisters paid their respects at the final resting place of Charles and Amy at Holy Trinity Anglican cemetery in Wavertree, their

Dennis and Beryl in front of Rose Cottage, 1971.
Beryl Potter personal collection. Reproduced with permission.

burials separated by forty-five years. Also buried there were their other two sisters, Peggy and Connie, taken in 1937 by diphtheria. To get to the gravesites, Dennis pushed his mother in her heavy metal wheelchair through the tall wild grasses behind the neoclassical cathedral. Joan and Beryl cried together, each clutching a wad of tissues, lamenting the loss of their mother as much as the many years they had been apart. Beryl probably regretted she wasn't there when her mother needed her most, consumed as she was with her own pain. In a photograph from the visit, Joan crouches low in the grass next to Beryl's chair. Joan sports a turquoise dress, her hair in neat blond curls, kind eyes above a mournful, reluctant smile. Beryl's brunette hair shimmers in the hot summer sun. In a light blue dress and white pearls, she drapes her left arm around her sister's shoulders, an obligatory smile masking her grief and likely some discomfort from the heavy gauze covering her right eye and tensor bandage around the stump of her right arm.

Beryl wrapped up her trip refreshed by the renewed connection with family. On July 12, she and Dennis boarded a plane bound for Toronto. Jet lagged though still feeling uplifted, they took a taxi to Avenue and Davenport, the roaring traffic quickly ushering them inside their apartment building. Exhausted from the journey, they were received by piles of bills and collection letters marked "PAST DUE" and "FINAL NOTICE" cluttering the entrance as they pushed open the door. Beryl paid little attention to finances given her focus on survival and healing. But her financial problems were not going anywhere. They could have moved further afield to a cheaper suburban neighbourhood, but their rent was reasonable for its downtown location and its proximity to hospitals and rehab clinics saved on transportation costs. Beryl was frugal by nature, a fastidious coupon collector who now made all her own clothes. Dennis, on the other hand, habitually overspent and ran up expenses on their credit cards, each month's bill another meticulously documented accounting of their spiralling problem with debt.

Canada's universal healthcare system and the Workers' Compensation Board had saved them from the potentially disastrous costs of Beryl's long hospital stays and rehabilitation expenses.

Beryl was supplied with an electric wheelchair and the bathroom in her apartment was retrofitted to make it more accessible. But it was the monthly benefit cheque she collected that proved their real lifeline. Her pension was calculated according to a predefined formula: 75 per cent pre-injury earnings multiplied by the type and duration of disability, including a supplement for permanent disability.[5] The final amount was largely determined by a detailed disability rating schedule that outlined entitlements for all manner of workplace injury. Known colloquially by injured workers as a "meat chart," the schedule stipulated that a missing finger might fetch 5 per cent of pre-injury earnings, whereas a thumb earned 10 per cent. Amputated arms and legs were considered the most serious of injuries given their likelihood of permanently affecting employability. A gruesome irony was that as Beryl's condition worsened, her benefits increased, each amputated limb traced back to the original workplace injury where it all started. Following her hip disarticulation procedure, Beryl found herself at the top of the "meat chart" pyramid, a summit no one in history has ever aspired to reach.[6]

Beryl may have had the Workers' Compensation Board to thank for retrofitting her living space and providing her with a wheelchair, but she had Canada's public healthcare system to thank for preventing her from falling into bankruptcy at the outset of her injury and recovery. Acute hospital care had been covered by the federal government since 1957, and in 1966 universal public healthcare was introduced with federal and provincial governments sharing the cost of hospital and doctors' services through a general tax levy.[7] Against stiff resistance from doctors and insurance companies, universal medical care was the brainchild of New Democratic Party leader Tommy Douglas, but it took the combined and extraordinary cooperation of the NDP, Progressive Conservative leader John Diefenbaker, and the Liberal minority government of Prime Minister Lester B. Pearson to finally make it happen. The adoption of universal healthcare coverage for all citizens and permanent residents quickly became a defining feature of Canadian society.

Even so, Beryl's benefits were not enough to keep the wolf at bay. Creditors began knocking on her door, which quickly escalated to a ceaseless hammering. Twenty-four-year-old Dennis returned to work as a bellboy at Sutton Place Hotel and Beryl did her best to stretch their budget. But it was not enough to keep their head above water. In 1972, Beryl filed for bankruptcy. She was devastated and ashamed. *Bankrupt.* The word was triggering for her. It dredged up memories of her childhood poverty, a personal history she literally just toured, the frantic moves to escape landlords, her feelings of homelessness. Had she really come this far only to circle back to the kind of life she had worked so hard to escape? Beryl wondered what her deceased mother would think of her now.

Undeterred and looking for a way out of their precarious situation, Beryl decided to return to England for good. Having freshly returned from a successful and emotional visit, this must have felt right, hopeful, and even exciting. She and Dennis would stay with Beryl's older brother Charles and sister-in-law Gwen, who ran "The Swan," a pub in West Derby. When she booked her plane tickets, Beryl learned she would have to buy a third seat due to her disability. Presumably there was a safety policy that only applied to people with disabilities, but there was no legislation preventing airlines from developing and enforcing such a discriminatory policy. "The person running the charter said these people were going on vacation, and anyone sitting by me would be sick," she later recalled.[8] It was one of the first times, but not the last, that she would encounter such bold-faced discrimination. In later years she would have vigorously fought such a prejudiced policy, but she wasn't yet ready to assert herself in this way. She could not afford it, but she ponied up the money and bought the extra ticket.

In the spring of 1972, Beryl's family and friends congregated at the Sutton Place Hotel to throw a send-off party in celebration of Beryl and Dennis's transatlantic move. Beryl was joyous, wearing an empire line dress with a sleeveless white bodice and flowing blue skirt, removing her eyeglasses for the camera to show off her blue eyeshadow and radiant smile. Little Michelle danced and twirled about in a white and pink dress, her blond pigtails done just like Diane's at that age, scrunching her nose as trails of curling cigarette smoke stung her eyes from the many people smoking around her. Victor showed up with his new wife, Eva, to toast Beryl. He was dressed well for the occasion, though especially sweaty and red-faced, the joyous, well-lubricated celebration likely rounding out any lingering awkwardness between them.

Following the send-off, Beryl terminated her lease and moved their belongings into a storage facility, hoping to send for them later when they had their own place in Liverpool. A few days later, George, Diane, Norman, and sister-in-law Eva drove them to the airport. At the departure gates, they stopped for one last photo. It was a hurried moment, everyone looking slightly perplexed and unfocused as they squint into the rising sun, their expressions also perhaps conveying a hint of unease. Once in Liverpool, Beryl and Dennis settled in with brother Charles and Gwen, grateful for their support and excited at the prospect of starting over, a phrase that now defined Beryl in so many ways. Charles helped Dennis find a job as a janitor in a local secondary school as Beryl figured out what to do next.

But this was not the city Beryl left behind twenty-five years earlier. In its place stood something far grimmer. In the early 1970s, Liverpool was hit hard by a lingering recession across the UK that marked the end of postwar economic recovery.[9] Well-paying jobs were still hard to come by and the labour market remained depressed. There were small-scale riots across the city among the poor, unemployed, and immigrant population that would steadily escalate, peaking in 1981 with the deadly Toxteth riots.[10] In this environment Beryl's prospects of finding a job, let alone a well-paying one, were slim. Dennis had found a job, but it was not clear that this was the best place for him to make a new start. Although the excitement of relocating back to the UK and her extended family had proven irresistible, leaving behind what seemed like insurmountable problems, it didn't take long for a new realization to dawn.

Beryl would have understood that her out-of-country absence might lead to the cancellation of her workers' compensation benefits, though it seems the prospect of relocating to the UK was driven more by emotion than a prudential plan with all the variables worked out. She might have eventually found paid work in her country of birth, but it seemed she did not have a plan for this, and it would have been a tough road ahead to find an employer willing to hire her.

Vacations and temporary absences were typically allowed for benefit recipients, but a permanent out-of-country move was different. If Beryl remained in England, her absence would trigger a complete payout scenario where she would receive a portion of her benefits in a lump sum and cancellation of any ongoing support.[11] This meant her sole source of income and access to subsidies for her assistive equipment would disappear, and she would be on her own, even if she later moved back to Canada. She was charting a precarious course for an unlikely future in her home city. After a few months trying to reclaim the life she had left behind, Beryl decided she had made a terrible mistake and could not jeopardize her and Dennis's futures. Whatever path lay before them, it would have to be in Canada.

With their bags packed and plane tickets booked, there was just one more thing to do. Before they left Liverpool, Beryl and Dennis attended a local courthouse to file for a legal name change. They appeared before a justice of the peace, just as they had done a year earlier when they became Canadian citizens. This time, however, they wanted to formally change Beryl's married surname "Carter" back to her maiden name "Potter." While they were there, Dennis also decided to change his last name to "Potter," later admitting "I never felt like a Carter."[12] In one sense, it was a poignant proclamation of a son's allegiance and love for his mother. But it may have also had more practical considerations. Credit reporting was never a perfect system, especially in the 1970s, and changing one's surname made it easier to reset one's credit history. Having declared bankruptcy before leaving Canada, with maxed-out credit cards following them as Beryl and Dennis "Carter," there was a new opportunity in them returning Beryl and Dennis "Potter" as they endeavoured to take control of their finances.

Once again, what kind of life awaited them once they touched down in Canada was very uncertain. Though Beryl and Dennis had left to escape their creditors, it wasn't long before Dennis returned to the same pattern of borrowing and spending. They opened new credit card accounts, each new influx of loaned cash another shovelful into a deepening hole of debt. It was a centrifuge from which they would never truly escape.

12.

A New Life

In 1973, Beryl and Dennis decided it was time to find a cheaper apartment in the suburbs of Scarborough. Beryl's case worker from the Workers' Compensation Board helped them find a subsidized rent-geared-to-income apartment with a local community housing provider. Located at the corner of Markham Road, the standard red-brick building at 2180 Ellesmere Road was built to provide sixteen floors of social housing in a transit-friendly corridor with plenty of nearby parks and amenities. Once again, the Workers' Compensation Board paid for the costly installation of accessible equipment throughout the apartment, including a ceiling track that ran from the bed to a fully accessible bathroom.

With an affordable, accessible space to call her own, Beryl felt empowered to begin building a new life for her and Dennis. One of the first things they did was adopt a couple of dogs; a dachshund and Shih Tzu. Beryl loved her dogs, calling them "her kids," lap dogs that easily hopped up and down from her wheelchair or cuddled with her in bed without causing too much discomfort. It was a daily ritual for Beryl and Dennis to visit the local park to let the dogs roam and play. They also often tagged along whenever they were out on appointments, hopping onto Beryl's lap after Dennis transferred her into their brown wood-panelled station wagon. At home, Dennis would bounce a ball down the hallway to entertain them, much to the displeasure of their white tabby cat. George and Diane had a 1960s-era cottage north of Peterborough on Lower Buckhorn Lake, and Beryl and Dennis would bring their dogs when they visited. The family would pass the days easily, swimming in the cool lake waters, boating its expanses, and enjoying the beautiful sunsets. One day at the cottage, however, a German Shepherd attacked and killed the Shih Tzu, an unexpectedly traumatizing event for Beryl that left her depressed for some time after.

In Scarborough, Beryl befriended her neighbours and regularly trekked to the newly constructed Scarborough Town Centre. Opened in 1973, the large, Y-shaped mall housed department stores, a grocery mart, and an array of retail stores. In the early 1970s, suburban shopping malls offered wheelchair users and others with mobility challenges a relatively barrier-free oasis in a sea of inaccessible streets and public spaces. This mall was purposefully constructed adjacent to the borough's civic centre to create a central plaza for the sprawling suburb. Beryl soon developed a new circle of friends that included mothers of disabled children, teens, adults, and seniors living with cerebral palsy, brain injury, intellectual disabilities, spinal cord injuries, epilepsy, polio survivors, and members of the Deaf community. Opportunities to participate in organized community activities in that part of the city were limited, so local meetups at the mall became an important part of daily life.

The reality of widespread inaccessibility in Canada did not happen by accident. Canada, like many Western nations, has a long history of confinement, oppression, and segregation of people with disabilities. From the earliest days as a colony of Great Britain, people with physical disabilities and mental illness were often stigmatized, kept separate from the rest of the community, and incarcerated by medical and religious institutions. Canadian officials imported old world attitudes and models of care built on fear, ignorance, and condescension. Residential hospitals were established outside major metropolitan centres where people with disabilities were deposited into the care of doctors, their needs deemed impossible to handle by ill-equipped parents and family. In these facilities, often located hundreds of miles away from their local communities, children born with congenital disabilities, physical deformities, and intellectual disabilities resided alongside youth, adults, and seniors living with mental illnesses and physical impairments.[1] Many spent their entire lives behind walls and locked doors.[2] Houses of Industry and sheltered workshops were set up to extract their labour for token wages, often disguised as occupational therapy or job training schemes.[3] To prevent the unwanted expansion of the disabled population, many inmates were sterilized by doctors upholding the fanaticism of the eugenics movement, and immigrants were screened for signs of disability to limit entry to those considered a burden on society.[4]

Following the Second World War, attitudes toward persons with disabilities shifted markedly thanks in large part to veterans' groups, community advocates, and parents of disabled children who organized themselves and lobbied to change the social and economic displacement of people with disabilities from mainstream society. Advocates established service agencies to make it easier for people with disabilities to leave institutions and lead fuller lives in the community.[5] Rehabilitation hospitals, such as Lyndhurst Lodge in Toronto, returned people home in partnership with agencies, such as War Amps and the Canadian Paraplegic Association, to provide a level of support that did not otherwise exist in the community.[6] Parents of children born during the polio epidemic of the 1950s joined other parents of children with intellectual disabilities in reframing permanent institutionalization as a problem rather than a solution. Extensive fundraising campaigns supported the development of community-run programs, including services of the Ontario March of Dimes and Easter Seals. These agencies pressured policymakers to shift public resources away from segregated facilities to support innovative community-based alternatives.[7]

Beryl's transition to her new life coincidentally overlapped with a new phase of disability activism. In the early 1970s, a wave of social activism was led by people with disabilities who asserted their human, civil, and consumer rights, with the goal of building a new social paradigm and legal system that would empower people with disabilities. Disability rights activists rejected the paternalism of many organizations led primarily by able-bodied people that, they argued, stood in the way of full independence for people with disabilities. They argued people with disabilities had rights as consumers to control their own services and resented how these organizations consumed the bulk of public funding and largely controlled the communication about the needs of the disability community to government and the wider public. Inspired by developments in the US and UK, disability rights groups started popping up across Canada and some formed allegiances through the Coalition of Provincial Organizations of the Handicapped, later Council of Canadians with Disabilities.

In Toronto, Beryl watched as a group of professionals, family advocates, and disability rights activists demanded newly elected populist mayor David Crombie work with reformers and consumer activists to create a special task force to investigate ways to improve the level of accessibility across the city.[8] As a prominent member of the reform movement, Crombie hoped to set an example to the larger Metropolitan Toronto area and the rest of the country on the matter of accessibility. By 1970, Toronto City Council endorsed a policy to ramp thousands of sidewalks and intersections across the city, and in 1973, the Metropolitan Toronto Social Services and Housing Committee began work on a public paratransit system. Wheel-Trans, as it was called, started in 1975 with the registration of two thousand users. It had limited weekday operating hours, prioritizing essential trips to work, school, and medical appointments. By 1977, one thousand sidewalks had been made accessible in the City of Toronto in high pedestrian traffic corridors and downtown transit hubs.[9]

Beryl was inspired by these developments, especially the concept that people with disabilities did not have to accept the way things were and could challenge the conditions that excluded them from participation in mainstream life. She drew a direct line between the lack of accessibility and the isolation of people she met in hospital, in rehabilitation programs, and at the mall where she commiserated and heard their stories. She decided she needed to do something to help. After all, she had returned to Canada to start over again and the inspiring words of the good Reverend Bob Rumball still rang in her ears. "The big guy up there did this to me for a reason. He's got a plan," she reminded herself. Maybe advocating for others was the plan.

Beryl started by supporting the Ontario March of Dimes, attending their programs in East York, and getting to know the clients and staff who worked there. It was also there that she learned about the serious lack of community programming for disabled adults in neighbourhoods further east in Scarborough. She witnessed firsthand how recreational programming brought disabled people together and enriched their lives. She approached Michael Coxon, then Community Development Officer at March of Dimes, and told him about her vision of creating a consumer-led club that would provide an accessible safe space for people with disabilities to gather.[10]

Before she could enact her plan, however, Beryl was confronted with yet another health crisis. The thrombophlebitis (deep vein thrombosis) that plagued her had returned. This time, the clot was in her left arm. The cause of its resurgence was unknown, but Beryl knew she would have to deal with it one way or another. Given her extensive medical history, the doctors wasted no time scheduling an operation to amputate Beryl's final limb. Shock quickly turned to defiance. "As I sat there and they were preparing for the operation, I became angry. I thought, 'This is going too far. I'm not taking any more of this.'" To claim her remaining limb just felt cruel, like some cosmic joke to rob every ounce of happiness from her. She worked so hard to adapt to life with a single arm and one eye, it wasn't clear to her how she would fare with no arms at all. There was so much she was determined to do despite her limitations, and she was not ready to have her independence stolen from her yet again. Against every opposition from the doctors who probably made her sign a release of liability form, she instructed Dennis to get the car and take her home. She knew she could not run from her poor health forever, but she could decide not to let them take her arm today.

As her anger dissolved, she contemplated a future without any limbs. Perhaps she would eventually lose her vision entirely. How would she survive? How could she help others if she could not help herself? "I thought of committing suicide that day. I had a bottle of sleeping pills in my hand. I was going to take them, but I don't know what happened. I ended up throwing them down the toilet instead."[11]

Against all medical advice, Beryl never went through with the operation to remove her left arm. Wrapped in a compression sleeve, her enflamed limb throbbed its angry drumbeat of relentless pain, each pulse reminding her of the major risk to her life she had accepted. If the clot dislodged, it could travel to her heart, killing her instantly. If it moved to her brain, she could experience a stroke. Each time she blinked could be the last thing she saw.

Miraculously, the inflammation cleared within weeks and never returned, as if it had all been a test of her will. Her elation was matched only by that same special feeling of invincibility she experienced when her family was spared during the blitz of Liverpool. But Beryl's resolve was fuelled by more than the power of positive thinking. Anger was a central feature of her motivation to carry on. Beryl had plenty to be angry about and could have easily let the emotion take over her life. Instead, she learned to harness her anger and channel it into something more productive. This mixture of anger and hope not only powered her resilience through an unworldly amount of pain and struggle, it also provided the fuel that pushed her to aspire to new heights beyond the anonymity of her pre-injury life or unwanted attention her disability attracted.

The result was a radical shift in her personality. Before her accident, Beryl presented to others as socially withdrawn and lacking confidence. Even though these could be explained as being the expression of someone who was deeply overwhelmed and depressed, it was nonetheless a radical transformation. Her "before" was nothing like the outspoken activist that emerged from the hospital. "The change in my mother's personality has been unreal," Diane told an interviewer. "It's amazing. She used to be so shy like me. If she had to meet my dad in a restaurant and she got there first, she'd be too scared to go inside alone. She'd wait outside." In an interview, Beryl described her life before her accident as "drab." "I had no special compassion for others, no special energy for life, no excitement in me. I was so introverted. I kept everything so bottled up inside that I got terrible migraines." Now, having come out the other side after years of her life hanging in the balance, powerful new shades of her personality were just beginning to show. Soon, a more empowered and confident person took centre stage.

———————

In 1975, once Beryl recovered from her latest health crisis, she was approached to launch her idea of creating more rec programming in her neighbourhood, discussions which led to the establishment of the Scarborough Recreation Club for Disabled Adults. In October, an eight-person steering committee led by Beryl, a few other people with disabilities, and representatives from the Ontario March of Dimes and Scarborough Parks and Recreation Department administered a twelve-week pilot project. "By January [1976], we had thirty-seven members," she proudly recalled. The group had no funds to rent a hall, so they met once a week to play cards and socialize at the Scarborough Town Centre, still one of the only free public spaces that was also accessible.

By 1977, the club became fully independent of the Ontario March of Dimes. "We only had $34.68 in the bank at this time. So, we could not afford $1,000 for a charter. Instead, I wrote the constitution and incorporation myself, with the help of a lawyer and several books. It cost us $20." Beryl approached Margaret Birch with an appeal for funding the club. Then Provincial Secretary for Social Development and first female Cabinet minister in Ontario history, Birch was a charismatic woman, then in her late fifties, who sported a massive beehive hairdo and hooded eyes that crinkled at the edges when she pursed her lips into a satisfied grin. Birch exuded a warmth and savvy confidence that paired well with her sharp wit, qualities that allowed her to slice through the chauvinistic culture of politics at the time. They were also qualities Beryl greatly admired and wanted to emulate. Birch later reflected on her first meeting with Beryl. "I thought it was an innovative idea at the time when most people were not thinking beyond disabled people's therapeutic needs. My first reaction to her was one of intense admiration. Her disability seemed so severe, I sort of gulped, stood back and wondered for a moment, what would I do if this happened to me? But once you start to talk to her, you become oblivious to her disability because there's something very comforting about her, a serenity that seems to radiate. There's no sense of embarrassment, no matter how the other person reacts."[12]

Beryl drove the early expansion of the group, using her magnetic personality to attract people with disabilities interested in new social opportunities and their families, though membership was open to anyone regardless of age or ability. As the club grew, they left the mall for a rented space at Bendale Secondary School, a former vocational school near Midland Avenue and Lawrence Avenue East. They printed a regular newsletter, held swimathons at the Centennial Recreation Centre, and fundraised through bake sales and bazaars so they could embark on monthly outings. They met in the school gymnasium, folding tables, wheelchairs, and walkers scattered across the glazed hardwood floor, arranging themselves in small groups. Some came just to chat, others played board games. In one scene from a documentary, Beryl sidled up to two men playing a game of checkers.

"I'm the champion of this game," the one man announces.

"Does he cheat?" Beryl jests.

"Yeah, totally," the other man laughs, as Beryl leans in to steal the winning move.

"I'll get you for that!" the first man laughs.

The group was surrounded by reminders that theirs was a rented space, the scoreboard, basketball nets, and other gym equipment making it clear this was a temporary clubhouse. But it did not matter. They had come to connect with each other, to forge relationships with others who understood them, the only requirement that it was accessible to everyone.

Community outings were integral to the founding philosophy of the club. "All our outings are aimed at integrating us into public places as much as possible, and this is all part of the process of getting back into society," Beryl explained. "Many of our members had been shut away and cut off, and this club has helped them back into normal living." Trips to amusement parks, restaurants, shopping malls, concert venues, and other public places became a lifeline for people with few alternatives to participate in the broader community. In 1979, thirty members even travelled as a group to the Bahamas. Each year the club sponsored fifty disabled people in need from across the province to take a week's holiday at the historic Rostrevor Lodge on Lake Rosseau in Ontario's Muskoka cottage country.

Early members of the rec club included Anne Abbott and Sam Savona. Anne joined the club when she was eighteen years old. A fair skinned young woman with large eyes, sharp features, and fine long brown hair, Anne carried her head tilted to the left, spastic cerebral palsy causing uncontrollable movement of her limbs. When amused, she grinned widely, squealing with delight as she threw her head back to reveal a long, slender neck. It was the first group Anne ever joined, and it represented an important step toward establishing a wider social circle and more independence in her life. "Before I joined the club, I was kind of in a bubble with my immediate family. I had a small circle of neighbourhood friends, but it wasn't a huge thing. The club broadened my view of life." Anne remembers the first meetings when only a few people came, but she kept coming back until it grew to around one hundred members. "There were swimming and card games. Oh yes, and my mom was voted in to organize outings. Beryl was very good at organizing things and soon became president of the club." On one of their outings in 1981 at Canada's Wonderland captured in a documentary, Anne rode the swinging pendulum shaped like a Viking ship, her unbridled joy obvious to all those around her.[13]

Sam, a handsome young man with curly brown hair and a fuzzy beard, also lived with cerebral palsy and remembers when some of the first meetings were held on weekends at Scarborough Town Centre and then every Tuesday from 7:00 p.m. to 9:00 p.m. at the school. "We did all the things that kids do. It was like our hangout space. Once a week, we'd go and hang out together like it was a college group or something." They would meet in the cafeteria to play games, swim, and dance. By 1980, growing demand in neighbouring municipalities led to the establishment of a sister club in East York to accommodate the overflow.[14]

Surrounded by club members, Beryl seemed especially joyful and playful. She loved to surprise people with the velocity of her electric wheelchair, rushing up on them and braking hard as they jumped back before being run over, laughingly reassuring she had no intentions of running them over. This playful side of her personality tended to emerge only in private, when she felt comfortable and secure in the company of family and friends. Years of building up the rec club and developing strong friendships with members made her feel as if she had a second family. She became protective of club members and genuinely cared about helping them solve their problems. As she became more self-confident, she learned to share more of this outgoing, playful side with others. In a 1989 documentary about Beryl's life, Diane expressed her delight in her mother's new commitments. "I'm very proud of what she's doing for other people and for herself because, I mean, it's really helped her. She's become a totally different person."[15]

Beryl wanted to bring people out of social isolation through recreation, but she soon discovered many disabled people in her community needed more than just a place to hang out. She learned about members' daily problems with transit, housing, social assistance, and discrimination. She experienced many of these same issues herself and knew how difficult it was to make social plans or keep appointments. When she wasn't visiting people in their homes or in hospital, she would be on the phone, responding to distressed calls from club members and advocating for them with taxi companies, landlords, welfare workers, and other officials. Missed pickups, late drop-offs, insecure housing, meagre welfare benefits, and daily experiences of prejudice and discrimination were among the main topics of these calls. Diane often found it difficult to get through to her mum on the phone because the line was always busy. "She spent a lot of time on the phone, reading what she could to help people, and typing up letters." Beryl troubleshooted problems with many individual members and, as such, increasingly acquainted herself with various policies and authority figures. It was the training ground for the escalation of her advocacy.

But she could not solve everyone's problems over the phone. Over time, she saw these were not a series of individual problems, but rather systemic issues that required a coordinated response. She decided the next step would be to form an organization to challenge these unacceptable conditions. In 1976, Beryl gathered a few people from the club interested in activism with the idea of empowering club members and other locals with information they could use to assert their rights. The result was the formation of an action committee within the club dedicated to helping people with disabilities navigate an inaccessible transit system and assist with applications to affordable housing and welfare benefits.

One issue that continually topped the list of problems was the lack of accessible transportation. Subways and buses were rarely fully accessible, and Beryl was one of many people with disabilities in the city reliant on a small fleet of accessible taxis. There were never enough taxis to meet demand and the cost was often prohibitive to people who lived on a fixed income. She wondered what was the point of encouraging people to get out and participate in the community if they had no access to reliable transportation? In 1976, Beryl joined a growing chorus of voices across Metro Toronto advocating for better public paratransit services. Wheel-Trans commenced operations the previous year, but the TTC contracted the service out to a private company called All-Way Transportation, a service that quickly proved woefully inadequate, especially in the suburban boroughs of

Scarborough. Beryl relied on Wheel-Trans to get around town and was disappointed in its many shortcomings. She argued a larger fleet of Wheel-Trans vans and buses was needed with a commitment to establish quality standards for paratransit riders across the city. She formed a coalition of disabled people dedicated to working with the TTC, local officials, and the Ontario government. But progress was slow and firm commitments were not materializing.

As Beryl stepped more confidently into the role of a disability advocate, she channelled the style of her mentor, Reverend Bob Rumball. His son Derek, who eventually took over the Bob Rumball Centre for the Deaf, described his father as being very much on the front lines of advocacy work. "He was boots on the ground, that's the way I describe him. He would never ask someone else to do the things that he would do. He would not say, 'If you want to change Queens Park [Ontario provincial legislature], this is what you've got to do.' He would say, 'Okay, what do we need to do? Let's go do it!' One of the things my dad did is he kept the doors open after hours, serving food seven days a week. I remember, as a young kid, four or five years old, always knowing that there would be someone different at dinner every single day. Over time, he essentially became the centre for the Deaf community. Not necessarily a community centre in the classic sense of the word, but very much a 'build it and they will come' approach."[16] Rumball developed relationships with politicians and decision makers but focused on accomplishing practical goals, leveraging his personal connections to bring about change. He was unafraid to exert pressure on decision makers through the media to attract attention to certain issues, steadily prodding his connections into action.

Rumball's example of advocacy demonstrated to Beryl that with enough grit and charisma, she could make things happen too. She decided she wanted to emulate his "boots on the ground" approach to disability advocacy. She had begun in that tradition by working to address people's problems one at a time, educating herself, and empowering others to challenge their situations and take back some measure of control. Now, she had to learn how to effectively communicate her message to key decision makers and get the broader public involved in changing attitudes to break down stereotypes about disability. This personalized, media-savvy approach would soon come to characterize the way many people were introduced to her.

13.
Ability Forum

The catalyst for the emergence of the disability rights movement in Canada occurred in 1973 when a group of consumer activists showed up at the annual conference of the Canadian Rehabilitation Council for the Disabled, the largest disability advocacy organization at the time. Activists demanded the council, led primarily by rehabilitation professionals, reconstitute itself with at least 50 per cent of its members being people with disabilities in line with the principle of consumer control. Unsurprisingly, the CRCD board rejected the petition, but it was this rejection that provided the impetus for the formation of their own organization. Huddling in the corner after the vote, activists left the conference disappointed but invigorated by the connections they made with one another and went on to establish their own advocacy organization, a national coalition of local activist groups that would become the forerunner to the Council of Canadians with Disabilities.[1]

Against the backdrop of this emerging world of disability rights, Beryl decided she wanted to reach out beyond those who regularly attended the rec club to engage community members about topics of interest to people with disabilities. Her medium of choice was television. In 1971, the Canadian Radio-television and Telecommunications Commission had changed its regulations governing the licensing of cable companies, requiring them to set aside a certain percentage of airtime to citizen-produced content.[2] Community-access programming gave individuals and community groups with little funding and limited access to expensive television equipment a platform to produce television shows targeted to local audiences. In Scarborough, CUC Broadcasting controlled Trillium Cable (later purchased by

Shaw Communications), which supplied residents with cable TV and the York Community Access Television program.[3] Sensing an opportunity to cast a wider net, Beryl approached Trillium Cable and applied to host a program geared toward educating viewers about disability issues. She pitched the concept to executive producers, sharing her ideas for the value and need for such programming. In 1977, her application was approved, and Beryl negotiated the hiring of an all-disabled production staff, creating jobs for producers and tech crews living with disabilities to ensure the program was produced *for* people with disabilities *by* people with disabilities.

And so, *Ability Forum* came to life with Beryl as the host. The set for the one-hour show had red carpeting, a large houseplant, and an old-fashioned winter landscape hanging on the wall. An armchair was positioned opposite Beryl where her guests sat, giving the impression that viewers had been invited into her home. Beryl dressed in a blue chemise with white lace collar, her soft English accent and gentle, entertaining approach completing the image. She was like the Agatha Christie character Miss Marple, the sharp detective, softened by the stereotype of the kindly older aunt come to share her thoughts on solving a problem or two. "I can go to a dinner and reach fifty people. But on television, one can reach thousands," she once told an interviewer.[4] The show covered a range of issues with each guest tailored to represent or speak about the weekly topic.

The show's concept was to invite people with disabilities of all ages from the community to discuss the daily realities of living with disability. These were not hard-hitting interviews, nor was that the point, but over time, things did get more political. She would invite politicians, employers, and other decision makers from all levels of government to discuss accessibility issues and other contemporary policy issues affecting the disability community, the arc of the show mirroring Beryl's progression into activism as she strode further into the public sphere. Behind the scenes, an all-disabled crew and team of producers kept things running smoothly. The technical director was a man who lived with cerebral palsy and wore a helmet mounted with a wand he wielded adeptly, switching between video sources with apparent ease. *Ability Forum* ran for more than two hundred episodes and provided a critical platform to project awareness of disability issues on a local scale to a broader audience. Most importantly, the show gave Beryl the opportunity to hone her public-speaking skills and on-screen persona, a blend of kindly grandparent and incisive advocate.

In addition to running the rec club, Beryl was becoming a consummate fundraiser. From the 1970s to 1990s, Dominion supermarkets ran a loyalty program that encouraged customers to turn their receipts over to volunteers.[5] The rolls were then tabulated, and the store would contribute two or three per cent of the total to charity. Volunteer receipt collectors representing different charities became a staple presence at supermarket doors across the country. Beryl spotted the opportunity to raise funds for wheelchairs and technical aids for those in need and began spending her weekends at the local Dominion store collecting receipts. She became a fixture at the store, parking her chair by the exit and chatting up the regulars. Over the course of six years, rain or shine, she collected $11 million in receipts that she exchanged for $66,000 used to purchase and distribute assistive equipment.[6] In 2022 currency, this would be $36.5 million collected in receipts, exchanged for $221,000.

In 1978, Beryl's volunteer contributions to the community were first recognized at the twenty-second annual Scarborough Recreation Night held at the Scarborough Centennial Recreation Centre. The evening honoured "the multitude of wonderful people who, without thought of remuneration, give generously of their time and talent in the cause of community recreation." Beryl was honoured for forming the Scarborough Recreation Club for Disabled Adults and her "knowledge related to the needs of the handicapped" as well as her leadership in assisting "many of the handicapped residents of Scarborough to live richer and fuller lives."[7] It would be the first of many honours she would receive over the coming years.

Recognition of her efforts emboldened Beryl to take a more assertive stance on disability rights. Calls from distressed club members and their families kept coming in, and she began to see how officials often failed to follow up on promises of action on long-standing issues that affected the lives of people with disabilities. Beryl believed discrimination was a problem primarily rooted in the attitudes and prejudices of others that reinforced systems that separated disabled people from the rest of society. She understood how ignorance and fear worked to perpetuate these attitudes, partly because she once held such attitudes herself as an able-bodied woman who never thought about disability and accessibility until she was forced to reckon with it herself. "Oh, I couldn't have cared less about the handicapped," she once said in a documentary, alluding to the invisibility of people with disabilities in the minds of ordinary people who have little knowledge or awareness of disability issues. "I did not even want to associate with them. I thought maybe they should be kept in their homes or locked away in institutions where they belonged. But you know, people don't think it could ever happen to them. I certainly did not think it would happen to me, that's for sure. There's no discrimination where disability is concerned. It can happen to anyone and at any time."[8] The ubiquity and inevitability that everyone would face disability in some way would come to define Beryl's message. She reasoned that if able-bodied people had a better understanding of their own fragility, they would see, as she now did, why people with disabilities needed to be empowered with greater rights and freedoms.

Beryl's style of advocacy would evolve to integrate elements of disability rights activism—including protesting and lobbying—alongside the more traditional approach of raising public recognition of disability through education and awareness workshops and presentations. Though not necessarily conflicting approaches, disability rights activists distinguished themselves from the people and organizations that received the bulk of public funding and political attention while claiming to speak *on behalf of* people with disabilities. Beryl's style of advocacy fell somewhere in the middle, inhabiting a unique liminal space in the broader disability rights movement that would eventually put her on a collision course with activists in both camps. But as her presence as a public figure grew, she would learn to use this middle ground to knit together activists, family advocates, service agencies, bureaucrats, politicians, and media figures.

By 1980, Beryl was at a crossroads. With the recreation club a great success, she could have doubled down on her efforts to expand the club and work on advocating incremental changes to local community issues. But she increasingly felt drawn toward the world of disability rights politics with its promise of overhauling systems that long excluded people with disabilities. Rapidly evolving events on multiple fronts would soon guide her ultimate direction. A major influence on her decision was a young man from British Columbia with an amputated leg who stepped in front of the news cameras and forever transformed the way Canadians saw the potential of people with disabilities.

14.
Aware Bear

In 1977, eighteen-year-old athlete Terry Fox was diagnosed with osteogenic sarcoma and his right leg was amputated six inches above the knee to prevent the bone cancer from spreading throughout his body. A strapping and strong-willed young man with boundless energy, Terry faced his amputation and recovery with extraordinary optimism, quickly adapting to life with a prosthetic leg. Convinced he was saved by recent advances in medical research, he formulated a plan to run eight thousand kilometres across Canada to raise awareness and funds for cancer research. He began a gruelling training program, appealing for seed funding from the Canadian Cancer Society. In a letter requesting support he declared the idealism that motivated him to undertake such an ambitious endeavour. "I'm not a dreamer, and I'm not saying this will initiate any kind of definitive answer or cure to cancer, but I believe in miracles. I have to."[1] Three years later, on April 12, 1980, Terry set out on his Marathon of Hope charity run across Canada. Starting in St. John's, Newfoundland, and trudging through Québec, where support was underwhelming, he entered Ottawa on Canada Day. Public attention skyrocketed. Greeting Terry was Prime Minister Pierre Elliot Trudeau, smartly dressed in a grey pinstripe suit with red carnation on his lapel. Terry was buoyed by all of the attention and demonstrated the workings of his artificial leg and showed off his completely beat-up running shoes.

Alongside millions of other Canadians, Beryl was enraptured by Terry's story and his youthful determination. On the morning of July 11, 1980, Terry entered Scarborough, followed by his ever-present Ford Econoline Van of Hope, and stopped long enough to deliver a moving speech at the Scarborough Civic Centre. Designed by Japanese

Canadian architect Raymond Moriyama, the centre's sharp geometric lines of concrete triangles and cylinders looked as if it were plucked from the pages of a modernist architecture magazine and dropped into the suburbs of Toronto. Inside, supporters packed the atrium, the large crowd peering down from four tiers of white balconies, raining down enthusiastic cheers on Terry as he took to a podium crammed with microphones. "I'm no different than anybody else. I'm no better and no lower. I'm equal with all of you." Terry choked back tears as he mentioned all his supporters, including his brother Darrell and friend Doug Alward, both of whom accompanied him on the marathon. "So when you're cheering and clapping for me, you're not just cheering and clapping for me, because there's so many other people involved in the run that nobody hears about."[2]

Beryl was one of those local organizers Terry was talking about who helped fundraise for the Marathon of Hope, and she turned up at the civic centre to see Terry in person. They met amid a surging throng of fans before he continued his whirlwind tour of downtown Toronto, where ten thousand people attended a ceremony in his honour at Nathan Phillips Square. That evening he threw the ceremonial first pitch at a Toronto Blue Jays game at Exhibition Stadium before continuing to Hamilton, where he was due to arrive three days later. Though they only met briefly, Terry kept in touch with Beryl, sometimes calling her from the road after he proceeded on his winding route into northern Ontario, their shared experience as amputees and belief about the power of public awareness at the core of their connection.[3]

Beryl's encounter with this eminently legendary Canadian strengthened her resolve to promote awareness of disability issues and to fight for the rights of people with disabilities. The world was at the cusp of an unprecedented moment in the advancement of disability rights, including international political developments designed to change the lives of people with disabilities across the globe. In 1975, the UN General Assembly passed the Declaration on the Rights of Disabled Persons to provide a legal framework for member nations to formulate progressive disability rights regulations.[4] The UN declared 1981 to be the International Year of Disabled Persons with the theme of "full participation and equality."[5] Governments around the world were called upon to undertake initiatives to enhance social, economic, and political opportunities for disabled people, including systems of rehabilitation and disability prevention. The international resolution promised to spur action that would comprehensively improve the lives of persons with disabilities.

Of course, much depended on holding political authorities accountable to their commitments, parsing feel-good rhetoric from actionable plans. Disability activists had already detected an emerging pattern in the political cycle that began with electoral promises, followed by the repackaging of old commitments, until the next round of election pledges began anew. It was a cycle most social activists understood as part of the work of political lobbying, but disability activists often had to work twice as hard to overcome the restrictions placed on them by an ableist system. Most people with disabilities during this period were invisible in mainstream society, so how were they to make their demands known? Beryl and her fellow activists, in their lobbying, drew on personal experiences and a deep well of resilience developed from being forced to confront a society failing to acknowledge even the existence of people with disabilities. Beryl and others were demanding more than simple recognition; they now demanded the rights and opportunities to be a part of the community, to live their lives with dignity, free of the control and oppression exerted by social and medical systems.

Some disability policy during this time also consisted of inadequate or insincere efforts to improve the lives of people with disabilities. In 1979, for example, the Ontario government attempted to introduce a Handicapped Persons' Rights Act, a piece of legislative duplicity that avoided the more serious and far-reaching task of amending the Ontario Human Rights Code.[6] In response, a coalition of disability activists and allies, including Beryl, protested at the Ontario Legislature until the bill was withdrawn. Under continued pressure from activists, the government amended the Code in December 1980 to include persons with disabilities as a protected category.[7] Significant accomplishments to disability rights like this were few and far between and always came after persistent lobbying.

By 1980, Beryl participated in this growing movement as her life shifted markedly toward public-speaking engagements. Primarily because of her television show and other public appearances, she began to develop a reputation as an engaging public speaker and was increasingly in demand by different organizations and media outlets. She wrote articles for magazines, attended conferences, and accepted invitations to speak at local schools, churches, hospitals, prisons, and service clubs. Beryl once told a *Toronto Sun* journalist that she often felt she was "stared at like something out of a circus,"[8] and that this motivated her to turn that curiosity into a discussion to change peoples' attitudes about disability. She organized a community forum called *I'll Meet You Halfway*, which brought together people with disabilities, employers, and community members at the Scarborough Civic Centre to discuss topics such as employment, housing, transportation, recreation, and accessibility. "We want people to come and get their anger and feelings out,"[9] the workshop's ad read, suggesting the forum was just as much about acknowledging disability issues as it was an outlet for people with disabilities to express their frustration publicly. It is uncertain whether the workshop was a success or if it was ever repeated.

Beryl was finding that some people became afraid if they got too close to her, they might "catch something." In an interview, she considered the countless times she was personally made to feel like an outlier: the people who crossed the street to avoid her; the woman in the subway who screamed when she encountered her; the mothers who ushered their children away as if to protect them from whatever potentially dangerous disease had afflicted her. In service of breaking down stereotypes, she began integrating physical contact with audience members. Children were invited to touch her stump. "See, nothing bad happened, did it?" she would say. Young adults were encouraged to hop onto the arm of her electric wheelchair and take a ride as she whirled around the stage. For Beryl, breaking down barriers and demystifying disability were just as much about imparting information as they were about making authentic personal connections, getting up close and personal with people to engage with them about their fears and ignorance, an approach that bred familiarity and understanding.

Over time, Beryl would hone her presentation style and content, typically opening with the story of her accident, hospitalization, and journey toward self-discovery. With older audiences, she would share her struggles with depression, addiction, and suicidal thoughts. Younger audiences met "Mr. Stumpy," a happy face drawn on the stump of her right arm with a marker. She got the idea from playing with her granddaughter Michelle, who would draw happy faces on her stump to perform mini puppet shows.[10] Beryl found it cathartic and empowering to share her story, and audiences were increasingly receptive to the style and content of her presentations. Most school workshops included a one-hour presentation with a question period and a slide presentation called "Look Beyond" that focused on breaking down stereotypes about disability. Her appearances were always free, funded by the provincial Office for Disability Issues.

Early on in her school presentations, Beryl decided she needed a special guest she could use as a prop to engage with younger children. On American television, Mr. Rogers had Daniel the Striped Tiger, and his Canadian counterpart, Mr. Dressup, had Casey and Finnegan, character foils used to approach kids at their own level, especially in service of teaching a lesson or making a broader moral argument. Beryl's answer to this was Mr. Grizzly the Aware Bear. Beryl used a portion of her government funding to build a custom life-size animatronic fuzzy teddy bear, complete with black bowtie. Mr. Grizzly had an amputated leg and arm and used a wheelchair that he magically self-propelled, the magic performed by Dennis, with a remote control and an inbuilt speaker. Mr. Grizzly would interact with children who would ask him questions about his chair or his missing limbs, or just to give him a big hug or kiss. The bear travelled everywhere with Beryl and Dennis. Sometimes for a few hours on a weekend, they would make appearances at the Eaton Centre. Mr. Grizzly would wheel around the cavernous shopping mall in the heart of busy downtown Toronto stopping to chat with kids and their families who showed interest. Most kids were magnetically drawn to the bear, kissing his furry cheeks, tweaking his nose, and giving him hugs. After a minute or two, Beryl would approach to engage the families in conversation, with Dennis off in a corner continuing to control the bear's movement and voice so as not to spoil the illusion. Beryl would then redirect the conversation to all the things a bear like Mr. Grizzly could do. "Do you know what he can do? He can do all sorts of things. He can play basketball, go skiing and other sports. Did you know he can do all that?" Beryl would say.

Beryl's school workshops were dynamically tailored to each age group with a focus on educating students and fostering sensitivity to disability issues. Her tour promotion materials described the first cohort ranging from kindergarten to grade three. "To remove the fear of the unknown, the visible disability plays a major role with these young students in promoting the need to play safe, prevention of unnecessary accidents and acceptance of persons with disabilities. At this impressionable age, given the opportunity to shake hands with 'Stumpy' (Ms. Potter's right stump with a face drawn on it), removes the fear of touch and at the same time, promotes parental teaching to the children. Mr. Grizzly, a life-size robot bear, operated by Ms. Potter's assistant, Dennis Potter, is registered as the only bear in Canada who manoeuvres his own wheelchair, sings, dances and interacts with the children regarding safety rules according to different geographic situations (i.e. playing in fields being plowed, busy city streets, railway tracks, drunk driving, etc.). Mr. Grizzly helps children to come forward with unusual questions that they may be too shy to ask Ms. Potter. Ms. Potter and Mr. Grizzly then bid farewell at the end of the presentation with a round of hugs and kisses from the children."

The next age group included students in grades four to eight. "This age group demands more specifics of how to cope with and acceptance of disability and often need visible proof of ability. They are encouraged to go into their community and face the barriers of several different disabilities such as physical access with a wheelchair, identifying raised numbers on elevator buttons with their eyes closed, identifying the need for flashing lights beside fire alarm systems, purchasing items at the store if they were developmentally handicapped or illiterate. The students are given the opportunity to operate Ms. Potter's wheelchair with environment control features, play basketball backwards while sitting in the wheelchair, dance with Ms. Potter, etc. They are informed of the many achievements of athletes with disabilities. They discuss drug use in their school and the effect it has on their grades and family life. They are encouraged to speak privately or write to Ms. Potter with any other questions or concerns."

The following age group included grades nine through thirteen. "This group is more curious as to why society should be responsible for services and programs necessary for persons with disabilities, such as who covers costs, who makes decisions, who knows what's best. They are particularly interested in sexual relations and how persons with disabilities can possibly bear and raise children. They often refer to real or hypothetical situations that may happen within their own families." The final group included university and professional studies students. "These groups are extremely interesting to speak with and a one-hour presentation often extends to more than two hours. A great deal of education is often necessary with these groups as they near their chosen occupations. They are anxious to discuss many issues pertaining to persons with disabilities and the possibility of removing barriers."[11]

One documentary followed Beryl into a classroom. At General Crerar Public School in Scarborough, a small two-storey brick building nestled in the suburban residential neighbourhood of McGregor Park, she entered the kindergarten class, her face immediately broadening into a wide smile as the group of children sat cross-legged on the floor staring up at her. She was elegantly dressed in a pastel blouse and black skirt with a large silver belt buckle, silver nail polish, pearls, and perfectly coiffed hair. Beryl was always well-groomed, her put-together appearance resembling that of a visiting elder dignitary but her demeanour more like a family relative or friend, the combination possibly helping put many kids at ease, as most of them looked shocked when she first entered a room. Some would lean forward with wide eyes, others crept back or slouched away. As she settled in front of this class, she looked at one boy and pointed out that his shoelace was untied.

"You know what happened to me?" she began, the boy hurriedly tying his shoelace with a sheepish grin. "Well, somebody dropped a candy wrapper on the floor, and I stepped on it and slipped."[12] The children listened with rapt attention, half of them with their mouths open as she told a version of her story.

"Would anyone be afraid if I let you see Stumpy here?" Most of the children mouthed "no" but one boy jerked his head down, covering his eyes in disbelief. "So, if I bring my sleeve up slowly here—" she began, cautiously pulling back her sleeve to reveal her stump. Her goal was to educate, not to frighten. Previous encounters shocked some kids into screaming or crying, so she learned how to avoid triggering a repeat of those situations. She invited one student named Andrew to stand up and shake Stumpy as if to say "Hello." "See, Andrew's arm did not fall off, did it?" she said, challenging the fear and prejudice of touching or getting too close to people with disabilities.[13]

In an earlier documentary, she visited another group of kindergarten students at West Rouge Public School in Scarborough. A boy named Jason looked up at her, his blue eyes peaking out beneath tousled brown hair that fell low over his raised eyebrows. "What would you do if you lost your two arms and two legs?" Jason asked her.

Beryl hesitated for a moment, remembering how close she came to precisely this scenario. "Well, I'd manage somehow. Every day we learn to do something that we never realized we could do. I hope it never happens, Jason, but I know if it ever did, I'd be able to manage."

As she prepared to leave, Jason stopped her. "Take care of your other arm!" he exclaimed with a smirk, squeezing in one more question. "Are you somebody's grandma?"

"Yes, I'm somebody's grandma. His name is Justin and he's just like you,"[14] Beryl said. As she prepared to leave, the children gathered for a round of hugs and kisses, the parting reminiscent of any adoring grandmother at the end of a visit with her grandchildren.

Beryl always loved children. She adored interacting with them in schools and was continually struck by the purity of their curiosity about disability. She told an interviewer that children's lack of judgement inspired her mission to promote awareness of people with disabilities and disability issues. "Children ask such genuine and honest questions. And if it means getting on the floor with them, I'll do it. The more embarrassing the questions, the better."[15] Beryl believed children had not yet been corrupted by society's attitudes and treatment of people with disabilities, and their lack of an adult's sense of social boundaries and a corresponding fear of the unknown meant it was easier for children to accept differences and learn about others. Within this youthful innocence she spotted space to implant positive representations of disability in developing young brains, which might make it harder for such children to internalize negative perspectives of disability later on in life.

15.
Leaning In

In 1980, Scarborough Mayor Gus Harris invited Beryl to be the chairperson of the Scarborough Action Committee for the International Year of Disabled Persons, a role that involved coordinating awareness initiatives across the city. Harris was an early fan of Beryl, generously opening doors for her and making introductions to advance her various initiatives. Harris was born in 1908 and, like Beryl, in Liverpool. He immigrated to Canada in 1929, a generation earlier than Beryl, and they shared many of the same motivations to escape poverty and build a new life in their adopted country. Extraordinarily fit for a man in his seventies, a snappy dresser with a luxurious crop of white hair, Harris lived up to his everyman image: a plain talking progressive socialist who always remembered his gritty roots. Beryl accepted his invitation and quickly got down to work. She took her new job seriously and immediately threw herself into the work of planning and organizing events across the city. She coordinated the first Awareness Day conference at Scarborough Town Centre, assembling representatives from service agencies, consumer groups, government offices, employers, and merchants. The connections made among these diverse participants were so successful that the event promised to become annual.

Harris later wrote to Beryl, thanking her for her work. "I can appreciate that you must feel frustrated at times with governments and staff at all levels not responding quickly enough to your programmes," a recognition of her sometimes strong, vociferous complaints about politicians not doing enough about disability issues. "But on the 'plus' side, I feel you can take great satisfaction in the tremendous progress you have made in Scarborough with your Committee, in a relatively short period of time. I seem to recall that five years ago, a number of people were floundering to work for the disabled, but it was not until you took hold . . . and started to 'wake' people up, and very clearly whatever progress has been made this year in the Awareness program, is totally due to your leadership and personal effort." Beryl also received a letter from the recently re-elected Prime Minister Pierre Trudeau, who commended her on efforts to promote recognition of disability issues. "Your Awareness Week program, focusing as it does on the abilities rather than the disabilities of the handicapped, will provide the citizens of your community with an understanding of the needs of their disabled, in the fields of employment, housing, support services and recreation."[1]

Trudeau created the Special Parliamentary Committee on the Disabled and Handicapped in 1980 to investigate and develop recommendations to overcome the many obstacles faced by people with disabilities in Canadian society. Chaired by veteran member of parliament Walter Dinsdale, a former social worker and parent of a child with disabilities, the committee travelled the country collecting depositions from Canadians with disabilities, their allies, interest groups, and officials from all levels of government. When the committee arrived in Toronto, Beryl showed up as a representative for the Scarborough Action Committee, alongside dozens of other delegates from different disability organizations. She submitted a statement that expressed her exasperation as well as her perspectives on disability rights at the time.

"Probably every concern possible has been heard and documented. So rather than repeat or overlap these genuine concerns, I present this not so much as a brief, but as an angry and frustrated statement." She carried on, outlining her views in straightforward language. "Why should it make any difference what part of the country we live in when it comes to God's given rights of being treated as human beings instead of rejects. . . . Maybe there's too much red tape, but not enough scissors to cut it with. . . . Our economy is supposed to be in poor shape, and yet hundreds of thousands of dollars are being wasted every day on mistakes made by the government. . . . We are not talking about separate countries here; we are talking about Canada."

She concluded with a list of basic rights that people with disabilities deserved:

- Safe and accessible transportation
- Access to family housing or residential group homes, instead of institutions
- Access to work that would earn a decent living
- To live above the poverty line
- Essential living aids
- Integrated education
- Integrated social and recreational development
- To marry without being penalized
- Support services
- Entry to any building of choice with dignity
- Accessible sidewalk curbs or road crossings at sidewalks
- Access to these necessities anywhere in Canada

"It is the responsibility of the Government of Canada to plan for the future of this ever-increasing minority, and to respect their rights as Canadian citizens. The Prime Minister is fighting for the Constitution of Canada," Beryl pointed out, referring to Prime Minister Pierre Trudeau's efforts to patriate the constitution after 113 years of British colonial rule. "Are we not Canadians and therefore entitled to be included in the Constitution as a people of Canada? It has taken years and many Prime Ministers to find the courage to fight for Canada's independence, but for what purpose if all Canadians are not given the freedom and independence to live and enjoy a normal life?"[2]

In 1981, the committee submitted their final report, *Obstacles*, that outlined more than one hundred and thirty recommendations to create equal access for people with disabilities living in communities and institutions across the country.[3] The report acknowledged what people with disabilities across Canada already knew, namely, that disability programs and benefits existed in administrative silos with constant jurisdictional jockeying between municipal, provincial, and federal governments creating gaps in the system into which many people with disabilities had fallen. A standing committee was established to implement the recommendations, cementing the *Obstacles* report as a foundational document in modern disability rights reform in Canada. It was a significant win for disability activists, but implementing it would require sustained attention, something Beryl and others would discover to be the true challenge.

In 1980, in recognition of her voluntarism and advocacy on behalf of people with disabilities, Beryl received the Ontario Medal for Good Citizenship. An official letter from the Lieutenant Governor of Ontario Pauline McGibbon invited Beryl and Dennis to attend the investiture ceremony. Letters of congratulations arrived from politicians and bureaucrats, including the Secretary for Social Development, Margaret Birch, who wrote, "You are most deserving of this recognition." Eric Cunningham, MP for Wentworth North, also offered his opinion. "It's about time the people of Ontario and the Government of Ontario recognized the hard work and dedication that you have devoted toward bettering the cause for the disabled."[4]

The ceremony at Ontario's Legislature in Queen's Park was held in the Music Room, the site of most official ceremonies, performances, and receptions, and the largest space in the lieutenant governor's suite. Towering windows brightened the otherwise dark oak-panelled room, originally built in 1893, with paintings of Queen Elizabeth II and previous lieutenant governors peering down from their canvases. Beryl wanted something to remember the ceremony, so when no one was looking, she quickly stuffed a few napkins stamped with the lieutenant governor's official gold seal into her purse, a small memento of the occasion. She wore her best homemade black dress overlaid with a patterned chiffon blouse and corsage, her hair cut short and blown back, as she mixed with Premier Bill Davis and other provincial officials. She could now add "OMC" to her post-nominals, a permanent recognition of the honour.

Awards would continue to roll in for Beryl in 1981. Rotary Toronto recognized her with the Citizen of the Year award and Scarborough Mayor Gus Harris awarded her the Civic Award of Merit. "Oh, not again," Beryl told a reporter. "This is getting embarrassing." Always the strategist, she graciously accepted the awards but used the attention to leverage her request for more funding. The Scarborough Action Committee survived on grants, and she remarked that she hoped her award would help her $2,400 application for funds from Scarborough City Council.

Public grants were crucial to the development and financing of many disability initiatives, but grants were only part of the picture. In

From left: Lieutenant Governor of Ontario Pauline McGibbon, Beryl, and Premier Bill Davis. Beryl pictured wearing her Ontario Medal for Good Citizenship and official framed certificate, Queen's Park, 1980.
Beryl Potter personal collection. Reproduced with permission.

February 1981, Beryl received a $50,000 grant from the federal government to establish an Independent Living Centre in Scarborough that would deliver information and resources in accordance with consumer movement principles of "for persons with a disability, by persons with a disability." The centre would help facilitate people's transition to independent living in the community through the provision of consumer-run services. But establishing an organization such as this was unprecedented in Canada. It soon became evident that the proportion and complexity of needs across the city were far more than one small, relatively inexperienced resource committee could handle. Beryl followed developments in the US, including the establishment of the first Independent Living Centre at UC Berkeley in California.[5] But there was little direction about how such a centre would operate in Canada, with multifaceted partnerships needed to help people with disabilities navigate the complex web of municipal housing, provincial income assistance, and various federal programs. In a December interview, Beryl seemed to be hedging her expectations about the centre. "*If* it succeeds," she emphasized, "all of society gains."

But it was not to be. In early 1982, plans for a Scarborough Independent Living Centre were scrapped. Another organization called the Centre for Independent Living Toronto or CILT, which serviced the needs of the entire Metro Toronto area and beyond, took shape in its place. CILT established a steering committee, directed by disability activist Sandra Carpenter, alongside consumers with disabilities and service agencies that operated under the trusteeship of the Community Occupational Therapy Association. Based at 182 Brunswick Avenue in downtown Toronto, CILT assisted people excluded from traditional group homes to find supportive housing, attendant services, and supported employment arrangements. CILT staff also conducted participatory action-based research to promote the full participation of persons with disabilities in all aspects of community life.[6] The success of CILT was found in its peer support networks, referrals, and networking with service providers to train individuals in independent living skills and promote the development of empowering service models. Beryl was disappointed that her Independent Living Centre experiment had not been successful, but she was happy to see the well-equipped operation at CILT take shape.

───────────

Throughout this time Beryl was lobbying endlessly to support her education campaigns. To that end, she headed to Niagara Falls in February 1981 to organize an international publicity event designed to demonstrate global commitment to the advancement of disability rights. The US State Department and the Canadian federal government agreed to participate in what was called Operation Horseshoe as twelve thousand Canadian and American volunteers assembled to form a giant human horseshoe around Niagara Falls to symbolize the international commitment to disability awareness. Beryl was the Canadian coordinator for the event, with participation from the executive director of the US Interagency Committee and US Ambassador to Canada, John W. McDonald. The official statement from these cross-border partners summarized the event, noting its significance in reaffirming international commitments to advancing rights and opportunities for people with disabilities.

"At twilight on the 8th of February 1981, 12,000 people, including many who are disabled, came from throughout the United States and Canada to join together in a unique event designed to bring attention to the International Year of Disabled Persons. The three-mile-long line of Canadians and Americans formed a human horseshoe reaching from Terrapin Point overlooking Niagara Falls on the United States side, across the Rainbow Bridge, and ending on the Canadian side at Table Rock. Each person carried a lamp which symbolized the world-wide commitment of help for disabled persons. The theme was 'Disability Has No Borders or Boundaries.'"[7]

Beryl led groups of people with disabilities to the falls, but it seemed not everyone was there for the same reasons. The *Globe and Mail* reported that many in attendance were groups of young people braving a steady snowfall and chilly winds to participate in the once-in-a-lifetime event and most participants were not persons with disabilities. A sixteen-year-old from Niagara Falls told a reporter, "It's just to show we care about the falls." His older friend stepped in to remind him the event was to "boost the Year of the Disabled." One of the organizers of the event, a general manager of a local Hilton Hotel, admitted the event helped attract attention to the falls during a sluggish tourist season, failing to mention anything about disability awareness. John Kellermen, a Toronto-based disability activist living with cerebral palsy, was also there and was interviewed by the *Globe and Mail*. "I'm very disappointed that there aren't more people from Toronto. I am annoyed that there are not more handicapped here. I'd like to know why." The temperature dipped below freezing by midday and grew progressively colder throughout the afternoon, especially around the falls, as bitterly cold winds picked up, gusting up to forty kilometres an hour.[8] Kellermen suggested the event be held again in warmer months because the winter weather made it inaccessible to many people with disabilities who might have otherwise participated. The international event was never repeated, but it did kickstart a busy year of organizing to raise public awareness of disability issues.

In May, at Queen's Park with Premier Bill Davis at her side, Beryl organized a ceremonial flag-raising for the International Year of Disabled Persons. "The next twelve months will make the disabled more visible to the public than ever before," she announced. The blue and white flag was adapted from the official United Nations flag. Two crossed olive branches representing peace encircled two stylized human figures, one black and one checkered, in a V-configuration appearing to hold hands with subscript lettering spelling out International Year of Disabled Persons 1981. The flags were flown across Canada and Beryl personally delivered many of them across Metro Toronto to be flown in front of public buildings. She also successfully petitioned Toronto Mayor Art Eggleton to declare May 1981 "Awareness Month" in Metro Toronto and secured limited funding to support a conference of more than one hundred and twenty booths and one thousand representatives. In an interview with the *Toronto Star* newspaper, Beryl outlined her plans for the event. "We plan to have 30,000 balloons with the Year of Disabled Persons logo, 30,000 buttons, T-shirts, and pins. Five hundred bumper stickers have already been ordered. I feel very positive about the response in Scarborough. I'm excited about the year and can see a lot of things happening."

But Beryl did not get everything she asked for. The Canadian Organizing Committee for the Year of Disabled Persons, working with a total budget of nearly $2 million to be divvied up across the country, turned down her request to fund a separate annual Awareness Week in Scarborough. Beryl was disgruntled by the rejection, and she let the *Toronto Star* journalist know it. "When we are finished, I'm going to Ottawa to tell them exactly what I think of them," one of the first public statements that showed a more combative side of her personality.[9] Despite the lack of funding, she raised over $38,500 through the sale of buttons, speaking fees, and a portion of ticket sales from the Canada Games for Disabled held in August at the Scarborough Variety Village Sports Training and Fitness Centre, which drew five thousand athletes and thousands of spectators.

By June, Beryl also became the public face of a campaign to promote the employability of people with disabilities, another major plank of the Year of Disabled Persons program. "If we can be accepted into the workforce, we can become useful citizens and pay taxes, too," she told the *Toronto Star*.[10] She argued that people with disabilities deserved greater access to the labour market to truly achieve full participation in society, pointing out that the addition of disabled taxpayers to the workforce would also help pay for affordable supported housing and other facilities. Beryl created a job for herself, sometimes being paid by grants that funded her organizations, but she likely would have found it difficult to find other forms of paid employment that wasn't directly related to her advocacy. Her visible impairments and perhaps even her age and limited recent work experience combined with employer prejudices about the capacity of people with disabilities to engage in productive work all would have interfered with her ability to gain access to the labour market. Consequently, she had a vested interest in trying to carve out more space for people with disabilities to find paid work at livable wages. Beryl travelled across Metro Toronto to malls and public plazas with an exhibit developed by the provincial Handicapped Employment Program within the Ontario Ministry of Labour that promoted the capacity of disabled people to engage in paid work.

The government commissioned a set of posters by renowned paper sculpture artist Jonathan Milne to travel with the exhibit. In a deliberate attempt to provide a diverse portrayal of workers with disabilities to audiences without much knowledge or experience dealing with working people with disabilities in their own communities, the posters featured a working man on crutches, a blind woman as a secretary, and a businesswoman of colour who used a wheelchair. Depictions of diverse people with disabilities were not widespread in the province at the time. The posters were independently sent to thousands of employers and industry groups across the province and received generally positive reactions. That is, until they reached the desk of Belinda Morin, Metro Toronto Coordinator for the Disabled and Elderly. Morin and other civil rights groups reacted negatively to the depiction of the woman in the wheelchair, which they argued insensitively portrayed race, given the "degree of blackness of the subject."[11] Although no known copies or images of the poster exist, Morin observed to the *Toronto Star* that the portrayal was "in extremely poor taste," and that it "looks more like something from the National Lampoon and does not elicit thoughts of competency in a job."[12] Milne received angry phone calls from activists arguing that he "did not understand how black people looked."[13] The Ontario Human Rights Commission responded by pulling its support of the government's awareness campaign. Ontario labour minister Dr. Robert Elgie instructed provincial officials to remove the offending poster from the travelling exhibit.

Beryl was not pleased. Antagonized by what she perceived as political interference in her tour, or perhaps angry and exhausted at all the work she put into the campaign, Beryl refused to remove the poster. In an extraordinary act of defiance, she scrawled "CENSORED—Not so proud are you, Dr. Elgie?" on the offending poster and displayed it in her poster arrangement for the rest of the tour.[14] Whether Beryl agreed with Morin and the critics isn't clear. Perhaps she resented the government intrusion in her campaign. Dr. Elgie and other government officials were upset with what Beryl had done. An internal memo between ministry officials discussed the incident and considered stopping her tour.

Beryl had already proven herself extremely committed to the campaign. The late announcement to change the poster would have been a blow. Perhaps she simply refused to help the government save face. Or maybe she resented the incursion of another social movement in her tour. It was becoming clear that the disability rights movement lacked racial inclusion and an intersectional dialogue on race and disability.[15] Her impulsive actions could be seen as insensitive to the wider racial politics of the 1980s. She was, after all, an older, white, working-class woman who grew up and spent half her life near the site of the infamous 1981 Toxteth riots, a civil disturbance in Liverpool that exposed long-simmering racial tensions among the city's working-class communities.[16] The probability is that Beryl's attitude reflected the general lack of attention to racial issues within the disability rights movement at the time. She often spoke of her lack of sensitivity to people with disabilities before she had become one herself. Her enlightenment to one set of injustices may not have extended to another. And she definitely was uncomfortable with what she considered to be the minister's heavy handed actions and was not content to sit back and accept a unilateral decision, especially given her devotion of every waking moment during this momentous year to the cause.

Justified or not, Beryl's impetuous actions revealed a few things about her at a time when she seemed to be fuelled increasingly by frustration and anger. Whether it was telling politicians what she really thought of them, or defying instructions to remove potentially offensive materials from a travelling exhibit, she was not to be mistaken for someone who was always going to toe the party line. Whatever her true motivations, the poster incident demonstrated the kind of audacity and rebelliousness that would soon come to define Beryl's evolving style of advocacy.

16.
Transit Activism

B eryl was especially bold whenever she dealt with transportation issues. She learned early on with rec club members and her own experiences on paratransit that building affordable and accessible transportation systems would be critical to the successful integration of people with disabilities. "I remember before my accident, I took transportation for granted. I was completely mobile, and if I wanted to go shopping, I hopped in my car or took a bus. But for so many of the disabled, it just isn't that easy. We have to be taken. We just can't race off across town whenever we want to. If we have an appointment with a doctor, we have to book a ride several days in advance."

Transportation consistently topped Beryl's list of priorities, which began with her fielding distressed calls from stranded people who missed paratransit rides. She knew from personal experience what it felt like to wait for hours for a ride that sometimes never showed up, the frustration and embarrassment in not being able to keep appointments, and the desperation of digging into a limited monthly budget to shell out cash for an expensive accessible taxi. She knew firsthand how the broken system of paratransit services undermined the ability of people with disabilities to make and keep appointments, to get a job, or to participate in community activities and events. Some employers who were open to hiring people with disabilities had their own reservations, as one such employer declared in a 1981 documentary. "One of the first questions we will ask a handicapped person when they apply for the job is their mode of transportation," explained the employer. "It's two strikes against him if he has to use Wheel-Trans."

Ever since paratransit services were introduced by the Toronto Transit Commission in 1975, there were problems. All-Way Transportation, the private subcontractor for Wheel-Trans, was proven not up to the task of ferrying passengers to and from their destinations in a safe and timely manner. Wheel-Trans service was highly subsidized by the province and municipality, providing riders with disabilities with essential door-to-door service for the price of a standard TTC fare. In 1981, TTC fares were $0.57 or $29.75 for a monthly Metropass, allowing unlimited travel.[1] Many Wheel-Trans passengers carried Metropasses but were charged extra for non-subsidized evening rides, with some passengers racking up additional bills over $980 per year, or nearly triple the rate of annual Metropass fares.

In September 1980, complaints of missed pickups and injuries on Wheel-Trans buses led Beryl to petition a local justice of the peace in Toronto. She charged that the TTC, All-Way Transportation, and its owner Nick Comsa Sr. should be charged with criminal negligence. The justice dismissed Beryl's petition, but she sought an appeal, hoping to raise contributions from the community to cover legal fees. In November, a passenger named Lynne Pyke died while getting out of a Wheel-Trans bus. The tragic incident prompted the TTC to open an official inquest to determine the cause of Pyke's death and any systemic shortcomings that required change. It was clear something was very wrong with paratransit in Toronto, and Beryl did her best to draw public attention to the problem while holding officials to account.

Reports also began to surface of disabled students forced to crawl to get into Wheel-Trans vehicles that lacked the capability to "kneel" (sink the entrance to the curb) or to deploy a lower step. Jill Cowie of the Iron Butterfly Parents' Association alerted Toronto public school board trustees to a range of problems with All-Way: drivers caught smoking while driving, arriving late for the opening of school, refusing to help students on and off the bus despite contract language stipulating that "in necessary cases, the driver will be obliged to assist students to and from the vehicle or dwelling." Despite these complaints, the Toronto school board lacked alternative paratransit options and renewed its $807,000 contract with All-Way to provide Wheel-Trans service to students with disabilities across the city.

As complaints about Wheel-Trans ballooned, Beryl responded by organizing to protest the TTC. She started by collecting signatures in a petition urging the TTC to cancel its private contract with All-Way and bring Wheel-Trans in-house to increase accountability, provide better public oversight, and improve quality of service. The march would head north along Yonge Street to the Davisville headquarters of the TTC where the petition was to be presented to officials. "I'm not a militant," Beryl told a reporter. "I won't be a militant until I start burning buses. Some people do not agree with me, but so far, the phone calls I have gotten from the people in distress who use Wheel-Trans support my actions." For her actions against the TTC, Beryl had been called a radical and a leftist activist, but she dismissed such labels. "All I am doing is simply taking a firm stand on the basic rights of the disabled."

The line between passion and militancy was one that she would continually traverse. Her brother Norman remembered when her personality shifted following her accident. "In fact, I think she's gone too much the other way," he told an interviewer. "She's too militant, and I've told her so. I hear her voice on the newscast and the timbre doesn't sound like my sister. I tell her, 'Tone down. If you get too enthused, you're going to hurt the people you're working for. You've got to know where to draw the line.' But you know, I've still got the best damn respect for her." Indeed, Norman was not the authority on how Beryl had evolved over the years, but he did have the longest perspective on how much she had changed since before her accident.

On the morning of June 25, 1981, trailed by a documentary film crew with cameras rolling, Beryl and a crowd of around seventy-five people using manual and electric wheelchairs, some with their personal care workers, met at Nathan Phillips Square in front of Toronto City Hall. Year of Disabled Persons flags were mounted high atop their wheelchairs and placards read "STOP using unsafe equipment!!" and "STOP injuring disabled!" Beryl presided over the demonstration, in a smart chiffon blouse and skirt, her purse pinned neatly to her armrest, as police arrived to escort the demonstrators along their route. Beryl deliberately chose rush hour to begin the demonstration to attract maximum attention by causing the biggest disruption along one of the busiest traffic corridors in Canada's largest city.

Car horns honked relentlessly, either in support or perhaps out of aggravation, as Beryl delivered interviews to reporters on the fly. "Naturally, yes, we need the special buses. Right? But I would like to see total accessibility. Our suggestions did not seem to be getting us anywhere, so ultimately, we were forced to bring them before the public." The *Toronto Star* reported that Wheel-Trans was allegedly responsible for lost jobs, missed appointments, and injured passengers. Later, Beryl reflected on the demonstration with a devilish sense of pride. "It was quite a sight. All those people in wheelchairs, motorized chairs as well as manual ones all making their way up the main street of the city. Why in the middle of the street? Well, we simply could not get our wheelchairs on and off the sidewalk."

On their arrival at TTC headquarters, they were met by TTC officials who invited Beryl into the building to discuss their proposals. Scarborough Controller Joyce Trimmer, who also marched alongside demonstrators, joined Beryl in the meeting. Born in London, England, Trimmer immigrated to Toronto around the same time as Beryl and had been involved in politics since the early 1970s, and in 1988 was the first female to become mayor of Scarborough. Before entering the building, Beryl turned back and spoke to the crowd, trailed by documentary cameras. "I wish we could all get in there, but I'm afraid it's not possible. These are some of the things we would like to read out to you, the things that we are going to ask. . . . People who have complained about the quality and quantity of the Wheel-Trans service will no longer be refused access to the service."

Beryl, Trimmer, another politician, and a few other Wheel-Trans users met with TTC Director of Operations Lloyd Berney and other board members for over two hours. Some riders gave personal accounts of their experiences, including missed and late pickups that led to missed appointments, poor scheduling, poor customer service, and inadequate levels of service to meet demand. Beryl shared some of her own experiences riding Wheel-Trans. "The bus arrived fifteen minutes early. I'm on the fourteenth floor, and by the time I got down there, the bus had left. I came up, and I phoned them and said, 'You were not there. I see you are fifteen minutes early.' They said, 'Well, that's not our fault.' 'Are you coming back for me?' I asked. 'No, forget it,' they said." These were just a handful of experiences that she argued pointed to larger systemic problems with Wheel-Trans operations.

Beryl later observed that they did not expect the meeting to last so long, but it was universally seen as a constructive exchange. She convinced Berney to come down and address the demonstrators himself. They were greeted by a round of applause in the packed lobby as people stood shoulder to shoulder and wheelchair to wheelchair to hear what had been discussed. "I think I was on the receiving end more than I was on the giving end," Berney admitted. "And we've heard the concerns of the group that came up here on this protest march today. . . . I've also indicated to your people that we will be taking a good look and that I will be recommending in September that the commission give consideration to taking over this service at the expiry date of the contract."

The announcement appeared to be a significant commitment to change. But as Beryl would repeatedly learn, verbal commitments did not always translate into meaningful action. Despite Berney's decisive words in front of the demonstrators, the TTC renewed its contract with All-Way, and problems with Wheel-Trans persisted throughout the 1980s. It would not be the last time Beryl would confront the TTC on the streets or behind closed doors, but each time her trust was betrayed by a politician or bureaucrat, she found herself more and more on the militant side of the line, a little more obstinate and a little less compromising.

—————

Beryl's decision to devote herself to disability activism and community organizing gave her a sense of purpose in her post-accident life. Beyond the anger that motivated part of her activism, she was also driven by the impression of divine intervention in her life. She reasoned there could be no other justification for testing her so severely. "It shocked us all," Diane commented to an interviewer about the extraordinary transformation of her mother's personality. "But it gave her a sense of purpose. She definitely realized that she was put on this earth and in this position to help everybody else."

Beryl once wrote, "I believe God allowed my accident to happen for the purpose of working through me." She later reiterated and expanded on this theme with an interviewer. "I figured, I'm alive, and there's some reason God has allowed this to happen to me, but kept me alive. He must want me to help other disabled people."[2] Religion and spirituality rarely featured in her writing and public speaking, but it clearly meant a great deal in her understanding of how and why she could possibly survive an ordeal that would have killed most others. If Beryl developed something of a "messiah complex" about being spared death by divine providence to help disabled people, it was not to proselytize for religious purposes, but rather to express her attempt to comprehend an incomprehensible situation. She decided she would take back control over her narrative and bookend a terrifying ordeal in her life with an explanation that made sense of it all. Inviting a supreme being into her story gave her survival a sense of higher purpose, a foundation on which she could return to recharge and remind herself what she was fighting for when exhaustion or the trials and tribulations of her life overtook her.

As if her life hadn't already been completely transformed by disability, Beryl's new path meant she would need a high level of support if she were to meet what seemed to be an ever-increasing number of obligations. She could no longer rely solely on Wheel-Trans and the odd accessible taxi to get her to appointments. She would need a full-time driver and assistant. Dennis, whose fate was increasingly tied to his mother, filled the role. "It hurt to just sit back and watch her

Beryl exiting a
Wheel-Trans van, ca. 1981.
Beryl Potter personal collection.
Reproduced with permission.

struggle," he confessed in an interview. As Dennis became a grown man, his stocky frame had filled in, his still large dark eyes were set in his now rounder, softer face, and like his mother, he always had his hair neatly combed and took pride in his appearance. He often sported leather loafers, beige slacks, and a collared shirt pulled tightly over his belly. Mother and son already lived together, and he facilitated her travel to and from appointments when she wasn't riding Wheel-Trans. But in the lead up to the Year of Disabled Persons, Dennis quit his job at the Sutton Place Hotel to become his mother's full-time assistant. "My mom and I work sixteen hours a day," he disclosed to a journalist.

Beryl could not afford to pay an attendant on her $631 monthly workers' compensation income. After allocating $184 to the rent of their subsidized Ontario Housing Corporation apartment, she was left with $508 for groceries, bills, and other sundry expenses. With Dennis as her personal attendant, he would earn an attendant's allowance of $490 monthly, which helped them stretch their limited budget. But with a combined annual income of nearly $13,000 to support herself and Dennis, they were living below Canada's official poverty line. They usually managed and were better off than others, but they did not have the budget for many extra expenses, including the kind of extensive daily personal support Beryl needed to accomplish all her ambitions.

Dennis was therefore essential to Beryl's development as an advocate, and his service to his mother defined his life in ways that highlight the dilemmas and struggles often faced by family caregivers. To Dennis, it seemed only logical that he would do everything he could to support his mother. But it was a lot of pressure on him, and he often felt overwhelmed. "My mom's accident happened when I was fifteen. I was so young, and I felt as though I was thrown too many hats. I was trying to be a husband, a doctor, her therapist when she came home, as well as a father and brother to my sister."[3]

The extraordinary sacrifice and dedication Dennis made to his mother was partly shaped by their already strong relationship. Beryl and Dennis figured out a caregiving relationship that worked for them. It may not have been perfect, and the extent to which their lives became tightly intertwined was not always considered healthy or appropriate by some. But in a letter to her brother Norman, Beryl defiantly asserted theirs was a mutually beneficial arrangement. "Regardless of what anyone thinks, I am more independent in the house than they think. I do all the cooking, cleaning, laundry, ironing, and Den does the vacuuming, windows, shopping, and driving. In other words, we share the responsibilities."[4]

In a world that values independence and self-reliance above all else, Beryl and Dennis chose a path of mutual support. Over time, this reciprocal interdependency verged on an unhealthy controlling relationship as both made choices and sacrifices that deeply affected the other. Dennis continued to have a problem with overspending. His extravagant purchases ate into their limited budget. Dennis was never good with money, prone to racking up credit card debt on travel, Rolex watches, and collectors' items such as guns, and model cars and trains. Prior to Beryl's death, whenever Dennis got into too much debt, he would lean on her pension income to make ends meet. As the bills piled up, he would become more and more possessive of his mother's income. "If I want to make a dress, I beg him to give me my money out of the bank," Beryl would complain to Diane, alluding to behaviour that could be described as elder abuse by Dennis. "And then he'd say, 'You have enough money and enough dresses. You don't need . . . anymore." Mother and son would often fight like this in later years. Beryl would sometimes call up her daughter, crying, saying she felt as if she were in jail.

And yet, with Dennis's world focused on supporting his mother, his employment and income increasingly revolved entirely around her. Beryl refused to accept help from personal support workers either at home or in the community, putting even more pressure on Dennis, and with her daily schedule requiring several transfers in and out of her wheelchair or up over a curb, the constant assistance eventually extracted a heavy toll on Dennis's body. If either of them recognized their arrangement as potentially unhealthy, they did not express that to anyone. Whatever his faults, Dennis proved himself a devoted caregiver to his mother, a situation particularly noteworthy considering his own intellectual disability and the stereotype that would have portrayed him as incapable of such strenuous caregiving. The true costs of this relationship would eventually come to a head, but for now, Beryl dived into the work of being an advocate and Dennis was happy to be his mother's constant companion.

Beryl at home working on projects for the Year of the Disabled, 1981.
© Erin Combs.

17.
Life Another Way

As Beryl became increasingly well-known in Toronto, she attracted the attention of writer, producer, and documentarian Alex Hamilton-Brown. Born in Glasgow, Scotland, a graduate of the New York University School of Film and Television, Alex was working on a documentary in 1980 about twelve-year-old wheelchair basketball player Jeff Adams whose team, the champion Toronto Spitfires, took on the Harlem Globetrotters in a game of wheelchair basketball. The story follows Jeff as he confronts the challenges of his disability, culminating in a decisive match. The film did well at the New York Film Festival where it was nominated for best film, and Alex for best director.

At the Toronto screening of the film, associate producer Fern Crawford told Alex about an amazing woman she met at a luncheon, a triple amputee and tireless disability advocate. Learning more about Beryl's story, Alex recognized the makings of another film. "I realized she was a very courageous woman who had overcome colossal difficulties. We all have to get over difficulties in our life. That's what life is all about, overcoming obstacles. She certainly did that." Fern put together a proposal to the Ontario government to produce a documentary profile of Beryl's life and work and secured a $115,000 grant through Wintario, a provincial lottery that raised funds for community projects.

Alex followed Beryl around with a film crew, capturing key moments of her life and work, including the Ontario Medal for Good Citizenship ceremony, the TTC demonstration, and activities of the Scarborough Recreation Club for Disabled Adults. He cherished the time he spent documenting Beryl in action. "I'll never forget, when we were filming, Beryl said: 'You must come along and make a film of all the people at the Scarborough Club for Disabled. We're holding a dance on Friday.' I got the cameraman and the sound man to come along. We went there in the afternoon and met some of the people to get a feel for the place. Beryl told me basically what would happen, which is essential for filmmakers to know what to expect. But some of the things, we did not expect. And those are the things that made the film memorable."

Earlier that year, a local troop of Girl Guides in Scarborough held a fundraiser fashion show and donated $450 to the club so they could purchase a sound system. "I was thrilled when they told me they had raised the money for something we need," Beryl told a reporter for the *Scarborough Mirror* newspaper. "Our members like to play bingo and make announcements. Until now it has been very difficult to do so because of the size of the room we hold our meetings in. We need a sound system so our voices will carry to the back of the room." The speakers were immediately used for a dance. Alex's cameras captured Anne Abbott as she joined in, and he recalls, "I'll never forget how a young fella came up and sort of swept her off her feet and began

Beryl, director Alex Hamilton-Brown, and cameraman Rob Rouveroy recording Beryl at her sewing machine, 1981. © Mike Slaughter.

dancing with her on the floor to some Beatles number. It was her expression of sheer joy, dancing as if for the first time, watching her slippered feet glide lightly across the floor."

Titled *Life Another Way*, the film projected positive, empowered representations of disability that Beryl tried to embody. The opening and closing music, "Look Beyond," was the official Year of Disabled Persons song for Canada with lyrics written and sung by Pat McKee of the University of Toronto. The lyrics captured the essence of the film's overarching theme.

> I am a person with dreams and ambitions
> And I have a song to be sung
> I am determined that when it is over
> I will have only begun
> To show to the world my potential
> To show to the world what I've done
> I am a child of the universe too
> Out of every seven, I'm one
> . . .
> I need so much more than just sheltered employment
> I need less than pity and tears
> I need your respect, and I need your compassion
> Lend me your eyes and your ears
> Then see me and touch me and feel as I feel
> Hear what I say can't you see I am real
> . . .
> So look beyond what I am not
> And you will see just what I am
> I'm a woman, I'm a child, I'm a man.[1]

Alex observed how the song fostered an emotional connection to the storyline. "It was a brilliant piece of music that fits into the film to absolute perfection. It could have been written for them." He remembers watching audience members at the premiere, including "macho 50-year-old men" who became teary-eyed as the credits rolled.

Life Another Way premiered in the lieutenant governor's suite at Queen's Park. This was the second time Beryl was there since being awarded the Ontario Medal for Good Citizenship. A reception in tribute to Beryl held by Lieutenant Governor John B. Aird followed. The film made waves when it was broadcast on television in Canada, US, England, New Zealand, Australia, and the Philippines. It won the Silver Screen Award at the Chicago Film Festival and the American Industrial Film Festival, the Judge's Award at the Yorkton Film Festival in Saskatchewan, and was played at the Montreal Film Festival.

One of the film's most important accomplishments was that it captured Beryl at a pivotal moment in her ascendant career and helped project her onto a national and international stage. Nothing would be the same for her after the film was released. It boosted her credibility as one of the leading advocates for the disability community, and she subsequently began to appear more frequently in the media, which she used to attract attention to support her various causes. Alex suggests intrigue about Beryl derived from not only the incredible story of her disability but also her unique personality. "She had that Old World feminine charm of an Englishwoman that appealed to Canadians. She did not have that aggressive or feisty streak much in her early life when she was raising her family, but when she became disabled, something clicked in her, and from some deep wellspring of her personality rose this amazing leader."[2] The line between gentle English housewife and outspoken determined advocate was one that Beryl would continually traverse. She learned to use this to her advantage, becoming increasingly adept at switching between these personas to achieve her goals in the public eye or behind closed doors as a lobbyist. But it was never an easy balance to maintain. As she took on an increasingly crushing load of responsibilities, she would find there was a price to pay when she was too far to one side.

Life Another Way was not the only film released during the Year of Disabled Persons depicting people with disabilities. In December 1981, the film *Whose Life Is It Anyway*, starring Academy Award winner Richard Dreyfuss, also premiered in Toronto. Adapted from a BBC television movie and Broadway play, the film features sculptor Ken Harrison (Dreyfuss) who becomes paralyzed below the neck as the result of a car accident. He struggles with depression and loss of self-identity as he is unable to enjoy life as he once did. He refuses to adapt, eventually petitioning for an assisted suicide, which his doctor flatly refuses. Harrison rejects this medical paternalism and hires a lawyer to argue the case in court where a judge decides whether

Harrison has the moral, ethical, and legal right to choose to die. The film opened to mixed reviews with some calling it "an engrossing drama" that "ambitiously and heroically" wrestled with the concept of death, while critics found it "shallow" and "depressing."[3] The film features some of the realities of living with quadriplegia and ultimately highlights how disabled people can be deprived of their agency by medical and legal authorities.

The timing of the film's release at the end of the Year of Disabled Persons was strategically significant as it was a moment meant to raise the profile of disability rights politics and acknowledge disability issues. It was unfortunate then, that the distributor chose to release the film at the inaccessible Toronto Famous Players Plaza Cinema in downtown Toronto at the corner of Yonge and Bloor. The two-screen, one thousand seat cinema, attached to the Hudson's Bay Centre, was newly constructed in 1976 but lacked any ramps or street-level access. The irony of screening a film about disability during the Year of Disabled Persons in a theatre that was inaccessible to many disabled people was not lost on Beryl and other disability activists. A group of approximately twenty-five people, led by Beryl and disability activist Pat Israel, descended on the theatre to protest their exclusion from the screening. Placards read, "Discrimination Towards Disabled Persons! This Movie Theatre Is Inaccessible For Disabled"; "1981 International Year of Disabled Persons. Truth Or?"; "A Film About Disabled Is Barred Accessibly [sic] To The Disabled."[4] News cameras captured the chaotic scene with photos showing Beryl defiantly pointing a finger while addressing reporters outside the cinema. Famous Players hastily arranged another special screening of the film at the accessible Skyway 6 cinema for the demonstrators before general release, but the alternate location was apparently not serviced by Wheel-Trans, nor was the arrangement of a special screening on point with the arguments about demanding greater inclusivity. Demonstrators indicated this was just one small, but glaring, example of how structural barriers continuously deny disabled people equal opportunity to fully participate in society.

But not everyone saw the demonstration as a positive affirmation against the discrimination faced by disabled people. Barbara Amiel, columnist for the conservative tabloid newspaper *Toronto Sun*, wrote an article entitled "Movies as a Human Right?" that repudiated the

Beryl, Pat Israel, and others protesting outside the Famous Players as news reporters interview them, 1981. © Frank Lennon.

protest and broader claims of accessibility being a human right. Amiel, who briefly served as editor of the tabloid, gained a controversial reputation for her right-wing conservative political views, despite having been a communist activist in her youth. She summed up the film as being about "a quadriplegic who wants to die" and admitted the cinema was inaccessible and compared this with the "virtual inaccessibility" experienced by able-bodied cinemagoers forced to queue alongside all those "horrid teenagers" who frequent the Bloor Street shopping mall.

The heart of her piece argued moviegoing was not a human right and that it was better to allow market forces to entice owners to make cinemas more accessible since compelling them to do so by legal authority would prove a slippery slope. Amiel was no stranger to writing in such a way that strained toward the extreme for comic or incendiary effect. "Would cinema owners have to provide facilities for people confined to beds? Or captioned movies for the deaf?" Fully aware of the political context of her writing during the Year of Disabled Persons, she lamented the loss of a charitable approach to disabled people with the advent of human rights activism. "This involved pretending that the disabled were *in no way* [original emphasis] different than the able-bodied." She mocked the phrase, "The Disabled Are Able," a slogan adopted by the provincial Handicapped Employment Program and championed by Beryl, comparing it to George Orwell's concept of doublespeak wherein the meaning of words and phrases are reversed for politically expedient reasons.

Echoing the *Toronto Sun*'s conservative values that tend to condemn high taxes and government waste, Amiel wondered why a private foundation could not raise money for wheelchair ramps rather than thrusting the accessibility demands of a disabled minority group upon the public purse. She said she would be first in line to donate, confirming her willingness to support disability issues as a matter of personal choice rather than being compelled to do so through taxes. Subsidizing disabled people's needs through taxation and legal rights was a key point of contention in her article. She wondered why able-bodied people should change their habits and spending "to accommodate the protesters' desires and ambitions as *a matter of right* [original emphasis]," dismissing such demands as "special privileges" to fit the "lifestyles" of a "special interest group." Such special privileges included, according to Amiel, the films being rescheduled "to fit your lifestyle, or taxi fleet owners be required to remodel their cabs for crippled drivers."

Amiel concluded her article in grand fashion, remembering a poster she saw during Ontario Mental Health Week. "It showed a man with the vacant look that sometimes distinguishes the retarded. The caption read: 'The only problem I have is in your mind.' Such a caption is more than mischievous. It is dangerous. The problem such a person has, alas, is that nature short-changed him. It is his problem and one that a prosperous, humane society like ours should try and alleviate. It becomes a danger to all our minds when governments and special interest groups try to convince us of such double-think as able = disabled and equality = special privileges and that my special tastes, problems or pigmentation confer a right on me to demand special treatment from someone else."[5]

Beryl was undoubtedly horrified by the poisonous invective she read in the newspaper that day. One would be hard pressed to find any published writing in Canada of the time (or since) as flagrantly disrespectful to people with disabilities and critical of disability rights, though Amiel did reprise parts of her arguments in a 1994 article, calling members of the newly created Ontario Advocacy Commission a pernicious "bureaucracy of commissars."[6] Beryl saved the original article, carefully filing it away in her personal papers alongside other clippings documenting her many initiatives and accomplishments. Perhaps it served as a reminder to her of the sort of attitudes she was working to challenge, the ignorance and prejudice that obstructed the path to full participation for people with disabilities. Maybe it served as fuel to motivate her to continue her fight to break down these kinds of barriers.

Beryl also remembered Terry Fox's inspirational words: "Even if I don't finish, we need others to continue." On September 1, 1980, after 143 days and 5,373 kilometres, Terry was forced to end his Marathon of Hope just east of Thunder Bay, Ontario. Cancer had spread to his lungs, and he returned to British Columbia to convalesce. Two weeks later in a swiftly organized ceremony, Governor General Edward Schreyer flew to Terry's hometown of Port Coquitlam to designate him a Companion of the Order of Canada, the youngest recipient of the country's highest honour. The following year, on June 28, 1981, Terry died, cementing his role as a martyr for cancer research and public consciousness of disability. An unprecedented outpouring of grief erupted across the country as Canadians of all ages mourned his death. Prime Minister Trudeau captured the mood in the House of Commons, speaking in his distinctively articulate style of elocution.

"It occurs very rarely in the life of a nation that the courageous spirit of one person unites all people in the celebration of his life and in the mourning of his death. . . . We do not think of him as one who was defeated by misfortune but as one who inspired us with the example of the triumph of the human spirit over adversity."[7]

Beryl was crushed by Terry's death and mourned alongside millions of others who considered him one of Canada's greatest heroes. Years later, she would be inducted into the Terry Fox Hall of Fame by the Canadian Foundation for Physically Disabled Persons next to her friend and mentor Bob Rumball. Clutching a bronze trophy in the shape of Terry, looking back over nearly twenty years of advocacy and education work, she remarked on how much she had looked up to him. She admired his ability to send a simple, clear message to attract the attention of the media, politicians, and the broader public. Above all, she hoped she had embodied Terry's example of steadfast resolve against overwhelming odds, and the many barriers that tested the limits of her own endurance.

The power to inspire was one thing, but Beryl found herself grappling with the increasingly complex problem of how not only to change attitudes, but systems and policies that kept many people with disabilities isolated, unemployed, and underhoused. She would learn to confront these challenges through tireless lobbying and networking, fighting for disabled people to take back control over their lives from the society that had denied them for so long, carrying on as Terry wished for others to do.

18.
Rights

A s the spotlight of the International Year of Disabled Persons faded, Beryl felt she was just getting started. The UN Decade of Disabled Persons (1983–1992) offered many opportunities to raise awareness of disability issues and held great promise to make substantive advancements for the rights of people with disabilities. Like other activists and advocates, Beryl was compelled to capitalize on this political moment by lobbying those in power to make lasting changes to the laws and policies that impacted the lives of people with disabilities. The lack of human rights legislation in Canada and deep-seated prejudices had already been exposed, but now it was up to national, provincial, and local governments to implement substantive change. It was fortuitous for disability activists, then, that the Canadian government was redefining its identity as a sovereign country with its own constitution and a new Charter of Rights and Freedoms.

In 1867, the British Parliament administered its colony of British North America through the BNA Act, which held ultimate authority over local, provincial, and national legislation. Since 1927, several Canadian prime ministers attempted to wrest greater control over the legislative process from London by patriating the constitution, but these efforts repeatedly failed to achieve the necessary cooperation of provincial governments. In 1980, a rise in separatist politics in the province of Québec led to a province-wide referendum on whether the province should become its own country separate from the rest of Canada. The motion was defeated, but the episode prompted Prime Minister Pierre Trudeau to "bring home the constitution" to help quell dissent and heal the divide. The "people's package," as the legislation was called, added an amendment formula to the constitution and a

Charter of Rights and Freedoms that promised to enshrine equality protections for every individual regardless of race, national or ethnic origin, colour, religion, age, or sex.

But what about disability? Disability rights activists were shocked to learn neither physical nor mental disability would be protected by the Charter. Activists across the country quickly assembled a frenzied lobbying campaign, urging Trudeau and then–minister of justice (future prime minister) Jean Chrétien to include disability in the Charter. But Chrétien felt the term *disability* was far too vague and open to legal interpretation. He wanted to limit "the grounds of non-discrimination to those few which have long been recognized and which do not require substantial qualification."[1]

The Parliamentary Special Committee on the Disabled and the Handicapped (or Obstacles Committee), the architects of the *Obstacles* report, disagreed with Chrétien and publicly endorsed the inclusion of disability in the Charter. The Coalition of Provincial Organizations of the Handicapped (later Council of Canadians with Disabilities) presented a brief to the Parliamentary Committee on the Constitution. Behind the scenes, David Smith, member of parliament for Don Valley East and chair of the Obstacles Committee, relentlessly lobbied his colleagues, delivering multiple speeches in caucus meetings on the topic and questioning why disability wasn't being considered for inclusion in the Charter. When Smith rose to deliver the same speech for the fourth or fifth time, Trudeau pre-empted him. "David, you can sit down. We're putting it in. We don't need to hear that speech again."[2]

On January 28, 1981, Chrétien announced that discrimination on the grounds of mental and physical disability would, in fact, be included in the equality clause of the Charter. On April 17, 1982, in a special ceremony held on Parliament Hill, Queen Elizabeth II officially transferred all legislative authority to Canada and proclaimed Canada's Constitution Act in force. The inclusion of disability as a protected category in the Charter of Rights and Freedoms provided a powerful new tool for an evolving disability rights movement to challenge discriminatory laws and policies across the nation and build up new case law to further protect the rights of persons with disabilities.

As part of its response to the Decade of Disabled Persons, the Ontario Ministry of Citizenship and Culture provided operational grants to various disability organizations. Hoping to enhance the informal support she provided out of her own apartment to rec club members, Beryl won a grant to establish an official office to provide support to the local disability community. The Scarborough Action Committee was dissolved, and, in its place, a new organization was created: the Scarborough Advocacy Centre for Disabled Persons and Their Families (also known as Action Awareness). Beryl rented a second-floor office at 305 Milner Avenue, a nondescript ten-storey office building in Scarborough in a predominantly commercial area just north of Highway 401. She was exhilarated but was also aware of the heavy burden this responsibility now carried as she strove to scale up her advocacy.

Action Awareness was to act as an information and advocacy hub for the disability community. Its basic function was to organize and implement community awareness tours, encourage networking, and assist people with disabilities and their families to access community resources. Beyond these practicalities, the larger goals of the organization were to stimulate and organize "collective action within the disability community" and promote the concept that persons with disabilities "can be active participants in the mainstream of Ontario's society."[3] Action Awareness created a strong footing for the expansion of Beryl's outreach mission. "Anyone who is disabled, either physically or mentally handicapped, and feels their rights are being infringed upon can contact our office and we will fight for them."[4] Action Awareness was led by a board of directors drawn largely from members and allies of the rec club, including Marilyn Currie, Barry King, Columba Nardella, Dennis Potter, Edith Rason, Sam Savona, and Zena Spurny. Beryl served as president and Dennis as her assistant, supported by a secretary/coordinator and rotations of summer students.

To educate people about the basic facts of living with a disability in modern Canada, Action Awareness published a guide booklet called *Open Doors* that was distributed at public events. Disability is ubiquitous, the booklet asserted, with three million Canadians across the country living with disability, in every community. "With a little love and understanding, a disabled person is capable of fitting into all society, providing the attitudinal barriers are removed." The book-let outlined essential etiquette when encountering a person with a disability, and attempted to answer some harder questions, including general feelings of fear and discomfort around disability. "Don't blame yourself. Until a few years ago, physical or mental disabilities were never publicly discussed. There was no place in society for disabled persons, and so they were locked away in an institution or kept out of sight. Consequently, the fear of the unknown has built a tremendous attitudinal barrier."[5]

Throughout the 1980s, Beryl found a true friend and ally in human rights lawyer David Baker. Baker established the Advocacy Resource Centre for the Handicapped or ARCH and assisted Beryl with various coalitions and initiatives over the years. A tall man with a shock of white hair, a boyish face, and glasses often pushed low on his nose, Baker remembers being a young law student studying at the University of Toronto in the late 1970s with a passion for social justice. His student legal aid program received a federal grant to start a new clinic at the Queen Street Mental Health Centre, modelled on a pioneering clinic at a psychiatric hospital in Washington, DC, where Baker learned about disability rights and the unique legal struggles of people with mental health issues and physical disabilities. While volunteering for activist attorney Ralph Nader on tax policy, he heard of a new disability rights centre called the Mental Health Law Project (later renamed the Bazelon Center) supported by the Rockefeller Foundation and staffed by top-tier lawyers.

Baker returned to Canada inspired to develop a similar disability law centre to aid Canadians with disabilities. The concept required willingness by service agency representatives, disability activists, and consumer groups to set aside their ideological differences to form a coalition to work together on a common project, no small achievement. Baker discovered he would not get funding for a specialty disability clinic if he could not corral all the major players in disability advocacy to the table. He began meeting with organizations to work toward building common ground, including service agencies such as the Ontario March of Dimes, the Association for the Mentally

Retarded (now Canadian Association for Community Living), and the Canadian Mental Health Association. On the consumer side, he met with groups such as the Canadian Association of the Deaf, DAWN (DisAbled Women's Network), BOOST (Blind Organization of Ontario with Selfhelp Tactics), On Our Own (a mental health group), People First (an intellectual disability group), and with Beryl as the representative of Action Awareness. For Baker, it was an emotional and momentous achievement when these different organizations from disparate parts of the advocacy world and disability rights movement came together with the common goal of providing legal support to people with disabilities to advance the cause of progressive legal reforms in the country. In 1979, ARCH was formed and opened its doors the following year. Each member organization could nominate a board member or two provided at least one member was a person with a disability to ensure the organization was controlled by people with disabilities. It was a breakthrough for the advancement of disability rights and the disability community in Canada.

Baker first met Beryl in the mid-1980s and was immediately impressed with her dedication, charisma, and influence. He identified her as one of the only people at the time who could get people with disabilities out to protest in the streets and march alongside her. "I remember that she had huge credibility and connections in the Liberal Party. [Ontario Liberal Leader and later premier] David Peterson was willing to meet with her, which meant huge access." Baker became Beryl's informal legal support whenever the occasion presented itself. "Whether it was a protest march or going into Peterson's office, I would be the guy in the suit with the briefcase walking along beside her as her legal vehicle." Beryl would continue to cross paths with Baker as he provided legal guidance for her various initiatives. "I can tell you if she wanted something, she was pretty good at getting it from ARCH. We operated on the basis that we received guidance as to what our priorities were in terms of litigation, in terms of law reform, and coalition building." Baker says Beryl had a huge role in helping move things forward. "If Beryl said something was a priority, it usually went to the front of the line because everyone agreed with her. She was able to pull everybody together."[6]

In 1982, Beryl was appointed to serve a six-year term with the Ontario Advisory Council on the Physically Handicapped where her consensus-building skills were put to the test. The council was established in 1975 by second-term Progressive Conservative Premier Bill Davis to fulfill his electoral promise of improving Ontario's relationship with the disability community. With his laid-back personality and charm, an image completed by the pipe or cigar he often smoked,[7] Davis was a famously moderate conservative leader who repeatedly won the hearts of Ontarians and is, to date, the second-longest serving premier in that province. The council was initially chaired by Edward Dunlop, president of the *Toronto Sun* newspaper and managing director of the Canadian Arthritis and Rheumatism Society, who also happened to be blind as the result of a wartime injury. The needs and concerns of over one million disabled Ontarians could finally be heard through a formal advisory body empowered to influence policy development at the provincial level on a wide range of issues including transportation, housing, income maintenance, assisted devices, and support services. Council members travelled across the province holding public hearings and then submitting reform recommendations to the government.

One of the inaugural members of the Advisory Council of the Physically Handicapped, later renamed the Advisory Council of Disabled Persons, was none other than Beryl's mentor, Bob Rumball. He had resigned from the council by 1982 to focus on other initiatives and Dunlop was succeeded as chair by Jack Longman, an insurance agent with tenure at several social agencies who lived with a congenital bone disease requiring him to use crutches and leg braces. Scarborough MPP and Provincial Secretary for Social Development Margaret Birch, who had marched with Beryl to TTC headquarters in 1980 and was now a close friend, oversaw the council and was responsible for nominating advocates to fulfill its mission. Naturally, when an opening came up in 1982, Birch jumped at the chance to appoint Beryl to the council. Beryl enthusiastically joined in April and began attending monthly meetings. Members of the public regularly appeared before the council to provide submissions about ways to improve the lives of Ontarians with disabilities, and though it was not required, Beryl would often stay afterward to personally connect with these folks.

Six months in, the first cracks in her relationship with the council began to appear and she was soon on a collision course with chair Longman. In her exchanges with the chair, Beryl revealed a new level of confidence and willingness to speak up against authority figures. In October, she crafted a letter to the chair outlining several grievances with how the council operated. She was apparently often the last to leave meetings, taking extra time to reassure people "what if anything would be done about their deputations." She also questioned the withholding of budgetary information from council members. "This leaves one feeling that we are very low in your estimation of trust. After all, these are public tax dollars being used." She argued council members with attendants should be reimbursed for the extra expense of having their support during council meetings, as these are "the true realities of life for some." She also suggested the council should not meet at the expensive Sutton Place Hotel and instead use their offices at 700 Bay Street. Beryl copied the Secretary for Social Development on the correspondence and noted, "Birch would not wish to see tax dollars being spent unnecessarily."

Longman was infuriated. In his terse reply letter, he suggested that as a new member, Beryl did not understand how the council worked. "It is very different from a club or an agency. There is nothing to hide." He continued that if she had suggested a private meeting, "it would have served a better purpose than your letter to me with copies to all members of Council." Another council member, Jim Gerrond, objected to the chair's reply in a separate letter dated November 18, 1982, arguing that Beryl's grievances were of concern to the whole council. "It is a healthy exercise leading to harmony among all Council members."

Beryl would not be pacified by her official position on the council; indeed, it seemed to have the opposite effect of emboldening her. The following year, she organized a demonstration held on October 13, 1983, to protest the poor state of social welfare for people with disabilities and called on the government to strike a parliamentary task force. She provided advance notice of the demonstration in a letter to MPP Bruce McCaffrey, the new Provincial Secretary for Social Development who succeeded Margaret Birch. It was clear Beryl did not share the same close relationship with McCaffrey as she had with Birch. Beryl wrote that she hoped McCaffrey would "overlook any personal feelings," possibly referencing past arguments between the two, and support her call for a task force. Beryl concluded with a stinger, if only to ensure her intentions were made crystal clear in a thinly veiled threat. "Hopefully, I can assure peace and control, providing we are not to be ignored. If, however, Premier Davis does not respond, I will not be held responsible for any outbursts of anger and bitterness that may arise from the frustration of a deeply hurting people."

The demonstration drew three hundred and fifty participants, including several prominent politicians and Professor David Symington, a well-known champion of vocational rehabilitation at the time. Demonstrators gathered in front of Toronto City Hall at Nathan Phillips Square and proceeded up University Avenue to the provincial capital at Queen's Park. Beryl complained to the *Toronto Star* that the Guaranteed Annual Income Supplement, a top up to the federal Canada Pension Plan, was 50 per cent lower for adult people with disabilities than seniors, an unacceptable ratio given the high unemployment rate in the disability community. Beryl proclaimed she was "ready to take to the streets again" because she had not seen the progress she had expected since 1981. She believed the government "thinks we are ready to crawl back into our holes. We are here to stay," she thundered.[8] Beryl acknowledged that she was developing a reputation as "a militant pain to many," but also asserted that she could not care less about her infamy within certain circles. "Being fortunate enough to have lived the life of an able-bodied and disabled person has taught me that having the ability to love and care for others is far more important, and certainly the most precious thing in my life."[9]

Beryl's life as an advocate provided her with opportunities she never dreamed of before her accident, including new connections with her native country. She coordinated a two-week visit of twenty people with disabilities from the United Kingdom to Canada to build international relationships with activists and learn best practices from the British context. A reception was held by Lieutenant Governor John B. Aird at Queen's Park. Though the viceregal position was largely ceremonial, Aird, a tall man with a friendly and almost aristocratic disposition, was a corporate lawyer guided by a deeply engrained sense of integrity who took a special interest in disability issues. Since his introduction to Beryl in 1981 during a special screening of *Life*

Another Way, Aird went on to champion fundraising efforts by the Hospital for Sick Children, learned sign language, and in association with the Canadian National Institute for the Blind hosted a summer retreat for blind children in Muskoka's cottage country.[10]

Aird was also there in 1984, when Beryl was invited to celebrate Ontario's Bicentennial with a reception and dinner at the Hilton Harbour Castle Convention Centre, a spacious ballroom facility with spectacular views of Toronto's harbour and cityscape. The area around the centre was flooded with onlookers and royal enthusiasts as the Queen arrived by the *HMY Britannia* (Her Majesty's Yacht) in Toronto Harbour on September 29, 1984, on her Royal Tour of Canada. Beryl was given the opportunity to meet the Queen and Prince Philip at the convention centre, and though she never mentioned what was said during their brief encounter, one can imagine Her Majesty's surprise not only at Beryl's appearance, but also when a Scouse accent greeted her in Toronto that afternoon.

Transportation continued to dominate Beryl's advocacy and lobbying agenda. In March 1985, she went to battle against the TTC again, leading a protest at the opening of the new Scarborough Rapid Transit (RT) line, an elevated light-rail track corridor connecting to Toronto's subway system at Kennedy station in the Scarborough Junction neighbourhood, extending rapid transit six stops east into the heart of Scarborough. The small rail cars painted in grey and red stripes ran on light gauge rail, usually two to three cars coupled together, giving riders the distinct feeling of being on an amusement park ride. Amazingly, the approximately $189 million rapid transit line was completely inaccessible to wheelchair users. In protest, Beryl quickly organized a demonstration at the Scarborough Centre Station RT hub, where both the civic centre and town centre were located. Reports surfaced of Wheel-Trans drivers refusing to take protesters to the demonstration, but enough people showed up to attract attention from the media about the egregious planning failure. "What happened to the Charter of Rights?" demanded placards held up by protesters. Beryl held up a large poster alleging the TTC chief general manager had been quoted in a news article stating, "It would be distasteful and inconvenient having the disabled on the TTC."[11] Unfortunately, attention to the issue was fleeting and the TTC made no commitments to making the line accessible. In fact, it would take another fifteen years for the Scarborough RT line to be made only partially accessible with the subsequent installation of elevators and platform modifications at Kennedy and Scarborough Centre Station.

Beryl did not get what she wanted from the TTC protest, but her leadership on the issue heading into the provincial election in the spring of 1985 attracted attention from both the incumbent Progressive Conservative Party and Liberal Party. Both party leaders valued her composure in front of the camera and experience as a lobbyist and invited her to run for their respective parties. David Peterson was a particularly big fan of Beryl and extended an open invitation for her to join the Liberals, knowing she would make a great candidate and how well her inclusion would reflect on the wider party's commitment to advancing disability rights. But Beryl was not yet ready to make the jump into politics, concluding there was far too much work to be done outside government. She simply had too many commitments that she would have to abandon to become a Member of the Provincial Parliament.

The Liberals won four fewer seats than the long-ruling Progressive Conservatives, but a motion of non-confidence soon after the election allowed Peterson to rise to power in a minority government with the New Democratic Party (NDP) holding the balance of power in a Liberal-NDP coalition that overturned the Progressive Conservatives. Peterson held out a standing offer for Beryl to join the Liberals in future elections should she ever change her mind.

The Ontario Liberal coalition government presented Beryl with fresh opportunities for the advancement of disability issues. By September 1985, Beryl took advantage of the International Youth Year to educate children about the realities of living with a disability in Canada. She secured funding from the Office of Disability Issues to embark on a month-long tour of northern Ontario schools. Her tour mate was young Margarita Buell, a polio survivor from Kingston and management trainee with the Ontario March of Dimes who would help Beryl bring the message of youth empowerment to students. They traversed the expanse of Ontario in an old beige Ford E-250 Econoline van—perhaps not coincidentally, the very same model and colour used by Terry Fox during his Marathon of Hope. Beryl must have felt a special communion with Terry, especially as she made her way north along the Trans-Canada Highway toward Thunder Bay. They likely stopped near mile marker 3,339 km just east of Thunder Bay where Terry ended his trek exactly five years earlier to pay homage at the memorial and lookout named in his honour.

The extended cargo van was graciously donated by the Cedar Brae Golf and Country Club and was specially outfitted with an automated side-entry ramp and two rows of tie-down hooks to secure Beryl's wheelchair during transit. Dennis was her driver and travelling assistant, navigating each inaccessible obstacle to get Beryl from door to door, even when her itinerary included several meetings and presentations a day, sometimes hundreds of kilometres apart. Beryl would sit behind Dennis so they could see each other through the rear-view mirror and communicate face to face. They would later acquire a customized blue Dodge minivan specially built with accessibility features that would make life for Dennis a little easier. But for now, they were stuck with "the beast," as Beryl's granddaughter Michelle called it.

Dennis standing next to the Ford E-250 Econoline van surrounded by a group of schoolchildren, ca. 1985. Beryl Potter personal collection. Reproduced with permission.

As dedicated as Dennis was, he wasn't known to be the best driver. His skills on the road sometimes got them into trouble, says Michelle. "Oh my gosh, he was the worst driver in the world! There were no seatbelts back then so she would have injuries on more than one occasion when Dennis would hit a curb and she would go flying out of her wheelchair." Once, they parked in a plaza so Dennis could go into a store while Beryl and her adoring little dachshund waited in the van. As the van rolled away, it became evident Dennis had forgotten to apply the parking brake. Terrified and helpless, Beryl cried out as the vehicle rolled backward into the parking lot. In the ensuing panic, the dog fell and injured its back, but Beryl escaped unharmed.

It was not the first, nor the last, mishap they would have on the road. "One time I remember we all went out for a function and Nana was all dressed up," Michelle recalls. "That was before the lift on the van was working properly, so my uncle had to carry her into the chair from the car. I don't know how he did that for all those years. It was wintertime and there was ice on the ground. Dennis slipped on the ice while he was transferring her, and she slipped right out of her dress and ended up under the van in her underwear! Nana said, 'Oh, whatever,' and we all burst out laughing. At that moment, a man happened to be walking by and all he saw was one arm waving out from under the van and all of us laughing. We must have traumatized him! But she was so easygoing that she could roll when things like that happened or when they did not go as planned."[12]

Beryl's schedule for the International Youth Year tour was gruelling. It began with a send-off press conference at Queen's Park. Before she took to the podium, Beryl was notified it was inaccessible so she would have to sit at the foot of the stage. Naturally, she deemed this unacceptable and told the press secretary as much, ironically forced to advocate for herself at the commencement of an advocacy tour. An internal memo from the secretary read, "Beryl has obviously said it is not okay to be at the foot of the stage, and they should build a ramp," which led to the installation of a temporary ramp at the rear of the stage.

Beryl, Dennis, and Margarita travelled the vast expanses of northern Ontario communities, including Bracebridge, Gravenhurst, Parry Sound, Lively, Thessalon, Thunder Bay, White River, Red Rock, Terrace Bay, Marathon, Wawa, Sault Ste. Marie, Blind River, Elliot Lake, Sudbury, Levacak, Garson, Val Caron, and the long return drive to Toronto. It was an ambitious and exhausting itinerary totalling approximately three thousand kilometres round trip, or more than half the distance between the Atlantic and Pacific coasts. Each stop consisted of multiple visits to schools, local malls, radio and television stations. She made appearances on Toronto's CFRB *Betty Kennedy Show*, CKFM with Pam Chiotti, CBC *Ontario Morning*, and City TV hosted by future Lieutenant Governor David Onley, including dozens of other media outlets across the north.

The tour attracted interest wherever she went and generated dozens of profiles of her life and work in local newspapers, each one with a slightly different accident story than the next. One account had her slipping on a piece of wax paper. Another reported it was a cigarette wrapper, perhaps having written the story after Beryl chain smoked in front of her. Some said it was a tissue paper, others a candy wrapper. Sometimes the accident happened at home, other times she was at the bakery. One placed her at a Laura Secord chocolate shop. Despite the garbled details, Beryl's story, and Margarita's example, clearly resonated with audiences. Beryl's personal journey was the centrepiece of presentations and served as a jumping off point to build personal connections with young audiences.

Enthusiastic feedback poured in from students and teachers. At the Muskoka Lakes Secondary School she received a mix of feedback that may have been equal parts encouraging and disheartening. Many students commented on how the presentation opened their eyes to the challenges of living with a disability. But there was a definite "them and us" paradigm that indicated people with disabilities were considered separate from the rest of the community. One student expressed her sadness about what Beryl lost but understood it "doesn't mean you have to treat them [people with disabilities] differently [because] they're just the same as you." Another student demonstrated their understanding of the primary message about people with disabilities deserving equal treatment, but added, "I feel the same about disabled people as I do my friends," an indication they did not have any friends with disabilities. Some students told her they could not live with themselves if they went through Beryl's experience. "I still don't know how you could be so high on life when you're a disabled person," one wrote to her. Another student remarked, "I do not think I could handle being disabled. Some people might be able to, but I could not." Another student confessed she cried during the presentation. Not from pity, but the frightening possibility that "an accident could happen to anyone."

Beryl picked up on this discordance, suggesting it was likely because people with disabilities were not yet as visible as they were becoming in larger urban centres. "I find the students in the north are far more reluctant to ask questions than those in Toronto," she told the Ontario March of Dimes. "They seemed really embarrassed and hesitant; I don't know why." But she was encouraged by the kind of curiosity she had come to expect from most students. "We got a great response everywhere. In one school, where the students were considered to be a tough bunch, the teachers who met us said they did not think the kids would sit and listen to us for forty minutes, but we were still talking to them three hours later. They wanted us to autograph the posters we gave out and invited us to their school dance that night. The teachers just did not give those kids enough credit!" She commented to a reporter that she believed she may have been the first person with a disability many of the students had ever interacted with. She felt youth were already beginning to internalize negative stereotypes about disability. Upon her return from the tour, Beryl concluded a return trip was necessary. "Our future professionals and frontline workers depend upon it."[13]

19.
Equity

Beryl was thinking of current and future workers when she co-founded the Coalition on Employment Equity for Persons with Disabilities, or CEEPD, in the autumn of 1984 to advance the rights and opportunities of people with disabilities in the labour market. Poverty and unemployment were chronic problems in the disability community. When the general unemployment rate peaked at 12 per cent in 1983 during a recession, most estimates put the unemployment rate in the disability community at around 50 per cent.[1] Fifty years earlier in the depths of the Great Depression when nearly 25 per cent of Canadians were out of work, more than half of disabled Canadians were unemployed and experienced far greater challenges in the labour market, especially those locked away in institutions. Beryl and her allies sought to change all that.

In October 1984, a showdown was brewing between the federal government and disability activists on the topic of unemployment and poverty. Judge Rosalie Abella, the sole commissioner for the Commission on Equality in Employment, released her report examining equality and discrimination issues in the workplace. Abella coined the term "employment equity" to address barriers to employment faced by women, visible minorities, people with disabilities, and Indigenous people. Employers were encouraged to redesign their recruitment and workplace practices to improve employment prospects for these groups. The federal government also tabled Bill C-62 to introduce an Employment Equity Act prohibiting discrimination against disadvantaged groups and encouraging more proactive recruitment measures. But the bill proved heavy on rhetoric and light on substance, including no enforceable regulations to ensure greater proportional representation of these groups in the workforce. Instead, employers were simply required to report workplace statistics to the federal government for tracking purposes, and the legislation applied only to federally regulated industries and Crown corporations, a relatively narrow range of the workforce. Ultimately, the bill bore little resemblance to the recommendations Abella outlined in her report. The lack of enforcement or real incentives for employers to reach target employment rates rendered the legislation an empty façade that failed to adequately address the intended goal of creating an equitable labour market.

In response, CEEPD (later Disabled Persons for Employment Equity) was formed as a coalition of consumer activists and service organizations co-chaired by Beryl and Judy Rebick. Rebick was already a vocal activist, NDP strategist, and later president of the National Action Committee on the Status of Women. A straight-talking campaigner with a mop of curly brown hair, Rebick was born in Reno, Nevada, but raised in Toronto since the age of nine. After her defence of Dr. Henry Morgentaler in a dramatic and highly publicized incident during an anti-abortion protest in which she blocked a man from attacking the doctor with garden shears outside his Toronto clinic, she developed a reputation as a fierce pro-choice advocate in the early 1980s. As a paid advocate for the Canadian Hearing Society, Rebick worked with Beryl on the fight for employment equity. "A story that never gets told is that disabled people led the fight for employment equity. They were the first ones to organize until it opened up to visible minorities and women, which is probably one of the few examples of people with disabilities leading a broader fight like that involving lots of other groups," said Rebick. CEEPD operated on grants from the Canada Action Fund to finance its lobbying efforts to promote employment equity for people with disabilities within the public and private sectors. When it became clear Bill C-62 had no teeth, the coalition quickly shifted its focus to pressure policymakers to amend the bill, particularly lobbying Progressive Conservative Prime Minister Brian Mulroney and minister of employment and immigration Flora MacDonald.

But the organization met with little success. In March 1986, Beryl, Rebick, Gary Malkowski (a leading activist in the Deaf community), and a few other members of CEEPD showed up at the offices of the prime minister and employment minister to secure promises to hear their concerns before going ahead with the legislation. The *Toronto Sun* later reported that the group "ambushed Mulroney in a Commons corridor three weeks ago and got him to promise he would listen to their concerns before going ahead with a bill on job equity legislation."[2] Rebick remembers confronting Mulroney with Beryl that day. "Lorne Nystrom from the NDP said we could confront Mulroney directly as he was walking from Question Period into a Cabinet meeting. There were four of us, including Beryl, waiting in the hallway. Mulroney came striding arrogantly down the hall. His staff had told him he had a group of disabled visitors, so he must have thought, 'It's going to be a great photo-op,' right? He strides right up to us until he sees Beryl, who he knows is very upset about the bill. Then he sees me, so he knows he's been trapped and can't get away. Suddenly, Beryl grabbed hold of him and would not let go! What are they going to do, tackle a woman in a wheelchair? 'You promised me,' she told him. 'You promised me you would listen to us.' He offered us a meeting with his top policy person. I told her, 'Beryl, just let go. It's the best we're going to get. You better let him go.' She just would not let go!"

Beryl had the meeting with Mulroney's policy advisors and made the coalition's concerns known personally before returning to Toronto. But when CEEPD later learned the bill was being tabled without any of the proposed amendments, they began organizing a major protest in Ottawa. Legal counsel for CEEPD, Shari Stein, remarked on the essential weakness of the bill. "How can anyone, the people, the provinces, the municipal governments take this legislation seriously when it has no teeth. It only requires voluntary compliance, and the federal government has exempted itself."[3]

Before dawn on Saturday April 14, 1986, Beryl, along with one hundred and fifty members of CEEPD from Toronto, Winnipeg, and Kingston, boarded buses, cars, and specially equipped accessible vans to form a convoy bound for Ottawa. The Canadian National Institute for the Blind had at least two buses that they allowed the coalition to use to bus people to Ottawa. After the nearly five-hour drive from Toronto, many demonstrators were already exhausted. Rebick remarked to a *Toronto Star* journalist that there was a serious lack of accessible public washrooms along the route that could handle more than one wheelchair user at a time. "I'm sure many people have no idea of the sacrifice these courageous people have made to come all this way. They can't just get in a car. Their wheelchairs have to be tied down in a special van, and many of them can barely stand the travelling."

Late in the morning, demonstrators began congregating in front of Parliament Hill, a complex of buildings that contain the House of Commons, Senate, and administrative departments. Their ultimate destination was Centre Block, a magnificent symmetrical Gothic Revival stone building dominated by the nearly one hundred-metre-high Peace Tower. It was a sunny but chilly day in early spring, a breeze unfurling their banners and rustling black balloons many of them tied to their wheelchairs. They also held or strapped placards to their wheelchairs and chanted slogans. "Dead Like Bill C-62," "No Penalties, No Justice," "Jobs When?" "Black Monday, Disabled Person, No Equality, No Jobs, No Justice." Sam Savona, one of Beryl's long-standing supporters who once attended the Scarborough rec club, also attended the protest.

"What do we want?" Rebick shouted into a megaphone.

"Jobs!" Sam answered in unison with others.

"When do we want them?"

"Now!" Sam shouted back, pumping his fist in the air.[4]

They moved together as a group, trailed by photographers and news cameras, past the Centennial Flame across the sprawling lawn until they were met with a set of stairs at the foot of the Peace Tower, the first of many inaccessible roadblocks to navigate. Outside Centre Block, Beryl addressed reporters. She wore a black patterned dress with white flowers and clear crystalline pearls. Caught up in the energy of the moment, she declared she was willing to be arrested to prove her strenuous opposition to the legislation. "The Mulroney government is trying to tell us the government doesn't need to ensure 'reasonable accommodation' for the handicapped in the workplace. But we can't even get into the most public place in the land."[5]

Inside the House of Commons, the First Session of the Thirty-Third Parliament was already underway. At 1:30 p.m., Beryl and other demonstrators began filtering into the sombre, cavernous halls to witness the ongoing debate of the proposed Employment Equity Bill. Judy remembers being there. "At first, Lorne [Nystrom] and I asked to be let onto the House floor because we knew the gallery wasn't wheelchair accessible, but the Speaker would not allow that. In comes Beryl and the guard told her, 'I'm sorry, madam, but there's no space for your chair.' So, Beryl says, 'That's okay, I'll sit in a regular chair.' I asked her if she'd ever sat in a regular chair and she said, 'No.' I suggested to the guard, 'Do you want to see her tumbling onto the floor?' And frankly, she probably would have risked that. All for the struggle! Because of that, they reluctantly made space for them."[6] But access to the gallery was also restricted by security with limited room for wheelchairs.

"There's only room for six," a guard shrugged, his authoritative tone carrying a hint of exasperation. "There's nothing I can do about it," the brim of his cap was pushed down especially low over his glasses to avoid the glare of documentary cameras, his shoulder patch identifying him as House of Commons Security.

It was not what Beryl had envisioned and she began questioning the officers. "How much room for able-bodied?" she snapped.

"In here? 487," the guard admitted.

"Okay," she began, as if the guard proved her point for her. "Have you got enough men to carry some people out of wheelchairs and put them in the seats and we can leave the wheelchairs lined up here?" Though framed as a question, Beryl was clearly making a demand, aware of the power of the cameras and attention surrounding the exchange. The guards did as she instructed, the hallway filled with empty wheelchairs belonging to demonstrators carried into the gallery seating. Later, Beryl remarked to the *Toronto Star* about the inaccessibility of the gallery. "It took more than forty-five minutes to seat about seventy-five protestors."[7]

At 2:30 p.m. Saskatchewan NDP MP Lorne Nystrom took to the floor. A clean-shaven forty-something man sharply dressed in a blue suit, Lorne opened a section of the debate requesting amendments to the bill.

Mr. Lorne Nystrom (Yorkton-Melville): Mr. Speaker, my question is directed to the Minister of Employment and Immigration. I think she is aware that today more than 100 disabled Canadians have come to Ottawa at considerable expense to tell parliament they want positive changes in the Employment Equity Bill. Why did the government not keep a promise that the Prime Minister's Office made to Beryl Potter and other disabled Canadians about three weeks ago and respond to three specific requests by disabled Canadians to strengthen the Employment Equity Bill before it came back to the House at report stage?

Hon. Flora MacDonald (Minister of Employment and Immigration): Mr. Speaker, as you will be aware, Bill C-62 on employment equity is before the House this very day for debate. We are debating a number of items. With regard to the Hon. Member's question, the Right Hon. Prime Minister responded to Miss Beryl Potter by writing to her at some length regarding the legislation. He pointed out that, among other things, the bill itself is the first piece of legislation ever brought before any Legislature in Canada dealing with employment equity and designed to improve the employment opportunities of disabled persons, visible minorities, native people and women.

Without warning, from the back of the gallery a voice cried out as heads turned to look up. "My name is Beryl Potter, and I've received no such letter, nor were any of my calls answered!" Speaker, PC MP John Wosley of Don Valley West, adorned in a black robe, rose from his oak lined green velvet chair, hammering his gavel. "Order! Order!" he shouted, signalling that the solemnity of the space had been unduly disrupted. A security guard leaned over and admonished Beryl for speaking out. Undeterred, she brushed him off and continued shouting back. "They can't get away with lying to the handicapped people. We're not going to stand for it!" Other demonstrators began cheering and yelling while security dragged Beryl toward the exit.

Sam Savona remembers the incident well. "We were in the gallery when Beryl yelled out and everyone looked to where we were. Then security told everyone to move out. It was a very small area. I was the last one in, so I had to be the first one out before anyone could leave. My friend next to me turned and whispered, 'Don't move.' I looked up at the security guard, looked down at his gun then turned to my friend. 'Yeah, he's got a gun, and I don't!'"

After finally regaining control over the proceedings, the Speaker returned the floor to Mr. Nystrom.

Mr. Lorne Nystrom (Yorkton-Melville): I think she said it for me, Mr. Speaker.

Some Hon. Members: Then sit down.

Mr. Nystrom: Disabled Canadians have asked me to ask when the government is going to move on its election promise to provide full-time permanent jobs in the federal Public Service for disabled Canadians? As of now, 75 percent of its disabled workers are on term contracts.

The President of the Treasury Board, Robert de Cotret, answered that the public service had an affirmative action program with an advisory committee. Nystrom interjected before he could go on. "Some 75 percent are on term contracts!" he retorted, referring again to the fact that most disabled workers were precariously employed and not in permanent jobs. The remaining demonstrators resumed shouting from the gallery as the annoyed Speaker hammered his gavel again. "Order! Order!" The floor then turned to Toronto Liberal MP Roland de Corneille, an ordained Anglican priest and human rights activist.

Mr. Roland de Corneille (Eglinton-Lawrence): Mr. Speaker, my question is directed to the Minister of Employment and Immigration. Recently the Prime Minister personally met Beryl Potter and promised her and a number of other disabled people that he would personally review his government's employment equity policy. That is why they are here demonstrating on the Hill today and that is why that voice has been crying out. There has been no answer, no reply to their phone calls—

[More shouting from the gallery . . .]

Mr. Speaker: Order, please. Does the Hon. Member have a question?

Mr. de Corneille: Yes. My question is to ask the minister what she has to say now to the hundreds of thousands of disabled Canadians who have called upon the government to act, and to say that this government's policy is toothless and phoney.

Minister MacDonald commented that the Liberal Party had failed to introduce employment equity legislation in the past when they were in power. "You are a phoney, Flora," responded Hamilton East MP Sheila Copps, an influential member of the Liberal Opposition and vocal critic of the bill.[8]

Outside Centre Block, the media stood waiting. Sweaty and red-faced, Beryl leaned toward the semi-circle of microphones thrust inches from her face as she spat her disapproval of what she had just witnessed. "He's a chicken!" Beryl shouted, referring to Prime Minister Mulroney. Visibly infuriated, she went on. "The bill, it isn't worth the paper it's printed on . . . I thought they were going to throw me out." The *Toronto Sun* reported that Mulroney had apparently conveniently "slipped out to the dentist and missed the rally."[9] Leaders of the opposing Liberal and NDP parties, John Turner and Ed Broadbent, followed Beryl outside, vowing to help her continue the fight. Cameras flashed as Beryl pulled Broadbent down to kiss his cheek.

20.
Access

Returning home from Ottawa, Beryl set aside one struggle for justice and equity for another. Just two days after leaving Ottawa, Beryl and other members of Trans-Action (a transportation activist group she co-founded in 1986) were determined to make themselves heard in a conflict between Wheel-Trans and the Toronto Transit Commission (TTC) when 185 striking Wheel-Trans drivers and mechanics set up a picket line outside the Scarborough headquarters of All-Way Transportation, the TTC's beleaguered contractor for Wheel-Trans. The strike began just a few days earlier in response to complaints of low wages and poor working conditions. Unlike their counterparts in the TTC, Wheel-Trans drivers and mechanics were subcontracted at a lower rate. Drivers earned $10 per hour while mechanics took $11.75 per hour. (In 2022, this would mean drivers earned $22.50 per hour and mechanics $26.49.) These wages were among the lowest of all TTC contractors, despite the arguably heightened responsibility of providing door-to-door transportation for disabled and vulnerable passengers.

The Amalgamated Transit Union Local 113 representing Wheel-Trans workers sought an immediate $4.05 per hour wage increase to achieve wage parity with TTC workers. All-Way countered with an offer of $1.37 per hour over two years. It was a far cry from what the workers wanted, but even the union endorsed the company's offer in the wake of mounting public pressure. As workers assembled at the Westbury Hotel on Yonge, one block north of Carlton Street, to cast their votes, Beryl arrived at the site with four members of Trans-Action hoping to persuade the workers to end the strike. "We too have rights. Let drivers drive, mechanics work and disabled persons travel to their jobs, homes & recreation," read one placard she held up.[1]

Beryl sympathized with Wheel-Trans workers, arguing they deserved a raise. But she also worried how fourteen thousand people with disabilities who relied on the service would suffer from a prolonged strike. Throughout the job action, Beryl fielded increasingly desperate and angry calls from people with disabilities literally trapped in their homes, unable to go to the grocery store and medical appointments, and forced to spend hundreds of dollars they did not have on the city's limited fleet of private accessible taxis. She met with Ontario MPP Tony Ruprecht on April 25, 1986. Ruprecht reported to the Ontario Legislature that he had met with leading disability organizations in the province "and Beryl Potter [who] were unanimous in their view that something had to be done quickly. . . . They do not support this legislation; they support the rights of their workers. As Beryl Potter put it to my staff this morning, 'It is symbolic that in a second-class system you pay your drivers and your workers second-class rates.'"[2]

The president of All-Way, Ray Hould, was "very distressed that people are being deprived of a needed transportation service." The chair of the Municipality of Metropolitan Toronto urged the province of Ontario to share the cost of a wage increase to bring a speedy end to the strike. They eventually came up with $377,000 in financing to end the strike, but it wasn't enough. Ultimately, workers rejected All-Way's offer. A photographer snapped a photo of Beryl outside the hotel weeping into her hand after learning the strike would continue indefinitely. "It was like waiting for a jury to come in, but I did not know we would be hung by it. That's how I feel now. We are prisoners in our own homes," she told the *Toronto Star*.

A Wheel-Trans driver who stood nearby offered his sympathy. "We want to drive you. We want to take care of you. We want to help you, but we can't take this [contract]."

Beryl blamed the government for failing to do enough to end the strike. "I know the government has put money in, but it's not enough. We appreciate them [the workers] because they treat us like human beings. I know how they feel. We can sympathize with them. But we are prisoners in our own homes. We can't condone the strike."

By day ten of the strike, her support was more fully behind the striking workers, arguing Wheel-Trans workers should be paid the same as other TTC workers. She led another protest with Trans-Action at Toronto City Hall with placards that read, "Give Us Our Freedom," "Why Are The Disabled Always At The Bottom Of The List?," and "Give Us Back Our Wheels." One protester who showed up pointed to the human cost of the strike. "This is becoming a real emotional issue for a lot of people. When you're looking at the same four walls every day, you get pretty damned tired of it."

Perhaps it was the time she spent on the picket lines, but Beryl's perspective had shifted, and she now saw the undervaluing of Wheel-Trans workers as yet another example of disabled people being treated as second-class citizens. "It's not only the inconvenience, it's the fear. Especially people with medical problems and appointments. Am I going to be able to get to my doctor? Am I going to be able to get that dialysis treatment that I need desperately? For young people, am I going to be able to write my exams at university this year?"

Beryl tried unsuccessfully to lobby Metro chair Dennis Flynn. "He said he has appointments. Politicians always have appointments when it comes to the disabled. These boys [Wheel-Trans drivers] push wheelchairs through the snow, they have to lift them up steps and into elevators. They're always down on their knees and stretching their backs. It's hard work." Even the bastion of tabloid conservatism, the *Toronto Sun*, agreed with her. "Metro [Toronto Council] clearly has an obligation to end the strike. . . . And if that means giving drivers another $2 an hour over two years or improving their benefit package, then so be it."

A Wheel-Trans driver who attended the demonstration acknowledged the human cost of the strike but illustrated the realities of his work. "We know that people can't get out of their houses. We know that some people might lose their jobs because they can't get to work. But we really felt we had to go on strike over this. This is a highly stressful job. We have to drive through two rush hours a day. We have to eat lunch on the bus because there's no time to stop for a break. And we get paid less than people who drive for courier services."

On day twelve, the Liberal government finally ordered an end to the strike with back-to-work legislation and an immediate fifty cent increase in the hourly wage, or $1.13 in 2022 dollars, while workers negotiated a new contract. Labour Minister Bill Wrye indicated to the *Toronto Star* that it was the potential of lasting damage to the employability of people with disabilities that finally prompted the government to intervene. "A prolonged strike could possibly add to the reluctance some employers might have about hiring disabled people."

Beryl argued the Wheel-Trans strike "illustrated the discrimination of the TTC's separate system. Thousands of disabled who rely on the service to get to work, school and everywhere else were stranded in their homes." Edith Rason, another member of Trans-Action, said it was common for her and others to wait two to three days for a trip. Once, she had to wait three weeks for a trip to the grocery store. "What I do is stockpile. Then, if I can't get out, I've got something in the house."

The strike also reignited long-standing debate about whether the TTC should take over Wheel-Trans. Beryl and other activists had been wanting a takeover since the introduction of the paratransit service. "We have been advocating for this since at least the Spadina line in the '70s," said Jerry Lucas of the Ontario March of Dimes. "Their argument then was that so much of the system would require retrofitting, that it wasn't economical. But if you look back, since then, twenty-five percent more of the system has been built." Neither the Spadina subway line (completed in 1978) nor the Scarborough RT (completed in 1985) were built to be accessible. TTC executives argued that a full retrofit of the system would cost nearly $343 million and disabled passengers would be blamed for delayed trains and buses as drivers would be required to tie down each wheelchair passenger.

Poor service levels plagued the city's paratransit system. The TTC's annual reports through the 1980s indicated that approximately 10 per cent of all ride requests were refused because of insufficient capacity. Wheel-Trans's annual report from 1985 registered upward of 180,000 refused and missed trips, nearly one-third of all 600,000 booked trips that year. The TTC continued to argue that a separate system was safer and more efficient: cost and logistics, however, seemed to be the real issue. According to a *Toronto Star* investigation, a TTC takeover of Wheel-Trans would cost $23 million in capital costs to build a custom garage and a custom radio communications system, inflating annual operating expenses by $578,000, compared to the $13 million spent annually to subcontract paratransit services to All-Way.

Finally, not long after the 1985 strike ended, the TTC decided it was time to cancel its contract with All-Way and take over the

Wheel-Trans service. The strike had exposed the hidden costs associated with savings from subcontracting out the service. All-Way paid lower wages to mostly part-time drivers and mechanics compared to mainly full-time TTC employees. Its vehicles were also subjected to a less rigorous maintenance schedule than TTC-owned vehicles, contributing to unsafe conditions for riders. By January 1, 1989, Wheel-Trans drivers and mechanics became TTC employees with a commensurate increase in wages. New vans were purchased to allow for safer and more reliable travel. And the move made paratransit more accountable to the public dollars that partially funded it. It was a happy ending for all, or so it seemed at the time.

Beryl and the Trans-Action Coalition celebrated the move as a victory but continued to push for greater accessibility in the broader public transportation system. David Baker of ARCH and lawyer for Trans-Action told the *Toronto Star* that he hoped the TTC would willingly embrace accessibility but asserted that legal protections in the Charter of Rights could be invoked against future building projects that don't accommodate people with disabilities. "I can assure you representatives of the disabled community will launch a Charter challenge before any sod is turned if [the TTC] does not include plans for full accessibility. We're not saying 'This (full accessibility) should be done tomorrow or else.' We're saying, 'Show a commitment to doing it for the future. 'It's a long-term proposition, and disabled people recognize that. They are just saying, 'Don't build any more inaccessible subways.'"

Subsequent media investigations revealed many of the same issues that plagued Wheel-Trans services simply continued under the TTC umbrella. "Wheel-Trans called a 'mess' since the TTC took over," read one *Toronto Star* headline from 1989. Late in the 1980s, Beryl stated she had been "flooded with calls" over ongoing problems with missed or late pickups, poor customer service, and limited availability.[3] She remained convinced the lack of reliable accessible transportation was one of the most critical factors perpetuating the ongoing segregation and oppression of disabled people.

In 1987, Action Awareness published a manifesto written by Beryl in its newsletter *G.O.* In it she pointed out that the Canadian Human Rights Act prohibits discrimination in the provision of goods, services, facilities, and accommodation. And yet, transportation systems were still largely inaccessible and tended to exclude people with disabilities, many of whom "live within a short distance of a transit service that they cannot use." She cited accessible transportation as one of the most essential commodities in modern society. "Why is it so difficult to transport persons with special transportation needs in a dignified manner and integrated in a system that transports other citizens, rather than segregate them with an inadequate and limited system?" Instead of waiting for an answer, Beryl took her question to the road, travelling to several major cities in southern Ontario, including Toronto, Hamilton, Sarnia, and Kingston. She delivered dozens of workshops on transportation, engaging audiences on the topic and highlighting the challenges faced by disabled people. "An entire social movement arose over the question of where certain people must sit when they ride the bus. I can't even get on the bus," she stated.[4]

The seventh annual Awareness Week held in 1987 at Scarborough Town Centre welcomed tens of thousands of people from across Canada, the US, and England, with the theme of accessible transportation. The event had a festival-like atmosphere with food stalls, games, and sixty-two booths that were both entertaining and informative. Ontario Premier David Peterson and four provincial ministers attended the opening with Beryl as their guide. A photo from the event printed in the *Toronto Sun* shows Peterson, neatly parted white hair, suit jacket off, and sleeves rolled up, with an expression of intense concentration as he attempts to manoeuvre through an obstacle course using a manual wheelchair, one of several demonstrations of what it was like for wheelchair users in the city.[5] Following the event, Peterson announced a provincial commitment of $85 million over the next five years to fund the development of paratransit services across the province.

As with previous wins, Beryl took little time to celebrate. She increasingly felt that solutions to local problems lay with policies and action at higher levels of government. With this conclusion she widened her mandate as she fought for the rights of all disabled Canadians, especially those outside urban centres.

21.
Order of Ontario

When a new Ontario Minister Responsible For Disabled Persons post was created in 1985, Beryl jumped at the chance to lobby the minister directly. Premier David Peterson came to power, creating the Cabinet position to acknowledge the province's obligations under the Charter of Rights and Freedoms and its commitment to the Decade of Disabled Persons. But Beryl traced the origins of the portfolio to earlier citizen activism. In 1981, Action Awareness demonstrated on Queen's Park alongside three hundred people with disabilities and disability rights groups from across the province, asking for a non-party committee to be set up to investigate the problems with provincial services and programs. At that time, they were told by Progressive Conservative Premier Bill Davis that such a committee was unnecessary, but the new Liberal Premier Peterson adopted the approach of dedicating a Cabinet position to address disability issues directly.

Peterson's choice for the minister responsible for disabled persons was thirty-six-year-old southwestern Ontario MPP Remo Mancini, a young man with thick black hair, a classic chevron moustache, and a dimpled chin. He was already a veteran in politics having first been elected in 1972 as a municipal councillor at age twenty-one and to the provincial legislature in Ontario's 1975 election. This was his first Cabinet position, and he would soon learn what it meant to be the point person on disability issues in the province. Beryl wasted no time getting to know Mancini firsthand and she made an impression. "The first time you see her, obviously, the first thing you see is the disability. I mean it's pretty obvious, but in no time, you saw way past that. And when I met Beryl the second, third and other times, I did not see the disability at all. I saw a person who had a busy life, a busy schedule, things to do, things to get done, people to meet."

Beryl first met Remo in her capacity as a member of the Advisory Council of Disabled Persons. She capitalized on this relationship, scheduling regular visits to his office to lobby him gently but persistently on numerous initiatives. Mancini realized early on that Beryl meant business. "She did not just come for tea and cookies." And yet, it was her unique approach that made each meeting amicable and productive. "You can have a list of issues and have a pleasant business meeting, and you can have the same list of issues, maybe with a different person, and the meeting could be very unpleasant. With Beryl, it was always pleasant." Others shared this sentiment. In the early 1980s, the assistant to the mayor of Toronto, Brian Ashton, similarly observed Beryl to be adept at getting what she wanted in meetings. "Good ol' Beryl, the type of person who'll park her wheelchair on your foot until she gets what she wants—and it works."[1]

Independent living, job opportunities, and shifting public attitudes toward disability were among the top issues Beryl and Mancini discussed. He described his office as a "hotbed of activity" and took pride in his accurate reading of the major concerns and needs of the disability community. "We were an advocacy ministry, so our job was to make presentations, proposals, and present ideas to the premier, attorney general, minister of transportation, and minister of community and social services. We were quite good at that."[2] Regular interactions with disability activists such as Beryl were an integral part of keeping the government informed and engaged on substantive issues.

———

On a windy, sun-drenched summer day in 1988, Mancini and Beryl appeared together on the popular call-in television talk show *Dini Petty's CityLine*, a show Dini hosted just prior to achieving national fame for her daytime talk show, *The Dini Petty Show*. *CityLine* was live and had an almost spontaneous energy. The day of Beryl and Mancini's appearance had a makeshift, "on the spot" feeling, with a temporary stage and folding chairs arranged almost haphazardly on a section of the asphalt parking lot of CityNews, also likely the only accessible area big enough to accommodate the audience that included many wheel-chair users. Cars and pedestrians passed by the fence demarcating the set from the bustle of downtown Toronto on Queen Street West, the ambient activity and commotion emblematic of the CityTV style. On *CityLine*, Dini would introduce each guest, then dart around the audience taking questions and gathering as many perspectives as possible on a given daily topic. That day, she commanded attention in her houndstooth pantsuit, classic eighties blazer with shoulder pads the width of a linebacker, and large aviator glasses that shielded her eyes from the unforgiving sun. She scurried back and forth in front of the audience, clipboard in hand, her confident, incisive style honed from years of interviewing people for news programs, the scripted pacing of commercial breaks and quick transitions typical of a talk show format.

Dini was acquainted with Beryl since her days as a daily reporter with CityNews, covering her at demonstrations and other events. Impressed by Beryl's determination and poise, Dini knew she was the perfect candidate to speak on disability issues when the occasion presented itself. Beryl seemed unbothered by the hot sun in her blue chemise and glasses, her relaxed posture and smile projecting the confidence of a pro in front of the audience and camera. Dini introduced Beryl as a former TAB: a Temporarily Able-Bodied person.

"So if you were a TAB before, what are you now?"

"I'm a person with a disability or a person who happens to have lost my limbs," Beryl responded. "I'm a person first, Dini. I came out of the hospital, and I was still the same person. I was still Beryl Potter, maybe not as much of me, but I was still warm flesh and blood, and all of a sudden, I found that the whole world was totally inaccessible to me." Dini asked what prompted Beryl to stop taking it.

"I was angry, Dini. Very angry because I realized the way I was being treated and I thought, my God, persons with disabilities are being treated like this all of their lives, so why aren't we doing something about it? Why aren't we letting people know that we are people, we are persons, we are warm human bodies that need to do the things that everybody else do, but a little differently. But we need to love, laugh, work, play and do all the normal things. We can do them but need to see a change in attitude and in the laws."

Mancini was there as a spokesperson for the provincial government's record on disability issues. He projected a cool self-assurance somewhat offset by a defensive posture, his legs crossed in a figure four position. But his smile, accentuated by that thick black moustache, was wide, his suit jacket off and sleeves rolled up, likely anticipating the grilling he would soon receive from parts of the audience. The hour-long program covered an ambitious range of topics, including discriminatory attitudes, disability rights, consumer activism, isolation, depression, etiquette, politically correct language and behaviour, family support, and media representation of disability. But it was when the topic of discussion turned to the lack of accessibility in public spaces that guests and audience members became most animated. A social worker in the audience commented about poor levels of accessibility across the city and questioned Mancini about laws governing businesses that claim to be accessible when they are not. "What about the buildings that have wheelchair accessible signs on them? The bank might be accessible inside, but there's a step or a very steep ramp to get in. A small step might not be a big thing to you or I, but it is to someone in a wheelchair."

"You mean they lie," Dini clarified. "They say they're accessible when they're not."

"We're talking about a lot of things that were done many years ago," Mancini responded somewhat defensively. "The question is what are we doing about it now."

"Excuse me," the social worker interrupted. "That was not my original question. I asked why they are allowed to have accessible signs on the buildings when they are not accessible."

"Can we have a round of applause for the inaccessibility of Toronto?" Dini quipped as the audience applauded in agreement. "Okay, let's answer this question: if I build a building and put an accessible sign out front, does anybody come and check it out?"

Beryl answered first, pointing out that most architects and city planners had little understanding of the needs of people with disabilities. "I've gone into a washroom with wheelchair accessible signs. My chair goes halfway in, and I have to leave the door open. Does anybody else agree with that? Would anybody else go to a toilet and leave the door open because the cubicle is not wide enough or big enough to take the wheelchair? That is not accessibility. We, disabled people, have to start speaking out and do what is necessary to bring all these things out into the open." While she had the floor, Beryl redirected the discussion to highlight the need to include disabled people in decision-making processes. "There isn't enough representation of persons with a disability on boards and committees. We [people with disabilities] are the experts. We know what needs to be done, but we need the architects to do it for us."

Mancini answered that his approach was to build relationships with owners of inaccessible buildings. He would start by sending a letter of introduction from the Office of Disabled Persons advising them of their infraction and offering guidance in barrier-free design. He asserted that the government made amendments to the human rights code and improved accessibility in the province by sponsoring training courses through the Barrier Free Design Centre. The Ontario Building Code required new buildings to be fully accessible and the government would provide nominal funding for non-profit organizations to undertake accessibility improvements.

"Once you send the letter, do they have 60 or 90 days to respond, or do you just keep waiting?" Dini asked.

"I find once these letters go out, people are very agreeable to start," Mancini said, alluding to the reality that much of his work was hamstrung by the lack of enforceable legislation, adding that egregious violations might end up in front of the Ontario Human Rights Commission.

After an energetic hour introducing disability issues far more complex than any phone-in chat show could effectively deal with, Dini brought the discussion to a close. "This is our first attempt. We'll have to try this again." Audience members received free passes to a stage production of the popular British sitcom *On The Buses* at the New Century Theatre. "And we absolutely guarantee it's accessible!"[3]

In 1988, in her final year as vice-chair of the Advisory Council of Disabled Persons, Beryl stepped down as president of the Scarborough Recreation Club for Disabled Adults. She was now in high demand as a public speaker, delivering hundreds of presentations to students, clubs, and other organizations across Metro Toronto and the Greater Toronto Area. With nearly $250,000 in provincial funding for Action Awareness, including a stipend for herself and a small staff, she dramatically escalated her itinerary and began travelling much further afield, including a repeat tour of northern Ontario. On the road again, meeting new people every day, she was constantly reminded of unrealized change—pervasive inaccessibility of transportation systems, sidewalks, doors, washrooms—despite years of commitments by policymakers during this long Decade of Disabled Persons. The tour helped her conclude that to effect real change in the lives of people with disabilities she would need to do so within the apparatus of government.

The tour also involved an experience that highlighted the potentially deadly consequences of inaccessibility. While in North Bay, Beryl was traversing a particularly treacherous stretch of sidewalk in the rain when she came upon two enormous holes filled with water. She did not know which way to go, trying to decipher which hole looked bigger and more dangerous. As she manoeuvred, it became clear that she chose the wrong hole. She pitched forward out of her wheelchair and landed awkwardly on her back. By the time she got to the local hospital, she knew something was terribly wrong. The fall cracked a vertebra at the top of her spine. The local hospital in North Bay was ill-equipped to assist someone with her injury and extensive medical history, so an emergency helicopter flew her nearly three hundred kilometres south, an approximately hour-and-a-half helicopter ride, to Sunnybrook Hospital in Toronto, where Dr. Hamilton Hall, an orthopedic surgeon, prepped to perform emergency spinal surgery. Coincidentally, Dr. Hall was a friend of Beryl's, and Diane had worked with him when he started the Canadian Back Institute (now CBI Health), running the first personal injury clinic with one kinesiologist and six staff that handled assessments for new patients. When Diane found out what had happened to her mother, she rushed to be with her at the hospital. Before Dr. Hall went into surgery, he reassured Diane he would do his best to save her. "Diane, I've never lost anybody on the table, and I don't want your mum to be the first one." Despite the extreme danger of spinal surgery for someone with such an extensive medical history, the operation ultimately proved successful. While she lay in recovery, Dr. Hall visited her in the evenings, ordering a beer to her room and putting his feet up to chat with her before eventually sending her back into the world to continue her work.[4]

In 1988, Beryl was appointed to the Order of Ontario. Created in 1986 by Lieutenant Governor Lincoln Alexander and modelled on the Order of Canada, the Order of Ontario is the highest civic honour conferred upon residents in the province of Ontario in recognition of extraordinary service, excellence, and achievement. Nominations from the public are submitted to the Ontario Honours and Awards Secretariat who form a committee including the chief justice of Ontario, Speaker of the Legislative Assembly, Secretary of Cabinet, and up to six members of the Order. The committee researches and reviews nominations and forwards their recommendations to the lieutenant governor of Ontario who makes the final decision.

Nominations for Beryl poured in from people she had worked with and influenced over the years. Vim Kochhar of the Canadian Foundation for Physically Disabled Adults was Beryl's primary nominator to the Order, including other organizations such as ARCH and the Association of Jewish Seniors, a non-denominational alliance of senior citizen groups in Ontario whose lobbying work often dovetailed with hers. One nomination read, "Beryl has been involved in virtually every major initiative which has advanced the interests of disabled people in Ontario. She has conveyed her message with dignity and humour. Her intensely personal approach has avoided stridency or self-righteousness. By honouring her, the province would be honouring the efforts of all disabled people to enter the mainstream of society." Another nomination read, "Beryl is totally committed and sincerely believes in her goal of integrating the handicapped into society. . . . She is extremely deserving of the Order of Ontario and in my humble opinion should be the first recipient of this award."[5]

The investiture ceremony was held on Monday May 9, 1988, at 11:00 a.m. in the lofty interiors at the Ontario legislative building. A Vice Regal Salute opened the ceremony followed by an invocation and welcoming remarks by the lieutenant governor and premier of Ontario, the singing of "O Canada," and a procession of the officials. The 7th Toronto Regiment of the Canadian Artillery Brass Octet provided the musical program. Seventeen highly esteemed recipients were inducted into the Order alongside Beryl, including singer Gordon Lightfoot, writers June Callwood and Roberston Davies, journalist Floyd Chalmers, psychologist Reva Gerstein, and architect John Parkin.

In a photograph taken at the ceremony, Beryl, wearing a pale blue dress and dangling gold earrings matching her gold-rimmed glasses, is next to Premier David Peterson, his hand resting on her shoulder, while Orillia-born folk singer Gordon Lightfoot stands behind, grasping Beryl's hand, all smiling for the cameras, both Beryl and Gordon with their medals' ribbons clearly visible around their necks. Later that evening, a reception was held at the Regency Ballroom of the Four Seasons Hotel where a French four-course dinner was served. Beryl stuffed the menu and special napkins into her purse as another memento to add to her growing memorabilia collection. She was elated at the honour and accompanying post-nominals. But once again, in her characteristically humble way, veered attention back to the work she could do with it. "It really does carry some weight with politicians. The government has always been really accessible to me. But I think there's a little extra attention paid now."[6]

From left: Premier David Peterson, Beryl, and folk singer Gordon Lightfoot at Order of Ontario ceremony, Queen's Park, 1988.
Beryl Potter personal collection. Reproduced with permission.

22.

Outside Looking In

B eryl's life began to shift toward a future in politics just as a major national constitutional battle was brewing in Canada. After years of acrimonious debate, the province of Québec refused to sign the 1982 Constitution Act shepherded by Liberal Prime Minister Pierre Trudeau. On April 30, 1987, Conservative Prime Minister Brian Mulroney attempted to broker a new deal to bring Québec into the "constitutional family" by hosting an exclusive, high-stakes conference of Canada's premiers at Meech Lake, thirty minutes northwest of Ottawa. After only nine hours of debate, Mulroney emerged and strode triumphantly to a podium to declare they had reached a consensus that proposed to greatly devolve power from the federal level to provincial governments, including recognition of Québec as a distinct society. The announcement shocked the Canadian public, bewilderment quickly yielding to disapproval when former Prime Minister Trudeau stepped forward in strong opposition to the Accord. Trudeau suggested the Accord would ultimately lead to further devolution of powers, fundamentally undermining both the Charter of Rights and Freedoms and national unity more broadly.

With the lynchpin of modern human rights legislation at stake, activists from various social movements across the country organized to oppose the Meech Lake Accord. Disability activists were especially concerned about the erosion of rights they had only recently won with the addition of disability as a protected category under the Charter. Just one year after Beryl had led a coalition of activists to Ottawa to protest federal employment equity legislation, she found herself joining another demonstration against constitutional amendments that further threatened the rights of people with disabilities.

Richard Dechter, who worked for People United for Self Help or PUSH, a disability rights activist group, attended the protest and remembers boarding buses with other activists and allies of the disability rights movement. "It was a little crazy to be honest. I'd never done anything like that before, but there were lots of people there who had been to demonstrations. We got on the buses and it's quite a long drive from Toronto." As some activists filed into the visitors' gallery, Richard became increasingly anxious. "I was getting more and more nervous about how this would actually work. The House of Commons is a solemn place, and you don't think that it'll affect you, but it did."

"I've got a question for the Prime Minister! What about people with disabilities in the Constitution!?" John Feld of ARCH shouted down from the gallery at the parliament members. Some of the members must have had a moment of déja vu after Beryl had interrupted the proceedings on the Employment Equity Act the previous year with a similar outburst, or perhaps it was just another day in the House of Commons. The Speaker hammered his gavel for order as a chorus of voices began shouting down from the gallery, throwing one-page political flyers that fluttered down onto the MPs below. Richard thought it was time to leave, but apparently, he was in the minority. "I was saying, 'Okay, we've made our point, quiet down, let's get out of here,' and some people were mad that I was trying to do that since we were there to protest. The RCMP showed up and started dragging people away."[1]

Beryl watched time and again as the rights and opportunities of disabled people were put on the chopping block. She thought the Decade of Disabled Persons was supposed to be about advancing disability rights. And yet, it seemed it was a constant struggle just to keep those rights and sustain the public's attention on disability issues. Over the next three years, public support for the Accord waned as many Canadians grew suspicious of backroom dealing and a general lack of transparency about the process. Critics worried about the consequences of granting Québec special status within the constitutional fold, and Quebecers believed English Canada's hostility to the deal was a symptom of wider anti-francophone sentiment in other parts of the country. In 1990, the Accord fell apart, fuelling further resentment and separatist politics in Québec that would eventually boil over in 1995 with a second referendum on that province's political independence from Canada.

At an age when most people consider retirement, the expectation of a meagre Old Age Security cheque, a thin buffer against poverty, Beryl began to reassess a standing offer from Liberal Premier David Peterson, first made in 1985, to run for the Liberal Party in the 1990 election. She had grown weary of constantly beating down the doors of the offices of elected officials. But was now the right time to join the political fold and push for reform within the system? Could she expect more results about the things she cared about? Might she expose herself to greater scrutiny and criticism? Did she have the energy to go all the way? Would it give her more time to spend with family or would she drift further into her hectic work life? Beryl knew her private life and professional relationships would change if she jumped from activist to elected official. The question was whether those sacrifices would outweigh the potential for good.

23.
Off the Record

As Beryl became busier over the course of the 1980s, she left little time to enjoy a rich personal life. But there were vacations to sunny destinations, family videos of Christmases, and holidays spent at Diane and George's cottage, one of Beryl's favourite places to visit. The cottage in Lakefield north of Peterborough backed onto Lower Buckhorn Lake, a deep expanse of water that flows into several neighbouring lakes in the Kawarthas, numerous rocky islands dotting the landscape in scenes that epitomize southern Ontario's cottage country. Beryl would visit every chance she got, lapping up the scent of pine and cool lake breezes, trails of cigarette smoke following her like an everlasting brushfire. There was a fully accessible washroom and ramp that led out to the lower dock so she could swim in the cool lake water, and she would pass the days sunbathing dockside, out on the boat, or playing cards with Justin and Dennis when it rained.

In one photo, Justin, Dennis, and Beryl sat around the breakfast nook, which was transformed into a card table, complete with ashtrays. Justin and Dennis conceal their cards while Beryl smiles for the camera, her customized card holder revealing what could be a winning hand. There were other funny moments too. One summer day, Michelle and Beryl were sitting, enjoying time out by the water, when a caterpillar fell right onto Beryl's head. They both started screaming and flailing trying to get it out of her hair. Beryl nearly flipped her wheelchair over into the water, taking her granddaughter down onto the dock as they both exploded into laughter.

These special family memories hide the reality that Beryl's calendar was otherwise filled with appointments dedicated to the mission of improving the lives of people with disabilities. She may have been

Beryl, Dennis, and Justin, ca. early 1990s.
Beryl Potter personal collection. Reproduced with permission.

aware of the stress and distance this created with her family, but Beryl always described this time in her life as happy and fulfilling. The tireless work of advocacy was never finished, and she never seemed to set any boundaries between work and home life. Or she may have been too wrapped up in the endless daily work of phone calls, meetings, presentations, and travelling to realize just how much her life had become dominated by her work. When an interviewer once confronted her with the idea that she never had much time to see Diane or spend time with her grandchildren, she became emotional, her meticulously painted metallic pink fingernails concealing her face as she cried with regret or embarrassment over all the lost time with her family.[1]

Diane once expressed her concern about her mother in an interview. "She doesn't seem to allow herself any personal life. I have told her, 'There's got to be a limit to how much you give other people.' I dropped by to see her on Easter afternoon, and she was sitting in her nightgown working at the typewriter. I asked her, 'Aren't you going to have Easter dinner?' but she said she was just too busy. Well, she's too busy to take care of herself. She got a kidney infection last year and the doctor wanted to put her in the hospital, but she would not even stay in bed. It's fine to be a workaholic, and I'm proud of her, and I'm glad she has all her work to keep her so happy, but sometimes I wonder if she's lonely. I'm not saying she's hiding behind all her activities, but I do wonder if it's a way for her to keep from thinking about anything that might make her depressed. Besides, I'd really like to see more of her. I think she'd enjoy seeing more of [her grandchildren]. She only comes to visit four or five times a year, but she seems to really love it here. She comes for dinner early and stays late and the kids love to play with her, and ride her wheelchair, and go swimming with help. We'd all like to see her more."[2]

Indiscernible in the many news clips, documentaries, and newspaper features of her as the firebrand activist is the very different private side of Beryl. Even if her timetable kept her regularly unavailable for social occasions, her heart was always open for her family. Every Christmas Eve after the children went to bed, Diane would leave a key under the mat so Beryl and Dennis could slip into the house and sleep in the living room. At daybreak, they would greet the family with hugs and kisses. "They were like Santa," Michelle remembers. In the intimate twinkling joy of Christmas morning, surrounded by presents and Dennis at her side, Beryl was completely at ease, reverting to the soft-spoken gentle grandmother she might have been if things had been different. She would sip coffee and chat while her energetic grandson, Justin, bounced around, quivering camcorder in hand, recording every angle of the festivities including the family cat, Meatball.

Beryl wasn't big on Christmas though she enjoyed the opportunity to spend time with her family. Diane describes her mother as hating the clutter of the decorations and wrapping paper. "I always remember waking up on New Year's Day, and there was no Christmas," Diane recalls. "My mother would stay up all night after the party. Everything wasn't even just taken down but put away in boxes and in the basement." Beryl also wasn't big on gift giving. Diane doesn't remember many Christmases with presents under the tree when she was a kid, possibly an upshot of Beryl's frugality, having survived the poverty of her childhood. "She never bought presents for Michelle and Justin. She used to say to me, 'I'm not going to buy gifts, I'll give the money to charity.'" Her charity of choice was the Jerry Lewis Muscular Dystrophy Association Telethon, which she saw as a more meaningful use of funds than buying her grandkids toys that they would ultimately throw away. "I would tell her, 'Mum, how are you going to tell a four-year-old and a seven-year-old you're not going to give them any presents?' And then she'd say, 'Well, then you buy a gift, wrap it up, say it's from me and I'll pay you.' I would do that, but she never paid for any of the presents." None of this pleased Diane. "I wanted that Christmas where the kids tear off the wrapping paper and it's a fire truck. I wanted them to have that. But it had to just be us as parents, because we did not get that from the grandparents."

There was a time when all Beryl wanted to do was dote on her grandchildren, which earned many cherished memories from her granddaughter, Michelle. "She taught me everything. She taught me how to sew, knit and crochet. She was very creative. We did crafts and put on little art shows. We did everything together." Beryl was just beginning to cultivate a more active public life in the mid-1970s when Michelle was still a young child, eagerly absorbing all Beryl's decreasing amount of free time. In 1972, from age three, Michelle revelled in her Nana's presence whenever she came to babysit. Michelle would push Beryl's wheelchair around the house, and they would do all sorts of crafts, and even put on mini art shows, constantly darting from one activity to the next. In one photo, Michelle is around three years old in a pink dress, stockings, and blond pigtails, a look of determination on her chubby cheeked face as she attempts to push Beryl's wheelchair forward across the carpeted floor. "Nana would babysit me and my baby brother, Justin, in the townhome we lived in. I don't remember her being immobile or not being able to do anything, because we were all creative in helping her move around. I would organize activities for us, so we would start at the top level of the house and make our way down during the day. To get down the stairs, she would plop down on a blanket, and I would help pull her down one step at a time. By the end of the day, I'd have pulled her on those blankets all the way out to the front lawn where we'd be playing when Mum and Dad returned."

"Later, when we had a pool, she would babysit us on weekends with my uncle Dennis when our parents were away. He would carry her out the back stairs and bring her to the pool. We would play baseball in the pool and tie her one arm to the railing, so she did not flip upside down because she was so bottom heavy. Oh my gosh, it was so much fun! My friends would come over and we would all play together. Getting her out of the pool was very difficult, so we had to stop that game, especially when it was only us with her there. But it was amazing fun."

Whenever Beryl was there to babysit, Dennis was close by. "Uncle Dennis was an oddball for sure. We never thought about where he fell on the spectrum, no labels or any of that. Maybe some people would say he was weird, but we thought he was all good because we were used to him. He was just our crazy, fun uncle. He loved kids just as much as Nana, probably because he was like a big kid. I always wanted them to come babysit. She could be silly, and we would always make a big mess with all our crafts and games. We would eat candies. She loved licorice and we would all sip our drinks with licorice straws. She was the kind of grandma where she always had something crazy and creative planned for our time together." Other times, Beryl would bring Michelle with her to the rec club. "There were times when I felt like I lived with Nana. I'd stay with her for a week or two at a time when my mum was working. I'd go down to the club and help out when people needed help with feeding. I remember going to the pool with them. There was a lot to learn."

Justin's earliest memories of Beryl are awash in the scent of smouldering tobacco wafting from the ashtray that seemed to follow her everywhere. "She smoked Peter Jacksons, and always had a smoke in her hand. No one in our family smoked, and I've never met anyone since who smoked so much!" Despite Beryl's aversion to gifting commercially bought items, she would often craft her own toys and garments. But whenever any of these homemade presents or knit clothing arrived, Diane would immediately send them to the dry cleaner. "The gifts that arrived always smelled of stinky smoke. [Beryl and Dennis] had to wash their apartment three times a year. The walls were stained orange." Once, Beryl knitted a plush toy for Michelle. "The stuffed bunny she made still smells of smoke even after all these years." If Diane ever commented about her mother's smoking habits, she got a defensive lecture. "I don't do drugs. I don't drink. I don't do this or do that. It's my only thing. That's the only bad thing I have, so I'm going to keep doing it. I don't care what people say about it." Before the days of smoke-free dining in restaurants, Beryl would get angry if someone told her she could not smoke after finishing her dessert, grumbling as she angrily stuffed the pack back into her purse.

Five years younger than his sister Michelle, Justin has fewer childhood memories of his Nana. He spent most of his time skateboarding and playing hockey. "And sulking," he adds, typical teen angst he eventually left behind. In one childhood photo, he's pictured next to his adoring grandmother outside Queen's Park in downtown Toronto, clutching a small paper Canadian flag, with a mischievous smile and windblown mop of brown hair. Justin realized later that Beryl taught him important lessons he would carry with him into adulthood. "She taught us about not putting up with shit from people. I always remember people staring at us when we were with her. She would often stop and question people. 'Hello, why are you staring at me?' Then she would get a conversation going with these complete strangers. Not in a combative way but in a firm way. That really made an impression on me."

The distinction between public and personal life became virtually inseparable for Beryl. Low-income, visually impaired, elderly, and a wheelchair user, Beryl was also a mother living in subsidized community housing with her son who had an intellectual disability. She *was* the subject of her advocacy. Not surprising, then, that it was hard for her to unplug from the issues she personally frequently encountered, refuelling her anger and refreshing her motivation to craft a different future for herself and others. Her pain and perseverance gave her a focus for her anger and bitterness, an anger that had been building inside since before her accident, now reinforced every time she travelled down the street. The invisibility she had shared with countless women of her generation had been replaced with the unwelcome attention that many with visible disabilities experience as they go about their lives. No longer invisible, her disabilities caused her to be seen in a new way. Beryl took that sharp and critical lens and redirected it toward issues she believed deserved attention, such as biased attitudes and accessibility in public spaces and the lack of it that daily confronted her.

Diane remembers every outing with her mother would become part of her crusade, sometimes putting her family in an awkward position.

"Mum, would you just stay right here please?" Diane would plead with her as they wheeled into the entrance of a restaurant.

"Show me your bathroom, please," Beryl would demand before the host had a chance to welcome them. Beryl would then ask to speak to the manager. She would proceed to the bathroom to complete an informal accessibility audit.

"You don't have a hook? How do you expect me to grab the little tiny hook on the back of the bathroom? Yes, it's a disabled door, but if my hands don't work how do I open the door?" she would explain as the manager would nod distractedly, politely accepting the advice so he could get back to work. If she could not get her chair in the door or if the bathroom was in the basement, she would get upset and they would all leave to find another restaurant.

"Really, we used to get embarrassed sometimes," says Diane.

"And we'd be sitting there as a family starving," adds Michelle.[3]

It was the same with acquaintances. In the early 1980s, Beryl once went to dinner with George Kavanaugh of the War Amps organization. George recalled the dinner to a *Toronto Star* reporter. "She's a 24-hour-a-day person, always on duty for the cause. My wife and I went out with Beryl for dinner one night to the Sheraton Centre, and at one point, Beryl headed off to the washroom. My wife asked if she needed any help, but Beryl said, 'No, I don't have to use the washroom myself; I just want to see if it's accessible to wheelchairs.' Sure enough, it wasn't, and Beryl complained to the management right then and there."

Beryl became ever more outspoken as time went on. Once, she and Dennis were at a cafeteria lineup and the chef turned to Dennis and asked what Beryl wanted. "Imagine!" Beryl recalled to an interviewer. "I just told that young man, don't you ever assume again that just because someone is in a wheelchair that they can't speak for themself. Of course, Dennis was off hiding in embarrassment by the time I finished my little speech."

Another time, Dennis remembered they were in a restaurant when she decided to intervene in a nearby commotion. "Once, we were at a restaurant at the Scarborough Town Centre and two drunks were arguing loudly with a policeman, and they were really swearing, and were really disrupting our dinner. So all of a sudden my mother goes over, runs over the cop's foot with her wheelchair—by accident, she says—and tells him to take the drunks away because, as a citizen, she has the right to eat without hearing that kind of language. It worked. They went away."[4]

24.
Dennis

I n 1983, Beryl and Dennis moved into a new apartment. The fully accessible subsidized unit was located on the ground floor of the newly built Kimroy Grove co-op complex at 4695 Sheppard Avenue East. The nondescript L-shaped red-brick low-rise complex was set against a small creek that weaved its way through Scarborough before emptying into Lake Ontario. She made the space her own with brown patterned drapes against beige walls, ornamental Japanese-style vases filled with artificial flowers, glazed wooden sculptures of a lion and other animals, and an assortment of gilded figurines, including a bird of prey perched on a rock. For all intents and purposes, it could have been any typical 1980s-era apartment. Beryl would leave the sliding door to their cement balcony open so her dogs could waltz in and out. This was also the entryway of choice for visiting family who would hop over the low balcony wall and straight into the living room. With the Toronto railyard for the Canadian Pacific Railway less than half a kilometre away, the location might have reminded her of her childhood in Liverpool as she listened to the occasional crash and tremor of hulking boxcars and locomotives ambling to life.

Before she moved in, the Workers' Compensation Board installed a state-of-the-art track system that enabled her to move seamlessly from her bed to the bathroom in a sling. She would pull herself up on a bar that hovered over her bed and remotely operate the track that would transport her to the bathroom. They also installed special cupboards and counters so she could access everything she needed from her wheelchair. The new apartment granted Beryl a high degree of independence, close to barrier-free living in her own home, at least as long as she remained healthy.

With Dennis as her personal assistant and most of Beryl's advocacy work outside the home, the new accessible living arrangements afforded mother and son the opportunity to realign parts of their relationship. Beryl could move around their living space more easily with the help of lifts and life hacks she learned.

"How about the tub?" an interviewer once asked her in a documentary.

"That's easy really. It's very, very simple. When I come up to the top, I can just slide over onto this mat. I leave the mat on the side and I slide into the top of it that way. I don't put the water in because if I went in with a bounce I could drown."

Despite the improvement in accessibility within their living space, Dennis continued to perform many of the tasks usually required of a personal support worker, and it wasn't always easy to maintain healthy boundaries. Showering, grooming, and dressing became increasingly difficult for Beryl to do on her own, especially as she aged and grappled with abscesses, pressure sores, and other ailments. She could have arranged for a nurse or personal support worker to come in and help her, but she never did. Whether it was from embarrassment, or a sense of her privacy being invaded by a procession of support workers, she preferred Dennis to help her.

Beryl's busy schedule of consultations with officials, meetings with other lobbyists, demonstrations, travel itineraries for public meetings, presentations, and workshops would have been impossible without the dedicated support of her son. Dennis willingly embraced his role as his mother's steadfast confidante and pillar of her support system having been drawn into the orbit of his mother's care during those long years in and out of the hospital. He was there for the bedside visits as Beryl recuperated from yet another surgery and her first shaky attempts at stepping out into the world, each time with fewer limbs. He helped her navigate through depression, suicide attempts, and the resurgence of suicidal thoughts and plans when she lost her arm and vision. He did his best to support her during times of financial distress even if he added his own pressure to the situation. He accompanied her when nostalgia led her back to Liverpool. And he was by her side when they returned to Toronto to build a new life together. He was an active participant in rec club activities and conveyed her to presentations, workshops, meetings, and demonstrations. He was also Mr. Aware Bear, delighting children wherever they appeared by operating the fuzzy mascot. In nearly every videoclip and newspaper snapshot, Dennis is always there shadowing his mother, often sitting or standing just out of frame.

When it became clear Dennis would assume much of Beryl's care, Diane tried to have a conversation with her brother about the situation. She told him how much support their mother would need in the months and years ahead, and Diane thought it might be a good idea for him to go and talk to a psychiatrist so he could express himself. But Dennis wasn't having any of this. "I'm not stupid. I don't have to see a psychiatrist," he would say. Diane soon realized whatever she said, her brother would react defensively. Perhaps he felt that people didn't give him credit for the competency he developed, especially as the years went by and he saw how much his mother relied on him. Or maybe he glimpsed what life was like for other people with intellectual disabilities and wanted to disassociate from them. "I remember one day in the hospital trying to have a conversation with him, trying to get through to him. But all he kept saying was that I was trying to make him feel stupid." It was no use.

Following the years after Beryl's accident when Diane began to step away from the role of family caregiver to build her own life, Dennis stepped in to take his sister's place, safeguarding and encouraging his mother the way she had for him over the years. "She's not a shy mom anymore," he admitted in a 1981 documentary interview. "And before her accident, here's a woman who was so shy to go into a restaurant for coffee and now I can't even keep her out of the damn restaurants." Beryl credited her son with helping her navigate life after disability. "Dennis became my therapist. He was tough, very tough, but the best therapist I could've ever had because that was the medicine I needed. I needed to be pushed. I needed to be shown that I could do things if I tried."[1]

As the years passed, Dennis became more attached and protective of his mother until the two were virtually inseparable. Diane recalls her brother's eagerness to defend their mother wherever they went. "If there was ever somebody in front of them on the sidewalk, Denny would yell out 'Get out of the way! Can't you see there's a wheelchair coming?' He'd do this even if the other people were quite a distance ahead. I would try to help him understand that not everyone knows.

'Denny, they don't have eyes in the back of their head.' But he would still get mad at people blocking sidewalks or staring."[2] For Dennis, all those years spent by his mother's bedside journeying alongside her bumpy road to recovery fostered an intense emotional identification with his mother's pain. "Seeing your mother cut, piece by piece, for six and a half years . . ." he once tearfully told an interviewer. "But I knew that someone was pulling me through all this."[3]

This mother-son tether led Dennis to commit himself to supporting her physically, emotionally, and logistically as Beryl turned toward a life of advocacy. She could not do it alone and she knew how isolated many people with disabilities were, given limited transportation options. Beryl took Wheel-Trans for ordinary daily activities, such as grocery shopping, but Dennis drove her to important appointments. Mobility and personal support were key ingredients to Beryl's success as an advocate, and most places on her weekly itinerary were not wheelchair accessible. At first, they used a classic wood-panelled station wagon. Beryl would drive her electric chair to the curb and grab hold of Dennis's neck while he lifted her with a bear hug and transferred her to the passenger seat. He would then push the heavy electric chair up two long metal ramps he stored in the back of the vehicle. When they reached their destination, the whole process unfolded in reverse. Since most buildings were still inaccessible, Beryl would switch the chair to manual mode so that Dennis could push her to a curb and pop a wheelie, pushing the backrest with his knee up and over the curb.

This procedure was repeated every time they left their apartment building and at schools, offices, meeting halls, and other buildings not designed for wheelchair users. Whenever there was a bathroom Beryl could not get into, which happened often in their travels, Dennis would hoist his mother up and carry her wherever she needed to go. Naturally, the physical strain of hauling his mother's heavy wheelchair and portable ramps in and out of vehicles, over curbs, and into inaccessible buildings dozens of times a day began to wear on Dennis's back and knees. He had surgeries on both of his knees, and eventually one kneecap was replaced. In the late 1970s, he began to take over-the-counter pain medications with codeine, such as Tylenol #1, Advil, and Aspirin, including the big bottles of 222s. The small pills temporarily relieved the pain, but over time carried serious consequences.

It wasn't all work, and in their shared life together, Dennis and Beryl also went on vacations. Beryl was a sun lover, so there were multiple trips to Florida, Bahamas, and other tropical destinations. Her sister Joan joined them on at least one trip south, during which an enormous rented yellow Lincoln Town Car carried them around in style. Beryl and Joan always enjoyed a strong relationship. Despite the distance between them and difference in age, their bond proved elastic, stretching out across the Atlantic through phone calls, letters, and visits. Beryl would park her wheelchair beside the hotel pool or find a patch of sand where she would plop down on a towel in a one-piece swimsuit, slather herself in Hawaiian Tropic tanning oil and bask in the warm rays, a pack of Peter Jackson's always within arm's reach. At night, she looked every bit the vacationing snowbird, dressed in a shimmering silver jacket and skirt, ready to hit the casino for an evening out. On more than one occasion, when she could not sleep at night, she would slip a dress over her nightgown and head down to

Beryl at the beach, ca. late 1970s.
Beryl Potter personal collection. Reproduced with permission.

the casino. She returned so regularly that she was on a first name basis with the man who dispensed buckets of quarters.

Beryl's family kept her grounded and provided the practical and emotional support she needed to sustain the relentlessly demanding nature of her mission. She would come to need her family more than ever as the political ground on which she had built a career as an advocate began to shift beneath her.

25.
Power of the Story

I n the latter half of the twentieth century, disability activism in Canada created space for people with disabilities in an inaccessible world. Beryl was a founder or participant in many advocacy groups, coalitions, and initiatives where she fought hard for legislative protections in employment, housing, and transportation. She was an expert at lobbying elected officials and leading demonstrations, and educational presentations and workshops remained at the core of her work. But, as time progressed, she appeared increasingly at odds with the wider disability rights movement in Canada.

Beryl's commitment to the transformational capacity of education never wavered, especially when it came to imprinting positive representations of disability on children. As the rest of the disability rights movement moved more intentionally toward issues of consumer control and the promotion and enforcement of legal rights, she remained convinced that changing attitudes, sometimes one small group at a time, was the best way to produce lasting change. She never disputed the importance of entrenching disability rights in law, but instead felt her priority was changing young minds to produce a generational shift in empathy for people with disabilities. As she explains in an instructional video produced by Action Awareness: "It has always been my priority that we reach out to children. It is through these children that we gain parental teaching, and it will be these children and the students who will create a brighter and better future for all people. It will be that next generation who ensure that the Charter of Rights and Freedom becomes a reality, and not just a hollow promise."[1]

Despite her charming and amicable demeanour, Beryl was also highly independent, preferring to establish and lead her own groups. This choice protected her from the kind of infighting that often afflicts activist groups as agendas and priorities are worked out, but it also may have insulated her from developments outside her perspective. Often a freestanding figure at the periphery despite heavy media coverage of her work, Beryl's detachment from the broader disability rights movement was the outcome of a constellation of factors, including her advocacy style, age, and nature of her disability.

Much of this distance owed to Beryl being a generation older than many other leading activists in the 1980s, drawing on different experiences, ideologies, and vernacular. When many disability activists were coming of age in the radical period of the 1960s, Beryl was an able-bodied forty-year-old mother of three. This generational gap made it increasingly difficult for her to fit in as a contemporary of other emerging leaders of the disability rights movement. Instead, she sometimes appeared slightly out of step with the vanguard, an echo of an earlier, perhaps less progressive time in disability rights activism.

Increasingly outspoken and media savvy, Beryl knew how to attract the attention of print and television media, recruiting journalists, television, and film producers as allies in her struggle. Her success in harnessing the power of media meant she was able to project an image of authority on disability issues far beyond what her limited resources allowed and many in the media presumed she occupied a leadership position as a spokesperson of the disability community writ large. When it came to changing public opinion of disability, Beryl knew how to leverage relationships with others to achieve her goals. The grassroots nature of her organizations required her to work tirelessly behind the scenes, lobbying people in positions of power to advance her goals. She cultivated relationships with authority figures and became a familiar figure within these circles of power.

Beryl believed in the power of storytelling to take complex issues and distill them into relatable narratives for audiences, building personal connections that challenged prejudices about disability, creating circles of awareness that expanded outward. She used curiosity about her physical appearance as a tool to drill down on substantive issues affecting the perception and treatment of people with disabilities. She once explained her strategy to an interviewer.

"Disabled persons are the ones who are looking for acceptance. We are the ones who are looking for our rightful place in today's society, and in order to do that, we have to be prepared to come out and tell you what being disabled is about and to help you to understand that you don't have to be afraid. I have to be able to come to you and say, 'Don't look at what's gone here, but look at what's left and what I can do.'"[2] Foregrounding presentations and workshops with her personal story allowed her to quickly connect with people, capturing their attention and redirecting it to where she wanted it to go. She endeavoured to present positive representations of disability to counter negative stereotypes that shrouded people with disabilities in a cloak of pity and fear.

But Beryl's personal style of advocacy increasingly diverged from the status quo in activist circles that frowned on exhibiting disabled bodies to engage others. Much of Beryl's advocacy began with a recounting of her accident story. She used her body as a tool for education and prefaced this with the concept that what happened to her could happen to anyone, an appeal to peoples' self-interest that forced them to re-evaluate the abilities many able-bodied people take for granted. As successful as this approach was in her connecting with audiences of all ages, other activists did not always see it as a progressive way to advance the rights and opportunities of people with disabilities. This was, in part, because of a legacy of charities that exploited disabled bodies to attract attention to their cause, often reinforcing negative stereotypes about disability in the process.

Disability activist Susan Peters observes that many mainstream charitable fundraisers of the day, such as the Jerry Lewis Muscular Dystrophy Labor Day Telethon, used disabled bodies as marketing tools.[3] From 1966 to 2010, the American telethon was broadcast annually, earning approximately 10 per cent of its nearly $2.5 billion dollar revenue from Canadians. Viewers were treated to the entertainment of the "King of Comedy," his guests singing, joking, and dancing, occasionally punctuated by heartfelt introductions of disadvantaged children with disabilities. With the telethon successfully motivating viewers to reach for their wallets, critics argued the show invoked potentially damaging stereotypes of disability by pitying, mocking, and infantilizing people with disabilities, who were called "Jerry's Kids" even if they were adults.

Beryl did not necessarily have a problem with Jerry Lewis. Though she would have frowned on his cruder jokes and comments about disability based on pity, fear, and ignorance, she felt he should be judged on the sum of his work and the money he raised for the disability community. She was likely more familiar with Lewis at the peak of his stardom in the 1950s when he teamed up with Dean Martin, and she admired his decision to use his celebrity to help others in need. For all his faults, Beryl saw Lewis as part of a system that helped promote public consciousness of disability issues and raised significant sums of money for research and programming, which ultimately trumped whatever personal feelings she may have had about his role in reinforcing the same damaging stereotypes she was working to dismantle.

Sensational media representations of disability with titillating stories of accident and injury also filled the newspapers and reinforced the idea that people with disabilities were objects of pity. Language and other choices used to depict people with disabilities in these stories did more than just sell papers; there were real-world consequences that shaped the daily lives of disabled people. In 1983, Barbara Turnbull sustained a spinal cord injury from a gunshot wound while working at a Brampton, Ontario, convenience store and was the subject of intense media coverage in the aftermath of the incident. In her memoir, *Looking in the Mirror*, she recalls one incident when she was dining in a restaurant. A woman walked up, confirmed Barbara's identity and said she wanted to donate to spinal cord injury research. "You never really know if the money goes where it's intended," the woman remarked, kissed Barbara on the head and left $100 on the table. "It left me feeling greatly embarrassed and like, well, like a charity case," Barbara wrote.[4]

"You don't need to know my story to understand that I deserve rights," asserts disability activist Tracy Odell. In the early 1980s, Tracy attended an educators' workshop at Frontier College in Scarborough where Beryl was the keynote speaker. "At the time, my disability politics were different than hers. So I had a little trouble with some of the messages in her talk because those were not the kinds of messages that I personally was promoting and the work that I was doing." Tracy explains that while many people were approaching the promotion of disability rights differently, Beryl's presentation of a "this could be you" scenario did not sit well with her. "It's not the message that I would use to promote that. Although people are going back to that now. They talk about the population being older, and this is why we need accessibility benefits. Everybody, even if you're eighty years old and you don't identify as someone with a disability, you still might need some support around vision, or hearing, or mobility."

Even if she disagreed with Beryl's style and parts of her message, Tracy understands why she attracted the media attention that she did. "She was quite a strong advocate at the time. She would do her own advocacy, but she was very outspoken. She would speak up. She would be on film. She was often someone that was on films because she was just so articulate." But the message Tracy took away from Beryl's presentation was that she was operating on a different wavelength despite their shared pursuit of promoting awareness of disability issues and the rights of people with disabilities. "For some people, that's life-changing to hear that kind of story for the first time. But I did not take that away from her talk at all. When I heard her speak, I did not think, 'Oh, that's someone that I should connect with because we're doing things the same way.'" For Tracy and others whose energies were devoted to achieving transformational change through policies, programs, and legal protections, Beryl's focus on education and building awareness of disability while using her body and personal story as a teaching tool did not seem like the most progressive way to achieve these shared goals. Nor did Tracy feel it was a solid basis from which to craft a strong rights framework, one where politicians only felt compelled to respect the rights of people with disabilities because of some personal connection or understanding of disability.

Disability activist and social worker Pat Israel also recognized Beryl as a somewhat free-floating figure in the disability rights community, and someone who seemed to follow her own path. "Beryl did her own thing," Pat concluded. Beryl was known for being highly independent, preferring to start and run her own groups rather than joining others in alliances or inserting herself into existing organizations. Co-founder of the DisAbled Women's Network, a national political network of women with disabilities, Pat appears in the 1981 documentary *Life Another Way* and worked alongside Beryl at various protests. Early on, however, Pat decided Beryl's concentration on education and awareness did not fit with the kind of frontline organizing and activism that interested her most. "She was more focused on working with children and teaching people how to go about in the world with a disability, which is fine. But I was focused on, 'How do we change the world?' If we can't get into every building and find transit, then we should change that." Beryl's message and approach did not necessarily complement or contradict the disability rights movement built by leading frontline activists like Pat, Tracy, and other trailblazers like Sandra Carpenter, Jim Derksen, Pat Danforth, David Lepofsky, and many others. "It was just different," Pat concludes.

Injured worker activist Steve Mantis worked for the Ontario March of Dimes' Thunder Bay chapter in the 1980s when Beryl embarked on her tour of northern Ontario. "I was around forty years old at the time. And frankly, she struck me as old-fashioned. We were developing the rights model at the time, and she seemed to me as being part of the charity model." A rights model focuses on putting the legal and policy protections at the centre of any advocacy work, ensuring people with disabilities are respected, free from discrimination, and empowered to protect themselves with legal rights. In contrast, the charity model, as an extension of the medical model, depicts people with disabilities as victims of circumstance (or fate, in the case of some religious charities) whose needs require services and supports often led by able-bodied people. "Being an insensitive white male, I sometimes formed these opinions too quickly," he chuckles. At the time, Steve was working with other activists to shut down sheltered workshops, and his energy was firmly oriented toward the future. "She was there with her bear. I'm guessing she was using the same approach as she would in the classroom, which was fine. But I thought, 'Hey, we're ahead of where you're at there, Beryl. Catch up!'" Steve understood that Beryl worked with others for years to lay the groundwork for the future but was frustrated with the slow pace of change. "But, because of my own biases at the time, I felt, 'She's the old guard, and we're the new guard.' Often, the 'new' feel they need to show how much smarter or better they are than the 'old.'"

If Beryl sometimes appeared at odds with a rapidly evolving disability rights movement in Canada, it's worth remembering that she was born in 1924, and the generational gap between her and other activists at the time meant she had different formative experiences than younger baby boomer activists. Younger activists coming of age in the 1960s and 1970s drew inspiration from other contemporary social movements that collectively transformed modern Canadian culture. By the time Beryl became heavily involved in disability politics in the early 1980s, she was already in her late fifties. She held many of the values and attitudes of an older generation that depicted people with disabilities as needing help and protection. This differed from the concept that people were disempowered by the very supports and services set up to help them and required legal agency and political rights. Beryl's generation included family advocates who led the deinstitutionalization movement and forged the very community service agencies that many younger disability activists fought against to project their own voice. To some, Beryl's close relationship with these agencies and her outmoded form of advocacy touched a nerve, harkening back to earlier eras when people with disabilities were not in control of their own lives or narratives, silenced by the advocacy of others who claimed to speak on their behalf.

Contemporary disability rights activism was a reaction to centuries of oppression of people with disabilities by religious and secular authorities. For most of Canadian history, people with disabilities were considered "unfortunates" in need of saving, protection, or punishment depending on the presentation of their physical or mental condition. From Victorian residential hospitals to the horrors of eugenics experiments, Canadian history is replete with stories of the varied ways persons with disabilities were oppressed and marginalized. Generations of Canadians with disabilities were incarcerated in residential institutions where they were removed from their families and communities, subjected to forced labour and experimental therapies, involuntarily sterilized, overmedicated, and ultimately abandoned when these institutions shut down without adequate replacement by alternative community arrangements. The act of separating individuals with disabilities from their families and communities, denying them their rightful place as valuable members of society, was deeply embedded in Canadian culture. However, people with disabilities, along with the organizations that advocated for them, started to push back against this damaging mindset.

In the 1950s, parents of children with polio and developmental disabilities sought to create opportunities for their children outside of residential schools and hospitals. Deinstitutionalization and the transition to community living required a significant shift in public attitudes and the treatment of people with disabilities. In cooperation with health and social services professionals, advocates lobbied government officials, held fundraisers, and established non-profit service agencies to serve people with disabilities in the community. Group homes and community-run programs managed largely by non-profit organizations started popping up across the country to fill a gap in services as governments slowly began to wind down residential institutions in the face of growing opposition and media exposés.

These non-profit organizations provided a critical stopgap to help people with disabilities transition to community living. But most did not involve their clientele in governing the homes in which they lived or the programs they relied on. When people with disabilities began to assert greater control over their lives in the 1970s and 1980s, many of these agencies pushed back as their leaders found the paradigm of consumer rights difficult to accept. Such organizations, started a generation earlier, were often reluctant to modify their governance structures to include disabled consumers on their boards of directors or in other positions of power. A significant reason for this unwillingness to give up control was the charitable model of disability of many service agencies, a paternalistic approach that often failed to account for an empowered consumer, a person with a disability who demanded greater control over their supportive services. "When the movement first started, we had to wrench the power away from them," Pat Israel explains. "They did not give it easily. Trust me." Many disability rights activists, often operating on bootstrap budgets with very little funding, strove to create consumer-led groups and resist the status quo that allowed advocacy organizations and agencies to gobble up most of the funding while claiming to speak on behalf of the disability community. Naturally, many developed animosities toward service agencies.

Beryl was more progressive than others of her generation who may have preferred a more paternalistic approach. But she did not harbour the same defensiveness as other disability rights activists when it came to dealing with service agencies. Her experiences were often positive, and she sought to leverage partnerships with relatively well-funded organizations such as the Ontario March of Dimes to support her grassroots advocacy work. "Beryl was more comfortable going to these service agencies," Pat explains. "Whereas I was normally more comfortable with fighting them. She was much more a part of them than she was a part of ours."

Beryl had a track record of speaking out against public officials, organizations, or policies that in her assessment failed the disability community, but she also believed she had found space between being a hardline activist seeking to tear down the dominant system to create something new, and someone who could use her connections with well-funded service agencies to improve the lives of people with disabilities. Whether or not Beryl successfully inhabited this borderland between activist educator and champion of service agencies and policymakers, the longer she lingered there, the more distance she created between her work and other disability activists, some of whom began to view her politics as out of step with the direction of the disability rights movement.

The fact that Beryl acquired her disability later in life was also a factor in complicating her relationship with disability rights groups. Within the disability community, a social phenomenon commonly referred to as a "hierarchy of disability" informally evaluates people with disabilities by the type of disability and when it is acquired in a person's life cycle. In this paradigm, ranking people based on how disability has influenced their formative experiences in life primarily serves to distinguish between people with congenital or childhood disabilities, whose self-identity is intertwined with the experience of disability, against others whose acquired disabilities clash with their worldview as formerly able-bodied selves. According to this reasoning, someone like Beryl who acquired her disability in her forties would have a harder time disentangling her sense of self built as an able-bodied person from the identity projected upon her by society as a disabled person. In other words, someone who is born with or acquires a disability in infancy develops an identity drawn from experiences and attitudes different from an able-bodied adult or senior who acquires the same disability later in life, even if both these people are ultimately subject to the same kinds of discrimination and prejudice in society. Though neither person's needs nor experiences of oppression are negated, there is seen to be a qualitative difference between the right to speak on behalf of the disability community since people with acquired disabilities are seen to potentially lack grounding in the realities of what it's "really like" to grow up and live with a disability.

In the contested world of disability politics where disability activists and able-bodied advocates often clashed on ideological terms, categorizing people by their experiences of disability became one of the distinguishing features in assessing legitimacy within the disability rights movement. Tracy Odell explains, "I think people who acquire their disabilities later in life, either because of an injury or an illness, have a certain perspective that someone like me would not share because I've had my disability all my life. I mean, from the time I was diagnosed, I was under two years old. I don't remember anything different. It's just a very different attitude that you have or a different outlook that you have around that."[5]

Beryl was aware of these qualitative distinctions within the disability community and always sought to highlight the ephemeral nature of ability to engage the broader able-bodied public on disability issues. If she was behind the curve when it came to an evolving disability rights discourse, by the end of the 1980s she did pick up some new language to express her perspective on the distinction. "I was a TAB," she told television host Dini Petty. "I was temporarily able-bodied."[6] The term "temporarily able-bodied" was popularized in the 1980s in reference to the likelihood that most people will become disabled at some point in their lives through accident, infirmity, or old age. The term perfectly encapsulated what Beryl had been saying for years about why the broader able-bodied public needed to pay heed to disability issues. The argument went, if nearly everyone would acquire a disability at some point in their lives, improving accessibility and opportunities for people with disabilities benefited all, giving everyone a personal stake in changing things for the better.

Notwithstanding the problems with this circular reasoning and its potential to change negative stereotypes, it did underscore where Beryl saw herself in relation to other people with disabilities. She felt that being an ordinary woman with visible disabilities gave her insight she could use to reach out to the larger "able-bodied" public. Whether or not her acquired disability affected her status within the disability rights community, or her approach seemed outdated and unnecessarily personal, seemed less important to her than her larger mission to change the hearts and minds of those whose prejudices reinforced the barriers and challenges she and many others faced daily.

26.

An Ordinary Hero

In 1989, producers from the Canadian Broadcasting Corporation approached Beryl to feature her on an episode of a popular weekly television documentary series called *Man Alive*. Hosted by veteran journalist Roy Bonisteel, the program offered a non-denominational spiritual analysis of faith, morality, and contemporary life on diverse topics, ranging from the Holocaust, nuclear war, "Third World" poverty, modern Buddhism, UFOs, and sexual abuse survivors. Produced since 1967, the program had yet to discuss the topic of disability. This omission appeared increasingly obvious as the Decade of Disabled Persons advanced. The show's producers began investigating potential sources for a program about disability. Beryl's name kept popping up in news clips, newspapers, documentaries, and interviews with politicians and other public figures. The 1981 documentary film *Life Another Way* was a hit featuring Beryl at the ascent of her public life. *Man Alive* would capture her at the peak of her influence, toward the end of an unprecedented decade of involvement in disability politics.

The episode was titled "An Ordinary Heroine" and aired on the CBC Network on the evening of Tuesday, January 24, 1989. "To be heroic, you must start out by being ordinary, and despite being ordinary, you must do extraordinary things," proclaimed Bonisteel in the show's introduction. Wearing a dark blazer and open-collared shirt, he suggested the cool confidence of a seasoned journalist with his baritone voice, perfectly styled white hair, and serious expression. "This is a story of a heroine. How great it is to be a heroine, and of the price she paid—is still paying." In the opening scene, we follow behind Beryl down a long hospital corridor, she with neatly coiffed white hair, floral blouse, pearl earrings and matching necklace. Viewers study the back of her head as her offscreen voice is accompanied by the soft purring of her electric wheelchair in motion gliding forward. The camera angle reverses as we continue moving backward facing her. Her blue eyes, their lids accented with blue eyeshadow, are framed with gold-rimmed glasses. Her left eye is fixed straight ahead as the pupil of her glass right eye stares off in a different direction. She wears a neutral, somewhat tired expression that contrasts the passionate energy in her offscreen voice. "I enjoy every minute of my life. My life is full! Have you ever woken up in the morning and thought, 'Oh God, this is a good day!' And it takes your breath away? I *can* feel like that every day. I *am* happy!"

She continues, quickly outlining her biographical details. "I was married, had three children. I had a job, and I would go to work in the morning and come home, prepare supper, and get the kids to bed. I would go to bed, and I would get up, go to work, and do the whole thing all over again. My life's not like that now." As Bonisteel resumes his narration, footage rolls from the employment equity protest in Ottawa showing Beryl and other activists on Parliament Hill and inside the House of Commons demanding accommodations for wheelchair users in the inaccessible gallery. "Now she's a battler, a champion for the disabled. Now she hammers on doors to let disabled people in, to wake Ontario up." The half-hour prime time feature captures Beryl's quiet charm, enthusiasm, influence, and resilience against all odds that had become a familiar part of her public profile. Beyond the public persona she had built up over the years, the documentary adds an entirely new side of her as Bonisteel takes viewers into the inner workings of her daily life and family relationships.

Beryl admits that her focus on community activism has had consequences for her personal relationships. "I lost sight of my social life."

Diane agrees. "She's either away, or if she is home, she's busy with somebody. You phone, and there's people there having meetings in the house or whatever. She doesn't have time." Diane adds that whenever they do find time together, it is enjoyable. "There just isn't enough of it. I'm very proud of what she's doing for other people and for herself because it's really helped her. She's become a totally different person. If she wasn't doing this, she might be sitting at home just depressed. I mean, maybe she might not even be around now," grimly alluding to the multiple suicide attempts that nearly claimed her life.

Beryl tearfully admits her biggest regret was not prioritizing more time with her family. "My daughter is healthy and has a good family. They have a good home, and I thought 'She is safe.' It's not that we don't love each other—I thought what I was doing out there was far too important to take time off for myself. People were in desperate need. People don't know how disabled people are hurting when they're on pensions that they can't live on, or they're in homes that are not accessible, or have families that don't want them and push them into institutions. To me, those are the people who need help."[1]

It's questionable if a similar documentary made about a man would have spent so much time focusing on the tragic costs of his activist work on his family relationships or domestic responsibilities. But if the CBC feature revealed anything new about Beryl's life that she hadn't already made public, it was the private struggle she endured to maintain her steadfast commitments to her advocacy goals. Following the broadcast, she arranged for two hundred copies of the feature to be sent to all boards of education across the province for use in classroom teaching, a stand-in for her when she could not be there in person.[2] Outwardly, she was the kindly but fearsome social reformer, but behind the scenes there was physical and emotional pain that would soon come to play a larger role in her life. In the stylized opening scene of the *Man Alive* feature, it is written on her face and in her choice of words. "I *can* feel like that every day." The statement lands hard, a self-affirmation against the physical and emotional obstacles she struggled with each day.

Whatever the struggles, Beryl had no intention of slowing down. The mission that had given her life meaning when she was ready to abandon all hope had now become an all-consuming obsession. People with disabilities deserved better opportunities in society, and she would not rest until she had changed enough minds to make a lasting difference. With a nationally televised introduction to a broader Canadian audience under her belt, coupled with a doubtful future in disability rights activism, Beryl felt she was on the cusp of a career as a politician. Years of lobbying and close connections with high-ranking officials taught her about how the government worked. Now it was time to enact these changes herself.

But could she transpose these experiences and connections to a career in politics? Would she muster enough support from her professional network and effusive personality on the campaign trail to lead her to victory? Beryl continually reinvented herself throughout life, picking up new skills along the way with each adventure or obstacle. By age sixty-five, she had learned a thing or two about grit and determination, personality traits that suited politicians with an agenda. She knew she could do whatever it took to get things done in government. But did she really understand what she was getting herself into? Whatever else was holding her back, Beryl finally took a deep breath and called up Liberal Premier David Peterson to accept his standing invitation for her to run in the 1990 Ontario provincial election.

27.
Politics

Liberal Premier David Peterson was a fan of Beryl since the early 1980s when, as Leader of the Opposition in Ontario, he encouraged her to run in the 1985 election. She turned down the endorsement offer to focus on her community work, but never closed the door on a future career in politics. The Progressive Conservatives won the 1985 election but were shortly defeated in a motion of non-confidence by a coalition of Liberals and the NDP. After forty-two years of PC rule in Ontario, the Liberals finally rose to power under Peterson. In 1987, at the expiration of the Liberal-NDP coalition government, Peterson called another election, giving Beryl a second opportunity to run. Still, the timing was not yet right for her. She worked so hard to get to where she was as a disability advocate that she decided not to risk it all for an election.

Three years later, with uncertainty sweeping the country in the wake of the disastrous Meech Lake Accord negotiations, Premier Peterson called an early election. At the opening press conference on July 30, 1990, environmental activist (and later Toronto city councillor) Gord Perks interrupted the proceedings when he stood up in front of Peterson and played a long, recorded message about the government's environmental record. The demonstration prompted Peterson to quip, "It's going to be an interesting campaign."[1] His words would soon prove prophetic. Mike Harris was recently installed as the right-wing leader of the Progressive Conservative Party. At the federal level, Conservative Prime Minister Brian Mulroney faced declining approval ratings. After being devastated in the polls in Ontario in

1987, NDP Leader Bob Rae privately considered retiring from politics if his party did not make a better showing next time around. The 1990 election would defy everyone's expectations.

On June 5, 1990, a few weeks after her sixty-sixth birthday, Beryl submitted her bid to run as a rookie Member of Provincial Parliament for the Liberal Party in Ontario. "I believe I can get more done for disabled people and improve everyone's quality of life by being in government," she told the *Toronto Star*.[2] Her campaign manager was Patrick Johnston. When the election was called, Patrick went to work in the campaign headquarters for the Liberal Party. A policy analyst on disability issues and later senior policy advisor with the Ontario government's Social Assistance Review Committee, Patrick was acquainted with Beryl since the early 1980s when he worked at the Canadian Council on Social Development. A wiry man with large glasses that did their best to camouflage tired eyes, Patrick became Beryl's right-hand man during her local campaign.

Beryl was selected to run in the Beaches-Woodbine riding of East York, a stronghold for the NDP. Despite being just east of downtown Toronto, the Beaches neighbourhood had a distinctly seaside small-town vibe, its leafy streets lined with Victorian houses, framed at the lakeside by a boardwalk that carried cyclists, pedestrians, and their dogs through a series of beaches along Lake Ontario. The good schools, low crime rate, and above-average income of its inhabitants distinguished this affluent and highly liberal lakeside community from its neighbours to the east where Beryl had lived for the past fifteen or so years, in the scruffier part of Scarborough. Regardless, Peterson hoped to turn the riding to the Liberals, deploying Beryl's trademark charisma to aid the party's prospects in the region. Peterson appeared at her campaign events as supporters waved pennants emblazoned with her name and the Liberal logo. One campaign pamphlet included a picture of Peterson hugging Beryl, alongside a ringing endorsement. "There's no better way for you to build a strong Ontario than to make Beryl Potter your representative at Queen's Park."[3]

Johnston knew that although Beryl had a good chance of resonating with many constituents, winning wasn't going to be a cakewalk. "That particular part of the city was a perfect riding for her in many ways to run in because it was really a progressive riding, generally speaking. The biggest challenge that the Liberal Party had in that riding is that it had consistently voted for NDP candidates." Long-serving incumbent NDP MPP Marion Bryden was retiring to be succeeded by Frances Lankin, who later went on to head the United Way and was appointed to the Senate by Prime Minister Justin Trudeau years later. She was a formidable opponent and very well-known in progressive circles in Toronto. "So you get a sense of what Beryl's competition was. It was going to be a tough campaign."

Some wondered why Beryl hadn't run in Scarborough where she was better known to the local community. "It's possible that by the time she indicated her interest in running, there might very well have already been a Liberal candidate nominated or somebody who had been working hard in that riding," Patrick explains. "It simply wasn't an option for her. It wasn't uncommon then for people to run in ridings that they did not necessarily live in, so finding an adjacent riding or a close riding in the general area was common."

At her acclamation assembly at the Kew Beach Junior Public School gymnasium, Beryl was in high spirits. She wore Liberal colours, including a red dress, white blazer, bright red lipstick, and newly manicured bright red nails. Fresh flowers, red and white streamers, and balloons framed the stage, and a live band played as she took to the microphone to thank her supporters. "This is the next logical step in my crusade for full participation, equality, and independence for all. I now feel confident that I can also represent other concerns just as effectively."[4]

One of Beryl's biggest challenges during the campaign was to avoid being seen as a one-issue candidate. She addressed this concern at Kew Beach School, knowing that she would spend most of her time discussing issues important to politically savvy Beaches residents. Disability may have defined her outward appearance and track record, but now she had to show people she also cared about local hot topics, such as education, daycare, and the environment. "I'm not going to be walking away from the disabled, but I'm going to be working for the whole community. I don't want people to look at my disability. They say when you lose one thing, you gain another. I may have lost my limbs, but I sure gained energy."[5]

Beryl threw herself into the campaign. Patrick remembers her boundless energy. "She was very hardworking. She would be out canvassing with volunteers. She could not get up to all the doors, but she would be out on the sidewalk as volunteers went up and knocked on doors. Some people would come out and talk to her, while others would wave. Despite all the obstacles she had encountered in her life, she was always upbeat, optimistic, and happy with a big smile on her face. And people responded to that right away. She had that gift of enabling people, a lot of whom were quite uncomfortable initially meeting her, to very quickly see past the disability and understand that she has all sorts of abilities."

Michelle, Diane's daughter, helped on the campaign trail. "I did a lot of the soliciting on the phone for her. And then when we would go door to door, nothing was accessible in the Beaches area. So I would run up to the door for her. Sometimes she would have arguments with people about political issues and I would be caught in the middle as the person who went up to the door. It was wild. They also would not let her smoke in public, which was hard since she was a big smoker. So she would have to hide in a closet so she could have a few puffs before moving on to the next house or event."

In mail outs to local Liberal members, Beryl's campaign finance manager declared the Beaches-Woodbine riding had an excellent opportunity to flip to the Liberals for the first time. "She now will use her experience and ability as an advocate to fight as the Liberal Member for Beaches-Woodbine for the issues that are important to the people of our riding, such as the environment, education, affordable housing, health and daycare."[6] Peterson was thrilled Beryl was running for the Liberal Party and planned to make the Ontario Legislative building fully accessible with a "very prominent seat" for her.[7] Victory for Beryl looked possible.

Prospects for a broader Liberal victory, though, were increasingly dodgy. As the thirty-six-day political race wore on, Peterson's prediction that it would be "an interesting campaign" turned out to be correct, but not in a good way for him or his party. Activist organizations and unions undertook a coordinated effort to disrupt the Liberals in response to Peterson's record on pension reform, privatization of public services, changes to worker's compensation, and medical billing practices. By their own admission, the Liberals did a poor job of messaging their achievements during the campaign and quickly tried to mount a defence. But as the NDP gained popularity, energy was sucked out of the Liberals' early lead.

Beryl's local campaign was not immune to controversy either. A year earlier, after becoming disillusioned with Trans-Action Coalition's allegedly narrow focus on Toronto transit issues at the expense of province-wide transportation problems for people with disabilities, she publicly quit as founding chair. In her tours of northern Ontario, Beryl had witnessed widespread inaccessibility, poor access to transportation and social services, crushing poverty, and a lack of understanding about disability issues in rural communities and First Nations reserves across the province. "I have talked to people in the streets and at public forums around the province. They don't want to see all the money poured into Toronto. Of Ontario's 839 communities, only 70 have any form of accessible transportation. I ask many (disabled) people on the street if they would use subways if they had lifts in them or if they would use accessible streetcars. Many say they would not; they have fears about safety." She started her own group, the Ontario User's Council on Transportation, with twelve consumer representatives and transit experts to liaise with the Ministry of Transportation to improve accessible transportation systems across the province.

Beryl's break with Trans-Action had played out publicly in the media. A bulletin in the *Toronto Star* read, "Beryl Potter, Canada's premier advocate for the disabled. Potter resigned as chairman of the Trans-Action Coalition because she no longer believes in its major objective—making the Toronto Transit System accessible to the disabled. After talking to people all over Ontario, Potter has concluded that such a narrow focus ignores the transportation needs of those who don't live in Toronto or who would not use the TTC in any event. Her resignation is a principled act that stands as an example to everyone in public life." Beryl followed up in an open letter emphasizing the need for accessible transit across the province. "The need to transport people from point A to B with adequate, safe and convenient transportation through various modes is far greater than demanding lifts on buses, streetcars and subways."

Remaining members of Trans-Action were infuriated, forced to defend the existence of their organization against Beryl's attacks. PUSH, one of the biggest activist groups in Ontario at the time and a member of Trans-Action, hoped their membership in the coalition would advance transportation equity in the province. PUSH's coordinator, Jonathan Batty, was both shocked and enraged when

Beryl seemed to unilaterally defy what they had been working toward as an organization for years. "Beryl wants to take the whole thing down with her. There is a sense of genuine outrage among members. There is a real disappointment."

Other activists' indignation was renewed when Beryl announced she would be running in the election for the incumbent Liberals. Some interpreted the announcement as Beryl's endorsement of the government's record on disability politics. Prior to the election, Ontario municipal affairs minister John Sweeney stated it was his intention to keep passengers with disabilities out of the subway system, citing safety concerns of the TTC fire marshal. If a train had to stop between stations, he argued, disabled passengers would not be able to make it to the surface quickly enough. His comments conflicted with a report of Metro Council and the TTC just weeks earlier that endorsed $50 million in upgrades to elevator service over the next ten years to permit passengers with disabilities access to the subway system. Disability rights activists saw the contradiction as an indication of the government's lack of commitment to building a fully accessible subway system. On May 9, the Trans-Action Coalition, now led by Francine Arsenault, protested at Queen's Park and spoke to the media about why they were there. "This little amendment would allow the Ontario government to get out of making stations accessible. We can't let that happen."

Before the official launch of her electoral campaign, Beryl released a statement in agreement with her former colleagues at Trans-Action. "We still haven't got a commitment, and we've been waiting for a long time. If Sweeney is looking to eliminate disabled people from the subway system, he's looking to get rid of about 75 percent of the riders. Not just people in wheelchairs, but people who are blind. These people have pacemakers and heart conditions and parents with strollers." While Beryl may have shared her colleagues' sense of outrage, as a candidate in the next election, she also could not afford to let it define her campaign. Patrick remembers the controversy but downplays any effect it may have had on her bid. "Concerning the campaign itself, it did not play any significant role or have any significant impact. Campaigns like that are just a blur, and there's so many issues that come up. Beryl had to respond. Although she was a disability activist, she was campaigning to be the MPP for everybody in the riding. The majority of discussion in the campaign would have no relationship to any of the disability issues."

But some disability activists felt that Beryl's decision to run as a Liberal was a betrayal to the disability rights movement. Even thirty years later, Pat Israel remembers it like it was yesterday. "Beryl fought for access to transportation for years. It was an issue she did fight. But she turned on our movement and [the Liberal Party] used her. We had to fight her and say, 'No, she does not speak for us. We still want accessible transportation.'" Even if the controversy failed to define the outcome of her campaign, Beryl's relationship with some disability rights circles was irrevocably damaged. "I knew Beryl for a long time, and we were close friends," Pat remembers. "No one appointed her spokesperson of the rights movement, but she was brought in like she was, and they [the provincial Liberal Party] always went to her."

When Beryl committed herself to run as a Liberal candidate, she was required to toe the party line. The Liberal government remained committed to accessible transportation, as confirmed in an August 25 party leader Q & A feature in the *Toronto Star*.[8] But the unresolved controversy with the TTC and Beryl's position as a candidate left to defend the government's record on accessible transportation damaged her reputation and reminded disability activists of her public break with the Trans-Action Coalition. "It exploded, and she was caught in the middle," says Pat. "If she did not say what the Liberal Party wanted her to say, they would not support her. When she did that, it was the death for her in the movement. She was not welcome anymore. It was tragic. And that was incredibly hard for her because she was used to coming to meetings." Unable to reconcile her personal political ambitions with her diminished standing in the disability rights community, Beryl spent less time with other disability activists in the coming years. Pat noticed that Beryl "hid for a long time because she knew what she had done."

As election day approached, a rising wave of support for the NDP was poised to crash down on the incumbent Liberals. Patrick knew about the unexpected nature of elections. "When you're working in that kind of environment, you hear a lot of rumours. You get a sense

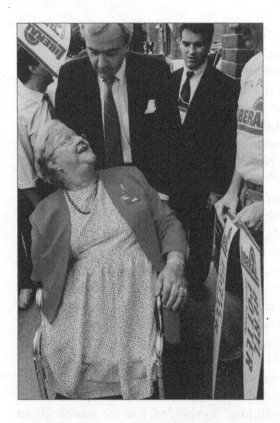

Beryl and David Peterson,
1990. Beryl Potter personal collection. Reproduced with permission.

of what's going on. It was pretty clear to everybody that it was becoming increasingly difficult throughout to see the Peterson government re-elected. That's difficult for those of us whose jobs depended on it. But that's politics. On the other hand, Beryl would not have had access to that information, and I could not divulge what I knew because it was speculation and rumours. But because people in the community received her so well, she did think that she was going to win."

Patrick calls it "the most difficult conversation you can have with a political candidate," as he describes the moment he told Beryl she probably wasn't going to win. "I was quite worried, to be honest, about how she might react on the day of the election, so I had a conversation with her. By the end of the campaign, I was pretty sure it was a foregone conclusion that she was going to lose. Any candidate has to believe they have a winning chance, or they could not sustain the time, energy and effort it takes to run a campaign. So, I did not want to put a damper on things for Beryl too soon. On the other hand, I

Beryl and Patrick on election night, 1990.
© Bernard Weil.

also did not want her to end election day without having some sense of what was likely to happen. The night before election day, I told her she was not going to win. And she was just devastated. She was. She'd worked so hard and built a positive response in the community."

"I think it's fair to say that Beryl was a bit naïve about the political process. She was kind of assuming that because people responded to her positively and said nice things, that meant they were going to vote for her. That isn't always the case, and it certainly wasn't there in her case. She went through election day and just carried on as if everything was fine. But there's a picture of me with her on election night where I was just hugging her. I think it's the only photograph I can think of where she wasn't smiling. She was trying to put on a game face. But you could tell she was just devastated." In the photo, Beryl offers a pained, mournful expression, barely able to contain her grief and disappointment for the cameras. Her face contorts into a mild grin as she hugs Patrick, her glass right eye defiantly staring down the camera, concealing the sadness in her left eye. Her obvious devastation is at odds with the cheerful but resigned expression she probably hoped to convey to others.

Michelle recalls Beryl being quite discouraged by the end of the campaign. "She felt that she could not be herself all the time, which was hard for her. There were all sorts of rules and having to always toe the party line and she struggled with that. She could not speak up and say whatever she wanted, and she did not like that at all. She was also very hurt by losing. I think there was a lot of psychological pain that eventually became physical pain."[9]

On Thursday, September 6, 1990, Ontario voters elected the province's first (and only, to date) NDP government led by Premier Bob Rae in a stunning victory for the social democrats. The final tally in Beaches-Woodbine put NDP candidate Frances Lankin in first place with 58.4 per cent of the vote, trailed by Beryl at 25.7 per cent, Progressive Conservative candidate Kevin Bruce at 14.3 per cent, and Independent Sam Vitulli at 1.3 per cent.[10] Thirty minutes after the polls closed, Beryl called Lankin to offer her congratulations. "I have great admiration for Beryl Potter and the work she has done," Lankin told the *Toronto Star*, adding, "I believe in this campaign that she was running for the wrong party."

A journalist called Beryl the following morning for comment on the election outcome. "I don't understand it. It's a weird, weird feeling. I tried so hard," Beryl stammered. Clearly still in a state of shock and used to making things happen through the power of her incredible force of will, Beryl no longer felt like the author of her own story. After this highly anticipated next chapter of her life was abruptly rewritten for her, she headed out to resume her activist work and public-speaking circuit.

If becoming a politician was off the table, she left no doubt to others that her plans were to continue much as she had done before. "If [Premier] Rae thinks he's had trouble with the disabled before, it's nothing compared to what I'm going to give him. I'm going to be hounding his doorstep."[11]

The 1980s were dead, but the 1990s would prove a radically different decade for Beryl with challenges that would push her to the brink.

28.

Common Sense

F ollowing the 1990 election, Beryl set aside her dream of making a difference in politics and decided to pick up where she left off. She secured one-year of funding from the Ministry of Transportation to further develop the Ontario Users Council on Transportation in support of her work with Ontario Action Awareness. But at the conclusion of the contract, OUCOT was in direct competition with the Trans-Action Coalition for funding. With Ontario moving into an economic recession, many advocacy groups were forced to compete against each other for a shrinking public purse, and few organizations shared such an acrimonious history.

In 1991, members of the Trans-Action Coalition were forced to defend their existence because of Beryl for the second time in as many years. PUSH Northwestern Ontario president Ron Ross, a member of Trans-Action, wrote to transport minister Ed Philip on February 28 to convince him that as a coalition of disability organizations, Trans-Action spoke with greater authority on the topic of accessible transportation. "We can agree there is an importance to having a Minister's Advisory Committee [such as OUCOT]. However, the persons who may be appointed to a Minister's Advisory Committee would present selected views and address specific agendas to the Minister's office. TransAction differs substantially in its mandate. It provides a forum for all disabled consumers to express their concerns throughout the province on issues related to accessible transportation."

On April 16, Minister Philip met with a delegation of Trans-Action members: Francine Arsenault, Anne Musgrave, Harry Fields, and David Baker. In his April 23 response to Trans-Action, Philip indicated the ministry had an existing relationship with Beryl. "Prior to any decision, it was felt appropriate that Mrs. [*sic*] Potter determine the expectations and nature of the contractual arrangements for this year between the Office for Disability Issues and the Ontario Action Awareness Association [Beryl's representative organization] in terms of ongoing community activities, particularly those at schools across the province."[1] It was possible to perceive a future where Trans-Action and OUCOT co-existed, but it was uncertain if Beryl would be able to rebuild the bridges she previously burned down.

Instead of haunting the steps of Queen's Park as she had defiantly warned, Beryl decamped to the road to resume her punishing schedule of public speaking. Less than a month after losing the election, she rolled into her reliable van with Dennis at the wheel, Mr. Grizzly safely tucked away in the back with the luggage and headed out to the peaceful environs of the Upper Ottawa Valley. "Mr. Dress Up and Sesame Street had better watch out if Beryl Potter ever decides to make working with children her full-time occupation," exclaimed the *North Renfrew Times*. "At the end of an hour with her, the lesson worked so well that teachers had to wait while their little students bade a reluctant farewell to their guest."[2] The following year, she increased the range of her tour, travelling almost nonstop. Scarborough,

Beryl with Mr. Grizzly
the Aware Bear, 1991.
© Jim Russell.

Kingston, Timmins, Cornwall, Ottawa, North Bay, London, Windsor, Brampton, Burlington. Her schedule was meticulously mapped out to coordinate with local school schedules and climatic conditions.

She worked like somebody running out of time, feverishly criss-crossing the map, reaching as many young people as possible with her message of hope. No longer welcome in the disability rights circles she formerly moved within, she decided to devote her time to the children's education programs that brought her joy for so many years. Her energy and determination were replenished at each stop by the children she visited, their curiosity feeding her ambition to transform the lives of people with disabilities by planting the seeds of acceptance and inclusivity in the next generation.

In 1992, the University of Waterloo conferred an honorary Doctor of Laws upon Beryl for her service to the disability community. Fumbling as she approached the microphone, Beryl appeared uncharacteristically nervous as she read from a prepared statement. "Your families and friends are rightfully very proud of you today," she said, expressing confidence in students' ability to make positive choices and use their love and strength to benefit all. "You are our tomorrows. Go forward and do what time has merit to do."[3]

To fulfill the equity plan that helped bring them to power two years earlier, the NDP government introduced the 1992 Advocacy Act. The legislation created a province-wide network of paid and volunteer advocates to assist the public to access resources, to understand and exercise their rights, and to express or act on their wishes when disability, illness, or infirmity interfered with their agency in healthcare or social services. Chaired by former NDP MPP David Reville, the Advocacy Commission struck an appointment committee, vetting candidates through two rounds of interviews at the Office of Disability Issues. Reville, who chose not to run in the 1990 provincial election that swept the NDP to power, attracted criticism as chair as his position was widely seen as a patronage appointment, which arguably undermined the legitimacy of the arms-length commission given his close ties to the premier and senior officials. Critics wondered how the commission could achieve its main task of holding the government to account when its chair was so closely associated with those in power.

Naturally, Beryl applied to sit on the commission. Given how long she and others fought for it to become a reality, she was overjoyed when it was finally established. Along with her extensive resume and numerous honours, her application package included a list of high-profile references, including *Toronto Sun* journalist Mona Winberg, CBC host Roy Bonisteel, and mayor of Scarborough Joyce Trimmer. Their endorsements portrayed a woman who was a "very strong guiding voice [who] doesn't take no for an answer nor allow her handicaps to get in the way," a "very goal-oriented person," and someone "people gravitate towards," someone who "puts audiences in the palm of her hand."

Beryl candidly discussed her state of mind with the interview panel at a time of painful transition in her life. She just lost the election and after competing with Trans-Action, OUCOT folded when its funding was cancelled for 1992, another casualty of dramatically shrinking government budgets and possibly a failed bid for funds. She also lost her funding for Action Awareness to tour the province, something that had given her joy and purpose in life for more than a decade. Her defiance in the wake of these setbacks was also marked by a sense of desperation. She vowed never to back away from advocating for others, admitting she could not enjoy life knowing what needs to be done to help others. "As long as there is breath in my body, I'll fight for people's rights," she told the panel in her first interview. She hoped the commission would empower disabled people to exercise their rights. "I was never given the opportunity for informed consent. I was only told what to do." Especially in the early days of her accident and hospitalization, she felt she did not have enough knowledge of her rights nor the confidence to assert herself and wanted to ensure that never happened to anyone else.

She received high marks in the first interview and was invited to the second round. "Rights are only as good as they are used," she told the panel, emphasizing the practical outlook she always took in her advocacy. "We should not tell people what to do. Let them know they have a right to decide if they want treatment or not." She observed that young people are becoming aware of their needs and rights, but community groups are too fragmented and "jealous of each other" to help them. She saw this as an opportunity for the commission to help people come together and break down silos. "We need to be clear on what we have now and make sure we still have it in five years from now."[4]

Despite her stellar performance in the interviews, Beryl was not selected to join the Advocacy Commission. She was not the only one disappointed. The announcement of the eight appointees chosen, only some of whom were persons with disabilities, caused an uproar in the disability rights community. Several groups representing people with disabilities and seniors issued a joint media statement denouncing the process to choose the commission. "Many disabled people and their groups are appalled by the recently announced eight appointees to the Ontario Advocacy Commission," Mona Winberg wrote in her weekly disability column in the *Toronto Sun*, pointing out as well that none had a developmental disability. Mona was particularly upset about the rejection of her good friend Beryl. "It is particularly appalling when highly regarded people like disability rights activist Beryl Potter were not selected," she wrote.[5]

In a return to commenting about disability rights after her vicious 1981 column in the *Toronto Sun* disparaged protesters at a Toronto cinema, Barbara Amiel chimed in and went one step further. In a *Maclean's* article titled "The New Enforcers for the Disabled," she called the Advocacy Commission a "vast bureaucracy of commissars." "The government is setting up a group of enforcers or commissars who have, intrinsically, a chip on their shoulder and will act as a battering ram of the state to interfere, under the guise of protecting vulnerable people, with any personal and professional structures within society that so far have managed to enjoy some modicum of autonomy."[6]

Critics of the Advocacy Commission would not have to wait long to witness its downfall. In the early 1990s Canada became mired in a global recession that hit Ontario hardest with more than an 8 per cent rise in unemployment, which significantly undermined its manufacturing sector. Grappling with a massive deficit and spiralling debt, the NDP government introduced a package of austerity measures that included wage freezes and mandatory unpaid days of leave, nicknamed "Rae Days," that sunk the party's popularity at the polls in the next election. The Advocacy Commission had barely begun its work when the NDP was swept out of office by the Progressive Conservatives led by Mike Harris.

Elected in a landslide, Harris immediately undertook a series of reforms to radically reduce spending. Styled after neoliberal conservative political ideology flowing from demagogues like Margaret Thatcher and Ronald Reagan, the reforms included tax cuts, reduced size and role of government, and a rollback of social welfare benefits. Branded by the party as a "Common Sense Revolution," Harris's policies were viewed much more harshly by critics. "A knife, an axe and a rusty saw" were how one CTV feature described the program of reforms.[7] Social assistance rates were cut by nearly 22 per cent. The Ontario Works "workfare" program incentivized the able-bodied working poor back to work. The healthcare system was radically restructured. Infrastructure projects were cancelled. Public utilities were divided up and leased out. Municipal governments were forced to amalgamate to reduce costs.

One of Harris's first acts as premier of Ontario was to revoke the Advocacy Act (1992) and dismantle the Advocacy Project. The provincial Office for Disability Issues was reorganized then disbanded. There ceased to be a minister responsible for disabled persons, and the Advocacy Council for Disabled Persons wound down. Funding for community programs and organizations that many people with disabilities relied on were clawed back or eliminated entirely. Many activist groups imploded in the face of bankruptcy, kneecapping the disability rights movement's ability to mount a campaign of resistance since many of these groups relied on public funds to survive.

Beryl was personally devastated by the political turn of events. She watched as decades of activism and hard-won victories were undone in an instant. Lacking the energy and resources to mount a major demonstration or lobbying campaign, she let her shock and anger ring out in the *Toronto Sun*. "Harris is not listening to us. He's not putting our priorities in order. I get the feeling he wants us to disappear. He has no feelings whatsoever. He doesn't give a damn."

Beryl could be forgiven for her despair. Beyond the larger existential challenge to the disability rights movement, her once powerful influence in government was greatly diminished as legislators and officials stopped answering her calls. She felt powerless to stem the tide. And yet, old habits die hard. "I'm going to go ahead and see them, even if I have to sit in front of their offices." She defiantly vowed to paper the doors of government offices with Mona Winberg's weekly disability column.

"I would not go back. I would not change," Beryl told *Toronto Sun* journalist Sandy Naiman, reflecting on her legacy as an advocate in an interview about the cuts. "But I thought it was time for me to step down. I thought the young people would take over, but they're not. Has Harris ever endured the discrimination a disabled person experiences every day? We've lost the Office for the Disabled. We're losing our subsidized housing. Is pulling the Wheel-Trans taxis the answer, so people ambulatory but unable to take the TTC are stuck? Yes, he's giving back 27% service until December 31st, then what? Where's his 'common sense' in all that?"[8]

29.
Order of Canada

S urrounded by turmoil, her blood boiling each time she picked up the newspaper filled with reports of the latest onslaught of cuts, Beryl watched as a lifetime of work was put on the chopping block. She sought to protect and uplift people with disabilities, but now they were being forced to the margins again by unrelenting and merciless public cuts. She felt as if decades of disability advocacy had failed to prevent the devastation that now unfolded before her. Dennis sought to remind his mother that nothing could deprive her of decades of tireless work to improve the lives of people with disabilities. For that he nominated her for the Order of Canada, the country's highest civilian honour.

Letters in support of Beryl's nomination poured into the Honours Directorate of Ottawa. The Order was created in 1967 to honour people who make extraordinary contributions to the country. An independent advisory council chaired by the chief justice of Canada researches and reviews all nominations, submitting its recommendations to the governor general. "Beryl's soft-spoken gentility, together with her extreme determination to create equality and accessibility (pensions, housing, education, transportation, medical care, etc.) for all persons has earned her the respect and admiration of everyone she comes in contact with regardless of their station in life," wrote Edith Rason, executive director of the Scarborough Recreation Club for Disabled Adults. "In my 40 years of community work, I have never been more moved or influenced than by my association and friendship with Beryl Potter," wrote Vim Kochhar, accomplished Rotarian, founder of the Canadian Foundation for Physically Disabled Persons, and later member of the Canadian Senate. "She is a shining star and guiding light, helping to make Canada the best place to live for people with physical disabilities." Kochhar had welcomed Beryl more than once to the Great Valentine Gala, an annual event in Toronto that raises millions of dollars to support causes that benefit people with disabilities. On one occasion, Ontario Lieutenant Governor Lincoln Alexander presented an award to Beryl and her good friend Mona Winberg at the gala.

David Onley, CityNews anchor and later lieutenant governor of Ontario, wrote of Beryl's influence. "Beryl is well-known and widely respected within Metro Toronto and area media as an expert and tireless crusader for the disabled. She is an inspiration to all who know her."[1] The list of supporters went on and on. Mona Winberg, journalist and activist; Michael Coxon formerly of the Ontario March of Dimes; Stan Walton of Scarborough Parks and Recreation; Adrienne Gilbert, associate professor at the University of Waterloo; John Aird, lawyer and former lieutenant governor of Ontario; Linda Crabtree, Order of Canada recipient and president of CMT International; Myron Angus, artist and member of the Association of Mouth and Foot Painting.

In 1996, convinced by the flood of accolades, Governor General Romeo LeBlanc appointed Beryl to become a Member of the Order of Canada. "For many years she has been a dynamic advocate for the rights of physically disabled people to education, employment, recreation, housing and transportation," read her honours statement. "Her indomitable spirit has been an inspiration to other disabled people, and her leadership in Ontario Action Awareness helped to focus on their needs and the many possibilities for solutions."[2]

Before the official investiture ceremony on November 13 at Rideau Hall in Ottawa, an awards ceremony was held on May 9 at the Royal Alexandra Theatre in downtown Toronto. Built in 1907 and purchased by Ed Mirvish in 1962, it was the oldest continuously operating theatre in the world. In 1986, Ed's son David assumed management of the building, securing its designation as a national historic site, which also protected it from costly accessibility upgrades.

Beryl attended the awards ceremony alongside Canadian country music star Stompin' Tom Connors, another inductee into the Order of Canada that year. Connors once told an interviewer a memory from the event that stood out in his mind. "Everything looked pretty straitlaced—people with tuxedos and all this stuff and little champagne glasses in their hands. So I went over and struck up a conversation with Beryl. I say, 'Do you ever give anybody a ride on that wheelchair?' And she says, 'Oh, yeah. Want a ride?' And I said, 'Sure.' So I thought maybe she'd just go a couple of feet and back up again. But she'd got quite a strong motor on that thing, and she just let her go. So I started hollering, 'Get out of the way! Hi-ho Silver! Here we come!' And so everybody had to get out of the road, and I'm waving my hands like the Lone Ranger with the cowboy hat and all, and she's just laughing her ass off. And before you knew it, it kind of broke the ice and everybody sort of let their hair down, and we had a party after that."[3]

As the ceremony ended, people began filtering out of the theatre onto King Street and headed next door to Ed's Warehouse restaurant for an elaborate reception. Located immediately west of the Royal Alexandra at 266 King Street West, the Reid Building was built in 1904 and purchased by Ed Mirvish in 1963 to service theatregoers, as there were few quality restaurants in the area at the time. Waiting in line to enter the restaurant, Beryl experienced a terrible but familiar feeling as she watched people climbing the steps into the building. Four stairs up from the sidewalk followed by two staircases meant the restaurant was completely inaccessible to wheelchair users.

Beryl was incredulous. How could the event planners not have considered that she would be unable to access the reception venue using a wheelchair? A celebrated disability activist being honoured for a lifetime of work, and nobody thought about accessibility. Shivering on the chilly sidewalk in an evening dress of her own creation, her anger melted into dispirited embarrassment as people filed past her into the building. As the long minutes passed, it became clear no one had arranged to accommodate her. "They wanted to carry me in. But I said no way. It was the indignity of being carried, of being wobbled up two flights of stairs by two people who are not steady and may fall and hurt their back and me at the same time."

To save herself from further humiliation, she whispered to Dennis to get the van and take her home. As Beryl was entering her van, a limousine pulled up behind them and out stepped Governor General LeBlanc. He witnessed Beryl being lifted into the van and questioned his aides why she was leaving so early. The next morning, Beryl received a call from the governor general's office apologizing for the oversight. "I just told them straight. The next time they made arrangements, to think of people in wheelchairs,"[4] her response expressing her pain and anger at being excluded yet again.

By the time she attended the investiture ceremony in November, any lingering resentment had vanished. The ceremony took place at Rideau Hall, the official residence of the governor general, in the ballroom, which sparkled under the light of its magnificent chandelier, gold columns, and blue walls rising to a coved ceiling lined with intricate plasterwork and crown moulding, a large portrait of Her Majesty Queen Elizabeth II presiding over the ceremony.

Beryl was radiant in a multi-coloured sequined blazer and black dress with a pearl necklace and earrings. Her companion that night was her close friend Mona Winberg, who would be inducted into the Order herself in 2002 for her journalistic achievements in disability advocacy and community service, including her role as former president of the Ontario Federation for Cerebral Palsy. Governor General LeBlanc pinned the badge on Beryl's blouse above her heart, a silver hexagonal snowflake insignia crested by a St. Edward's Crown, confirming her as a Member of the Order of Canada. As LeBlanc leaned down to congratulate her, he clasped both his hands around hers as she grinned ear-to-ear in a moment of pure joy.

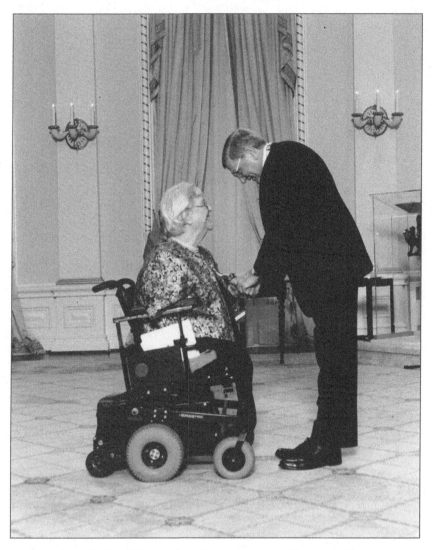

Beryl receiving Order of Canada from Governor General Romeo LeBlanc at
Rideau Hall, 1996. Beryl Potter personal collection. Reproduced with permission.

30.
Final Stop

Beryl's health declined throughout the 1990s. She was always good at hiding pain and ailments, but by the mid-1990s, the façade began to crack. In 1994, she confessed to Mona that she was in constant pain, a consequence of sitting on the stumps of her legs for long periods of time. "My problems began almost five years ago. At first, I thought it was indigestion. There was constant pressure in my stomach and vagina. I had pressure sores and skin irritation. Finally, I went to see a woman gynecologist at a downtown Toronto hospital."

But the medical appointment did not go as planned. "I could not get up on the examination table. No one in the hospital could help me, including the six nurses in the cubicle, because they are not taught how to lift a person without legs. I had to lie down and slide forward in my wheelchair so the doctor could examine me and do a Pap test. I was most embarrassed because the nurses all stood around watching me. Neither the doctor nor the nurses seemed to realize the indignity of the situation. Disabled people have feelings. We are not on public display."[1] She ended up going to Women's College Hospital, where there were accessible hydraulic examination tables.

In 1996, Beryl temporarily lost the remaining vision in her left eye, a complication due to type 2 diabetes. She began experiencing severe vertigo and was tortured by the constant sensation of falling out of her wheelchair. She had no depth perception and would consequently bump into walls and knock over objects. Diane remembers her mother becoming very frustrated during this time. "When we all went out to eat, she would get so frustrated, and found it very hard, not having control of when she would put down her glass or coffee cup and it would almost drop on the floor." Her electric wheelchair became a bumper car, every forward or backward thrust of the joy-stick ramming her into unseen obstacles. She frequently found herself caught between the bed and dresser and needed someone to rescue her. Navigating the world with vision loss while coping with constant pain was something she had feared most when a blood clot stole the vision from her right eye twenty-five years earlier. Now it was happening all over again.

She learned to adapt, as she had done so many times before, and did her best to keep up with her speaking circuit. Several months after losing her vision, Diane and Michelle went with Beryl to a presentation at the University of Toronto at Mississauga campus. "She was onstage when we walked in the back door. There were a lot of students already sitting down. Suddenly, she cried out, 'Oh my god, I can see my daughter and granddaughter walking through the door! My vision is back!' She saw a green circle, and as it cleared, she could see us walking in. Then the kids started yelling for us to come up and help her."

Beryl's vision may have been restored, but her pain became ever more excruciating. She abstained from pain medication for as long as possible, fearing the return of her earlier addictions that drove her suicidal thoughts. Now she had to take up to six Percocet (oxycodone) tablets just to get out of bed in the morning. In her personal papers, she stopped tracking her accomplishments, although one document reads as a declaration of her hopes for the future. She saw elderly people confined to understaffed nursing homes or struggling with cutbacks to homecare, and young people striving to contend with student debt while adapting to a changing job market. "There is a great deal of fear and frustration within these target groups. They are fearful about what the future holds for them as the programs and services they had are becoming less available. Canada owes them more than this. We owe it to them to give them the education they need." Against these challenges, she concluded with a solemn pledge. "I will continue with my work for as long as I can reach the people."[2] Her words read like an reaffirmation of her commitment to Terry Fox so many years earlier to carry on the work of raising awareness of disability.

In those final years, Beryl grew undeniably weary. As her health conditions worsened, she acquired the physical appearance of someone beyond that of an early septuagenarian. She became pale, jaundiced, and puffy, one of many side effects of the cocktail of medications she needed to function every day. She started wearing copper tinted glasses to combat her deteriorating visual acuity. But she still knew how to put on a good face, and her commitment to educating people about disability issues and advocating for the rights of people with disabilities never wavered.

By the mid-1990s, Beryl understood she was nearing the end of her life and she began to put her affairs in order. Naturally, her thoughts turned toward what the future might hold for Dennis. Their lives were intertwined for so long, it was unclear how he would fare without her. Now in his late forties, the last job Dennis had before he committed himself to assisting his mother full-time was in the early 1980s as a bellboy. He collected a small caregiver supplement to Beryl's workers' compensation pension, and their subsidized rental apartment at 4695 Sheppard Avenue was in her name.

In her desperation to safeguard her son's future, Beryl wrote to her estranged brother Norman, pleading for his help. Norman lived not far away in Scarborough, but their fractured relationship kept them apart. "I know you are holding a grudge against me, a grudge

From left: Arnold Boldt, Bob Rumball, Beryl Potter, and Peggy Cameron, recipients of the Terry Fox Hall of Fame, 1994. © Boris Spremo.

that could only have been drawn from your conclusion that you do not understand, nor are you willing to discuss openly. . . . I am more concerned with the fact that you are apparently including Dennis in this grudge by cutting him out of your life also. Is it because you think I have given him a rough time and have done nothing to provide for him or cover the cost of my funeral? If so, then you are wrong on all accounts. . . . Norman, I don't know what else I can do except what I am doing right now, and that is to *beg you* if necessary not to cut Dennis out of your life."[3] Diane felt Norman did hold a grudge against Beryl and quietly resented her for decades for what he perceived as Dennis being forced into a life of personal servitude. "He was very hard-headed. Norman detested my mother when Dennis started to have all his knee problems from lifting her all the time. He thinks that my mother took his life away. He never got over the fact that she would not let him adopt Dennis when he told her his wife could not bear children." Beryl hoped that a final letter to her brother would, if not clear the air between them as siblings, at least create room for him to keep an eye out for Dennis after she was gone. But it's uncertain whether Norman ever replied to Beryl to reassure her he would look after his nephew.

———————

It was an unseasonably cool spring in southern Ontario in 1998, with average daily temperatures in cottage country north of Peterborough hovering around six degrees Celsius. Traditionally, Diane and George would host a family gathering on Easter Sunday at the cottage in Lakefield but decided to delay the celebration a couple weeks hoping for warmer weather. Beryl had been at the cottage the previous Thanksgiving. The outdoor table was set with roast turkey, baked acorn squash, cranberries, and fresh rolls, the aroma of the feast mingling with the gentle perfume of autumn, fallen leaves crunching underfoot when they made their way down to the lakeside. By spring, Beryl was too sick to make the journey to celebrate Easter. Just a few weeks earlier, she learned that her worsening health put her remaining arm at risk of amputation once more. The news left her crushed and exhausted. "I just don't want to live anymore," she told Diane, her voice heavy and battle weary. Thirty years of digesting bad news from doctors and learning to survive finally pushed her to the edge. When Diane telephoned her mother to announce their return from the cottage, Beryl asked that her grandchildren not see her like this, her uncharacteristically faint voice softly crackling through the line. As Beryl's intake of pain medication increased, her appetite faded, and she grew weaker by the day.

Diane and George arrived with a plate of leftovers to warm in the oven. Dennis was in hospital recovering from stomach surgery, a consequence of his heavy intake of painkillers, so Beryl was alone in the apartment. "Come on, Mum, just eat some mashed potatoes," Diane pleaded.

"I don't even want tea anymore," Beryl sighed, excusing herself to the bedroom to slip into her nightgown. Moments later, she began hyperventilating and breathlessly wheeled out into the kitchen. "Can't—breathe," she gasped.

George dialled 911. An ambulance arrived so quickly it seemed as if it was idling just around the corner. In no time, the living room was filled with paramedics. Two of them laid out a stretcher while another fitted Beryl with an oxygen mask, peppering her with questions while they read her pulse and quickly worked through a list of diagnostic tests essential for assisting with respiratory distress. Single-use medical products littered the floor as Diane and George hovered in the corner holding each other as they watched the shocking scene unfold before them.

Diane, Michelle, and Beryl. Thanksgiving at the Juda cottage, ca. early 1990s.
Beryl Potter personal collection. Reproduced with permission.

Neighbours crowded windows that looked onto the front of the building, alarmed by the pulsing light that cast an urgent red shadow over the monochrome cul-de-sac. They watched as Beryl was loaded into the ambulance on a stretcher, many of them unaware of the woman's identity and what she had given to the world. The short journey down McCowan Road to Scarborough General Hospital was over in an instant. Emergency doctors said that Beryl's lungs had "filled with water," *pleural effusion*, which involved excessive accumulation of fluid between the lungs and chest commonly caused by pulmonary emboli. A blood clot was likely pumped through her heart to her lungs causing the respiratory impairment, an infarction of the lungs. The blood clots that plagued Beryl throughout her life finally returned to claim her.

Beryl was admitted to the Intensive Care Unit. Her water intake was restricted, an order enforced by teams of uncompromising ICU nurses. But Beryl's defiance was unyielding, even at this stage. As soon as the nurse's back was turned, she would plead with her eye to Diane and Michelle for water, her unbearably parched throat unable to offer up any speech. A sigh of temporary relief accompanied each stolen moment with a moistened sponge or tube of lip gloss that caressed her cracked lips. The horror of her mother's forced dehydration haunted Diane for years afterward. "It must have been torture to lie there without water for so long." Even now, Diane finds comfort wherever she sleeps in a tall glass of water that sits on her nightstand in memory of her mother.

Days passed as Beryl slowly slipped away against the backdrop of beeping, buzzing, whirring, and pumping machines, the soundtrack of her life for so many years. Sometimes she would tug at all the lines criss-crossing her body as if tearing herself out of a giant spider's web that inextricably entangled her. A constant parade of visitors, nurses, and doctors marched by while Diane and Michelle kept vigil at her bedside. Diane signed the hospital's do-not-resuscitate documents to confirm Beryl wanted to die naturally. They took turns holding her hand and softly whispered reassuring, loving words in her ear.

Beryl's boys, Victor Jr. and Dennis, did not respond well to the situation. Victor Jr., Beryl's eldest son, was given leave from the addiction centre where he was staying to visit his dying mother. Victor Jr. never spent much time at home after joining the Navy and was dealing with his own demons. As his mother lay dying in her bed, Victor Jr. was unable to offer much comfort and wandered the brightly lit hospital corridors alone in private contemplation. Recovering from his own stomach surgery, Dennis's shock and fear registered outwardly as anger and denial. "I'm sick too and nobody ever pays attention to me!" he would shout at Diane.[4] In the waiting room, he steered conversations away from the current situation in a vain attempt to distract himself from the terrifying prospect of losing his mother and confidante. Now, as before, the women of the family provided a steady hand in rough waters.

Beryl died on Friday, May 1, 1998, from kidney failure and cardiac arrest, nearly one month shy of her seventy-fourth birthday. She drew her last breath with the dawning sun that welcomed another calm spring morning. In her youth in Liverpool, she would have spent the day celebrating May Day, the ancient pagan festival that evolved into the observance of workers. May Queens would march down Liverpool streets alongside horses festooned with elaborate laurel flowers. It was a day of release from the toil and strain of everyday life, a fitting moment for Beryl's final deliverance from the hardships that wracked her body with a lifetime of battle scars.

31.
Remembrance

C P24 News ran multiple stories on Beryl the day she died, announced by the alliterative tagline "Dynamic Disability Defender Dies." Archival footage shows Beryl meeting people on the street during her 1990 run for government. "A triple amputee following an accident, Beryl was the force behind many projects designed to make the world more accessible for able-bodied and the disabled alike," announced anchorman Mark Dailey, who added a personal note of condolence to family and friends.[1] Dailey was there when Beryl received her Order of Ontario and personally covered her 1990 campaign in his home riding of Beaches-Woodbine.

Beryl's funeral service was upbeat, just as she would have wanted it. Her son, Victor Jr., delivered the eulogy at the downtown Toronto Rosar Morrison Funeral Home, once a large Victorian house, its interiors now filled with calming beige antique furniture and nondescript wallpaper. By his own admission, Victor Jr. did not "see or feel a lot of the pain/agony and suffering that she went through at the start," having joined the Navy at age eighteen. "But I sure did during the latter part of her life." He remembered her early dedication to all her volunteer causes, including the countless days she'd sit in front of supermarkets in the rain and cold collecting sales receipts for charity. He told a story about one Halloween at a Shoppers Drug Mart, where candy boxes were piled so high that it blocked the aisles for wheelchair access. "When Mom saw this, she sure had a message to send to the manager. She put her electric chair into high-speed mode and sat there poised at the end of the aisle, just like a dragster, revving up and waiting for the green light to rip up the track. She had fire in her eyes. She shot down the aisle, and boxes went flying everywhere. I don't think she missed too many, although I'm not sure because I took off. I did not want them to know she was with me."

He remembered how infuriated she became at cars parked in accessible spots that did not belong. "Woe betide you if you were one of the unfortunate or irresponsible people that she caught. She had these peel off stickers made to put on your windshield as a friendly reminder. But these were not your normal friendly reminders. They were embarrassing, somewhat nasty reminders of the sin you had just committed. To make it more unpleasant, they were the metallic type, like the license plate sticker, that don't peel off. So you wore the shame even longer, and you could not forget about it because you had to stare at it as you quickly drove away. It was always conveniently stuck onto the driver's front window."[2] Victor Jr. summarized his mother as he and others knew her. "In a nutshell, mom was a lady devoted and dedicated to the needs of others."

CP24 also covered the funeral service on May 4 as Dennis, George, Justin, and other pallbearers carried Beryl's casket out of the funeral home.

Beryl was cremated at the Forest Lawn Crematorium. Diane never liked the idea of interring her mother's ashes in a cemetery vault or crypt. And yet, she remained uncertain where they might be scattered. At their cottage where Beryl loved to spend summer vacations and holidays? If they sold the cottage, they would no longer be able to visit that special spot. In Liverpool where she grew up and her mother, father, and sisters were buried? Beryl moved around so much as a child and it had been so long since she lived there, there wasn't an obvious place for her in England. In the absence of any one special spot, Diane ultimately decided the best place for Beryl's cremains was with her family. Beryl always regretted that she was unable to spend more time with her family because of the rhythm of life she adopted following her accident, so it seemed fitting that she remain in the care of her loving daughter and granddaughter.

32.
Aftermath

Only five years after Beryl's death, in 2003, someone else would stand in Victor Jr.'s spot at the same funeral home where his mother's service had taken place. Following another tumultuous relationship and still battling his addictions, at fifty-six years old, Victor took his life in a motel in Scarborough.

In many ways, Victor Jr. followed in his father's footsteps. In the years after they divorced, Victor's addiction continued to spiral out of control. Once in the early 1970s, when Victor was on a return trip to Toronto after visiting family in Belfast, Northern Ireland, Diane received a call from security at Pearson International Airport in Toronto. Victor was too intoxicated to leave the airport on his own and had no taxi or bus fare to get him to where he needed to go. Similar interventions reoccurred over the next twenty years. When Diane and George started a family, Diane would invite her father to babysit on the strict condition he stay sober. He would carry around a mug pretending he was drinking coffee all day long. One day, Diane received a call from home. "Grandad's face is in the soup! He passed out and his face is in the soup. What'll I do?" Diane raced home, but by the time she got there, Victor had woken up, left the children, and gone to an Italian bar down the street.

Eva, Victor's second wife, eventually divorced him, and when she died, the family made it clear he was not welcome at her funeral. Over the years, there were multiple car rides to and from Lakeshore Psychiatric Hospital where either Diane or George, listed as next of kin, would ferry Victor in and out of detox and rehab clinics. Diane remembers the sleepless nights when her father would barge into her life. "He would call from all sorts of places in the middle of the night. If he had nowhere to go at three o'clock in the morning, we'd hear banging on the front door. 'Let me in! Let me in!' George was always very good to him." Sometimes he would get kicked out of a residential treatment program for breaking the rules. Whenever this happened, George would collect him, and he would spend a few days with Diane's family until they could find him another place to go. Eventually, Diane got her father an apartment in Toronto Community Housing, so he always had his own place to go back to when he was in and out of treatment. Victor bounced around from Yonge and College to the Esplanade, endlessly shuffling from one community housing building to the next.

For the last twenty years of his life, Victor floated from halfway houses to detox and back until he died three years before Beryl on November 15, 1995. Attempting to account for how her husband's life turned out, Beryl always pointed the finger at herself. "He just never got over it," she asserted again and again, referring to her medical journey. Of course, the truth was much more complicated than that, but casting Victor as collateral damage of her own physical trans-formation was, perhaps, Beryl's way of offering him forgiveness, abso-lution for a broken soul.

Family friend Mona Winberg knew Beryl's death would be tough on Dennis. Perhaps Beryl also asked Mona to look out for her son because soon after she died, Mona wrote to Dennis. "Dennis, Beryl could not have made the wonderful contribution she did without your support. She realized this and was always very proud of what you and she were able to accomplish. I ask you not to make import-ant, life-changing decisions at this time. It is difficult to think clearly at a time of grief, and things that seem impossible now may look more hopeful six months from now. I know this from personal experience. If you feel like talking at any time, I am here."[1]

Mona's concerns were well-founded. Without his mother as an anchor in his life, Dennis soon began to drift. For years, he struggled with a debilitating addiction to codeine. He took copious amounts of ASA-222s and Tylenol #1 for his chronic knee pain and stomach problems. The effect of codeine on the body is like morphine and often considered a "gateway drug" to more powerful opiates. While the codeine in Tylenol #1 attacked his liver, acetylsalicylic acid in the ASA-222 and the Aspirins ate away at his stomach lining, causing severe digestive issues even if it did temporarily alleviate the inflammation in his back and knees. Years of poor diet and habitual consumption of fistfuls of pills wreaked havoc on Dennis's digestive system, causing painful bleeding ulcers.

Diane knew her brother needed someone to keep an eye on him. "The first conversation we got into was, 'Okay, who's going to watch Denny and all the pills he takes?'" She would try to get Dennis to eat better, cut down on the pills, and talk to a doctor, but her pleas were always met with his common refrain. "I'm not stupid. I don't need to talk to anybody." Eventually, Dennis would undergo a partial gastrectomy, losing half of his stomach to mitigate the damage to his severely corroded gut.

Beryl never left a will. Instead, she designated Dennis as the sole beneficiary of her survivors' benefits from the Workers' Compensation Board (renamed the Workplace Safety and Insurance Board). Diane pleaded with him to be careful with the money. "Okay, Denny, you can only take out so much a month to make it last." But he did not listen. He would go on vacation, rent expensive cars, and frequent casinos. Dennis stopped receiving his caregiver benefit when Beryl died, and within ten months of her death, he exhausted the $6,400 to $9,600 lump sum survivor benefits. Later, he borrowed money from his family and sold most of his mother's belongings to pay his debts. Beryl's pearl earrings, a Rolex watch (an extravagant present he had given her), and a collection of Franklin Mint all went to pawn shops or unscrupulous neighbours who often took advantage of him. He would show up to Diane and George's office begging for money because he could not afford to keep the van. More than fifty years after he once requested to adopt Dennis as his own, Norman tried to honour his sister's plea to look after her son, but he was in no position to support anyone and did little to prevent Dennis's death spiral.

Soon after Beryl died, Dennis moved into another subsidized apartment with Toronto Community Housing. He continued eating poorly. His fridge was packed full of ice cream and the cupboards overflowed with junk food. He never cleaned the apartment, which quickly deteriorated. He also found increasingly creative ways to acquire the codeine he craved daily. He ended up back in hospital in Mississauga, repeatedly sneaking across the road in violation of the rules to buy large bottles of pills or to convince people visiting the hospital to get them for him. Diane remembers one incident when she went to visit her brother in hospital. "I was attending physio across the street from the Mississauga Hospital. We had visited before this, so it was a regular thing. But I did not know he had been using our visits as an excuse to access the pharmacy, which he normally would not have been allowed to do. Of course, the pharmacy staff had no idea who he was, so he would go in there, 'Can I get a bottle of 300 pills?' get his stuff and come visit with me as if nothing had happened. After that happened once or twice, they placed him in a locked ward."

For months, Dennis was bleeding internally from the ulcers and other damage to his gastrointestinal tract, which led surgeons to perform a full gastrectomy. As his next of kin, Diane was advised Dennis needed to be moved to a long-term care home. She was powerless to stop her brother's slow decay. Diane recalls her last visit with him. "We walked in, and he was sitting there by the window, just skin and bone. He was like a zombie, drool dripping out of his mouth. He had a hell of a last few years. He died because he just stopped taking care of himself."[2]

Dennis Potter died in 2005, aged fifty-seven. The date was Sunday May 8, Mother's Day.

Epilogue
Finding Meaning in Loss

The life of Beryl Potter contains lessons about how identity is constructed in the face of loss. Beryl lost a great many things in her life. The opportunity to know her birth father; childhood and adolescent years free from poverty and the terror of war; a viable future in her homeland; a stable marriage. From these and other experiences, she learned about endurance and adaptation, skills that would prepare her for the most profound losses of her life—her health, mobility, independence, and agency. When confronted with the dilemma of adapting to a world no longer designed for her needs and abilities, she worked to find meaning in the aftermath of her personal trauma. She learned to adapt, and even thrive, using her hardships to elevate her to something unimaginable before her accident, discovering a new sense of purpose, a mission to change the world by building a new identity as a crusader against injustice.

In 1888, German philosopher Friedrich Nietzsche reflected on his experience of pain. Like Beryl, Nietzsche knew about pain. He endured lifelong bouts of vision loss, migraine headaches, and abdominal pain that forced him to live in near isolation toward the end of his life. He would take large doses of opium to mute his symptoms. Before his death, he suffered mental breakdowns, manic and depressive episodes, psychosis, dementia, and at least two strokes. In his philosophy of pain, Nietzsche argues that because pain and suffering are a universal human experience, it can teach us about the meaning of life, a theory that led him to write the famous phrase *"Aus der Kriegsschule des Lebens—Was mich nicht umbringt macht mich stärker."*[1] In English: "Out of life's school of war—What does not kill me makes me stronger." The phrase was often interpreted to express optimism and determination in the face of hardship, but Nietzsche's original meaning was to identify a person who had succeeded in learning to turn injury and misfortune to their advantage.

Beryl's life was an example of self-affirmation in the face of loss, proof that uncontrollable situations causing pain and suffering can be transformed into a vehicle for promoting change in the world. She did not take this philosophy to people with disabilities; they, like her, were already living in a world that segregated them. Instead, she talked about her own personal journey to lead the "able-bodied" public, especially children, toward normalizing people with disabilities, and arguably, their own disabilities later in life. Beryl taught that most people would experience illness or disability at some point in their lives whether through accident, circumstance, or with age. She did not argue that this was necessarily a prerequisite or justification for accessibility and inclusion, but rather an appeal for empathy and understanding, warm emotions capable of melting prejudicial reactions from a place of fear and ignorance.

When people first encountered Beryl, they were shocked and captivated by her missing limbs, her blindness, and electric wheelchair. But those who looked beyond what she had lost, beyond what she was not, quickly grasped the extraordinary depth of her character. What disability took from Beryl was returned to her many times over. She gained a new source of motivation to change the world, anchored by her unique experience and perspective on life, such as she could never have imagined before her accident. She used her pain, grief, and loss as fuel to make a difference in the world.

Beryl knew none of us live in isolation. As independent as we may seem, we largely construct our lives and sense of self in relation to others. As many families and friends of people with disabilities learn when someone reclaims an identity from a place of loss, others are often drawn into their orbit, an expanding circle that holds the potential to transform more lives in the process. Beryl's family were all impacted by her transformation, especially her son Dennis. Privately, the "old" Beryl would resurface when surrounded by family, and she would continually traverse these contrasting parts of herself, sometimes strategically deploying them at will in her public works.

Despite how she may have felt about her legacy toward the end of her journey, Beryl's impact on the world resonated well beyond her lifetime. Condolences rang out from officials, colleagues, advocates, and admirers across Canada. "This country has lost a great Canadian," wrote Governor General of Canada Romeo LeBlanc. "We are certain that her indomitable spirit will not be forgotten."[2] Toronto City Council observed a moment of silence in respect for Beryl, moved by councillor Anne Johnston, seconded by councillor (and future mayor) David Miller.[3] On May 14, 1998, deputy house leader for the Liberal Party and MPP for Scarborough North, Alvin Curling, rose in the Ontario Legislature "to honour Beryl Potter, a great woman who selflessly served her community and the citizens of Ontario in a long life of public service. With her passing early this month . . . Ontario has lost a woman who truly demonstrated the spirit of sharing. . . . On behalf of the Legislative Assembly, I extend condolences to her children, Dianne [sic], Victor and Dennis, her grandchildren, her brother Norman, and all those whose lives have been touched by the remarkable accomplishments of a truly remarkable woman."[4]

And Beryl touched many peoples' lives. For those who knew her professionally, she was a doer who made things happen. Disability activist David Lepofsky wrote, "I knew her as an outspoken advocate. The kind our community desperately needs to bring attention to the many unfair and irrational barriers that people with disabilities routinely face."[5] David Baker, whose work founding ARCH Disability Law Centre transformed the state of disability rights in Canada, remembers Beryl as a true leader. "She was the one person who could get the message to the top. She could get the issues on the news and in the paper. She could get people to march. Even if she did not head this or that organization or coalition, she was the one who could say, 'Let's move!'"

A strong supporter of Beryl throughout the 1980s, former Ontario Premier David Peterson first met her when he was Leader of the Opposition and quickly developed a working relationship with her. "We would see each other at different times, and there were people in politics who you loved to see and some you did not. She was always someone you looked forward to seeing. She was an incredibly warm person who could easily talk to anyone. She would have made a fantastic politician but still had a positive impact on public policy like few others. She was a whirling dervish, involved in so many different things. I always had an open ear for her."

Beryl taught former minister responsible for disabled persons Remo Mancini some important lessons in life and politics. "I found her to be a person who was able to transmit to whoever she was with immediately that there was more, a lot more to her than what you may have first noticed. She was able to get people almost immediately to see past her disability. It was wonderful to be able to see and hear her talk about everything that she was going to be doing and getting done. There was no visible remorse or reflection on both this, that or the other. It's just like, 'Hey, I'm here, I need to talk to you. These are my thoughts, my concerns, my issues.' And then she was off. 'I'm busy. I got three or four meetings to get to, and I've got to go.'"

Vim Kochhar, a former senator and founder of the Canadian Foundation for Physically Disabled Persons, had a close working relationship with Beryl and always held her in high regard. "Being in the promotion of people with disabilities, I often came in contact with Beryl. She was a great human being. She was a great promoter of people with disabilities. She played a big role in making Canada the best country in the world for people with disabilities." Vim feels her legacy as a "boots-on-the-ground" advocate is the defining aspect of her legacy. "If you asked her to do something and she said she would do it, it was done. She was a doer and not a dreamer or thinker. Whatever she dreamt and thought up, *she* made it happen."

"I admired what she did and how she overcame adversity," said former lieutenant governor of Ontario, The Honourable David Onley. "She certainly had more adversity than most people have in three or four lifetimes. She was very intense; I think she ran at one speed in life, which was overdrive." A polio survivor and disability advocate, Onley recalls Beryl's grand entrance during her induction into the Terry Fox Hall of Fame. "There was a fairly steep ramp up to the stage, and she decided to make a full-speed entrance. When she hit the ramp, there was an audible gasp in the room. I thought she was going to springboard, or the ramp would not hold. She did not need to go that fast, but she was making an entrance. People like Rick Hansen and Terry Fox had higher profiles. But Beryl certainly blazed trails. First, as an advocate raising awareness of disability, and second, as a person who truly did not allow her disability to stop her from achieving what she wanted."

Journalist, reporter, and author Wendy Murphy was similarly inspired by Beryl's ability to get things done. "I became a paraplegic in 1984, and I would see Beryl everywhere, very active and determined to make a change. She was someone I became drawn to in terms of her strength and tenacity. I had never encountered many consumer activists. But I did often see Beryl in the media, combating this or that issue." Wendy had never seen a person with a disability portrayed in public in such a way. "She was in your face but not in an angry way. Always very poised in her delivery and got the job done. She did well in getting what she wanted done. That was very inspiring to me. She made the world a much better place, especially her work with children." Television host Dini Petty remembers Beryl's tenacity. "I interviewed her three or four times, and we became friendly. I admired her so much. She spoke softly but was a very determined woman."

Anne Abbott, who had joined the Scarborough Recreation Club for Disabled Adults, remembers Beryl as a positive influence. "She was a powerhouse of a person, and I truly admired her for that. She was instrumental in fighting to make my dreams come true and fighting for other disabled people's rights. I remember when she was at Toronto City Hall, and the mayor brushed past her, she yelled at him, 'I voted for you! When are you going to do something for the disabled community!?'" Anne admits Beryl was a complicated person. "I have mixed feelings about her. Certainly, she did a lot of good things for the disabled community, but she also had a difficult personality. I think that people will only remember the good that she did, and perhaps that's just as well. The disability community needs an icon to show us that we can be strong and implement positive change. That's what's important. Everybody has clay feet. I can hear Beryl laughing at that last remark. She was always making fun of her disability."

Sam Savona also met Beryl through the Scarborough Recreation Club for Disabled Adults and went on to follow her example by dedicating his life to disability activism. "She was my role model. When I was growing up, I always advocated for myself when people would try to tell me, 'No, you've got to accept where you are.' When I looked at Beryl, she was the opposite. She was saying, 'You have every right like anyone else. You need to go and get it.' Recently, I was tired of advocating and wanted out. But when I was out and had nothing to do, I realized my life was activism now." Beryl similarly affected the life of Mona Winberg who wrote a touching tribute to her "mentor" and close friend. "Because she was such an independent soul herself, Beryl understood and encouraged my desire to be as independent as I can for as long as I can." Mona argues no one will ever replace her enthusiasm, dedication, and understanding. "It was an honour to be her friend."

Beryl's death struck her family hard. Her oldest sister, Marjorie, already in her eighties, came to believe Beryl was invincible. "It's so hard to start writing this letter. I just cannot believe my dear sister Beryl passed away so suddenly. She had battled so much for so long, that one thinks 'Oh Beryl won't give up, she will fight on. She will fight on.'" The two sisters carried on a close relationship despite being separated by the Atlantic Ocean for more than forty years. "She will be a great loss to her country. She worked so hard for the disabled. I think she will be remembered for a long time."[6] Eric Potter, Beryl's beloved oldest brother, who died in 1990, admired her greatly throughout her life. "He was so proud of her achievements," relays Eric's daughter, Pauline. "He was thrilled when he and my mum were able to stay and visit with her and Dennis in Toronto and see firsthand how she was championing accessibility rights and highlighting the disgraceful prejudice that disabled people faced. Mum and Dad visited some of the schools with Beryl and Dennis and saw how she interacted with the young pupils."

Through all the pain, struggling to strike a balance between her public and private life, Beryl's family always kept her centred. Beryl's daughter Diane was immeasurably proud of her mother's accomplishments. Their relationship evolved over the years through several painful transitions. By age seventeen, Diane recognized her mother's care needs, but refused to allow her own life to be forever defined by them. Ultimately, Diane returned to Beryl what she so desperately feared she had lost at the onset of her deteriorating health. Beryl loved being a mother. It was a role she fully inhabited, having grown up surrounded by ideals of womanhood that primarily revolved around the role of mother. She cherished the work of providing for her family, creating a safe and nurturing environment. But she could not reconcile that vision with the one implanted in her about the lives of people with disabilities. There were no one-armed, blind, or wheelchair-using mothers for her to consider when she unexpectedly found herself in a similar position. But as Beryl moved toward a life of advocacy and community work, with the assistance of Diane, she found a way to restore her role as the family matriarch while transcending the ideals she held in her own mind.

Beryl delighted in being a grandmother to Michelle and Justin. Michelle loved spending time with Beryl. "She was an activist out in the streets, but it was not how she was at home. Family time gave her freedom from that. I spent a lot of time with her as a baby through my teen years. She changed my life." Whether it was spending time during the holidays, hanging out with her at the rec club, or helping her on the campaign trail, Beryl left an indelible mark on Michelle's life. Grit, courage, and determination were all characteristics often used to describe Beryl. But they could just as easily be applied to all the women in her family, from her mother Amy to daughter Diane. "They were all strong women," admits Michelle, a legacy of resilience she feels will continue with her own children. Diane regrets that Beryl never got to meet her great-grandchildren so they could have a direct relationship with her and learn firsthand what a unique and wonderful person she was.

———————

Perhaps the most important influence Beryl had on others was the generations of students from the mid-1970s to mid-1990s who were introduced to a positive representation of disability at a young age. Over the course of more than twenty years, she addressed tens of thousands of students in presentations and workshops. Elvira Muffolini is one such student who remembers her first encounter with Beryl in the 1980s at a high school presentation. "Seeing and meeting her changed my life. In any situation where I found myself down and out about anything, I had to say to myself, 'Forget about it.' There's a woman who raised a family, faced challenges, and became an advocate for others. It was a transformative experience to meet this person who did not let her disability stop her from making changes on the planet. I would tell friends about her, and even today, I still tell young women about her. She's been with me my whole life. She affected me and probably lots of other people."[7]

How many more fleeting, but powerful, encounters did Beryl have on thousands of young minds, helping them course correct away from negative stereotypes, toward basic principles of respect, understanding, and inclusion? What effect might this have had on general attitudes toward people with disabilities? How might her positive example have filtered out into the broader Canadian consciousness?

It is perhaps impossible to measure the true extent of Beryl's impact as children grow up and move out into the world, exposed to all sorts of experiences and influences. But Beryl never lost sight of the role children play in transforming society and came to believe that true systemic change was generational. She bet her life's work that helping children understand their responsibilities to people with disabilities was the answer to chronic poverty, unemployment, and isolation in the disability community. It was a project that necessarily outlived her, the product of which she could never expect to personally witness.

Like any social movement, the work of promoting disability rights activism and recognition of people with disabilities is never complete, nor does it rest with any one person. People forget, political leaders change, and the fragile edifice of hard-won rights and public consciousness of the issues soon begins to crumble. Crafting a progressive, liberal society that respects human and civil rights is an ongoing process of raising public awareness, lobbying decision-makers and, when necessary, taking to the streets to protect and advance those rights.

Beryl understood this. At some point, she realized the kind of change she sought wasn't necessarily located in the halls of power. Rather, it was buried deep in the psyche of the average person. By tapping into the early education of children, she was hoping to access something much more powerful, and her approach can serve as an example for future generations of people who witness oppression and seek change.

Beryl addressing an assembly of schoolchildren, ca. late 1980s.

Beryl Potter personal collection. Reproduced with permission.

Author's Note

I must have been five or six years old, sitting cross-legged on the cold gymnasium floor with my classmates, all of us in neat rows. We waited as the older grades filed in behind, our teachers posted all around us, their watchful eyes silently keeping order. As the principal finished his introduction, the special guest speaker enthusiastically zoomed into the room. She looked like my grandma, in her sixties with elegantly styled white hair, thick oblong glasses, and a kind, broad smile. "Hello, kids! My name is Beryl Potter," she greeted us enthusiastically in her soft English accent. She was somehow immediately familiar, despite her obvious physical differences and electric wheelchair, which was still a curious and uncommon thing to see in those days.

Beryl told us about the accident that claimed her limbs, pointing out her missing arm that she nicknamed 'Stumpy.' Frankly, I was a little scared at first. Then my attention was drawn to a life-size animatronic bear next to her, also missing limbs. She invited us to ask questions. Nothing was off limits. "How do you get dressed?" "Who takes you to the store?" "How do you take a bath?" "Are you in pain?" "Do you miss your legs?" "What happens if your chair runs out of batteries?" We were filled with questions about her body and daily routine, comparing her answers with our own experiences.

My understanding and experience of people with disabilities was very limited at that age. I had never seen an electric wheelchair before, let alone anyone with missing limbs, and it was uncommon where I grew up to see any wheelchairs outside hospitals or nursing homes. I knew about Terry Fox and his run across Canada with an artificial leg, his legacy solidified by the annual marathon fundraisers in his name. I used to play with a friend who was Deaf. We would communicate by writing messages back and forth on a pad of paper he carried with him everywhere.

Growing up in the 1980s, I watched a lot of television. There was one commercial during afternoon programming sponsored by the War Amps featuring "Astar the Robot from Planet Danger." I was mesmerized when the android jumped and somersaulted through spinning gears, ultimately falling on a buzzsaw and reattaching a severed arm. "I can put my arm back on, but you can't. So, play safe!" I watched the show *Life Goes On*, with "Corky," one of the first major characters in a television series featuring an actor living with Down syndrome. I was always interested in the fact that Corky took regular classes with other students when the kids like him in my school were kept separate in their own classroom. Even in the schoolyard, we were instructed to be extra careful around these kids, which usually meant they played on their own.

From the late 1970s to the 1990s, Beryl Potter toured the province of Ontario talking to thousands of schoolchildren like me. I don't remember thinking much about Beryl after the day of her presentation. But more than twenty years later, during one particularly long day at the archives, I turned over a picture of her and Mr. Grizzly the Aware Bear. In a flash, my memories of that day in the gymnasium came back to me. Perhaps it was the mental connection I made between her and my late grandma. Maybe it was her Mr. Rogers-style approach and personal touch that stuck with me.

A key element of Beryl's story is that we rarely think about disability until it happens to us. She is right about that. When my sister sustained a traumatic brain injury due to a life-altering car accident along a wet stretch of an infamously dangerous highway, my family was completely unprepared. Facing almost every obstacle one can imagine, she clawed her way back to a new life as we journeyed alongside her. As a brother and caregiver, I quickly learned how much of our world is constructed for normative minds and bodies. A web of previously unseen barriers revealed itself, and I began to ask how and why we live in a society where being able-bodied is a prerequisite for inclusion. These questions led me to advanced studies in disability history and into the archives where I rediscovered the photo and memory of Beryl.

Her brief lesson left a light fingerprint on my mind, like other school presentations about road safety or "stranger danger." Beryl took that part of my five-year-old imagination about disability that could have been struck with fear and instead filled it with empathy. She knew what it was like to go about life blissfully ignorant of the daily struggles of people with disabilities, struggles to be included and accepted. She taught that disability is not something to be feared but to be understood, and with enough compassion, we can work toward dissolving negative attitudes and practices that oppress people with disabilities. We must understand how these fears are reinforced by the culture and built environment, and only then can we begin to repair the damage by constructing a new set of norms that include everyone, regardless of ability.

Beryl's goal to imprint a positive representation of disability on young minds represents a critical step in building a more equitable world. In retelling her life story—her joy and pain, success and struggle—my hope is that her mission to change attitudes about disability may continue, one reader at a time.

Dustin Galer
Toronto, 2023

Acknowledgements

I have such sincere gratitude for the many people who have helped make this book possible. First, thank you to the family of Beryl Potter, and in particular, the Juda family: Michelle, Diane, George, and Justin. Your support and willingness to share your memories and insights about Beryl have been invaluable to me, and I am honoured to have had the opportunity to get to know you. I would like to give a special acknowledgement to Michelle, without whom this project would have been impossible. I cannot thank you enough for your dedication and generosity. Thank you for believing in me and for being such an important part of telling Beryl's story to the world.

I would also like to thank the many interview participants who generously shared their time and stories with me: Michelle, Diane, Justin, Sam Savona, Tracy Odell, Richard Dechter, Steve Mantis, Pat Israel, David Baker, Dini Petty, Wendy Murphy, Mary Dartis, Alex Hamilton-Brown, Anne Abbott, the late great David Onley, Derek Rumball, Judy Rebick, Leen Naji, Faysal Naji, Patrick Johnston, Remo Mancini, Richard Hudon, and Vim Kochhar. Your contributions have enriched this book and helped bring Beryl's life and work to light.

I am deeply grateful to all those who helped me access and navigate the many archives and collections that were instrumental in researching this book. The late Pauline Barnes shared many valuable photographs and Susan Goodridge provided invaluable genealogical insights on Beryl's family background. Your expertise and guidance were invaluable, and I thank you for your dedication to preserving and sharing Beryl's history.

I owe a debt of gratitude to my fine editors, Kendra Ward and Mary Newberry, whose sharp eyes and insightful feedback helped me shape and refine this book. I feel fortunate to have had the opportunity to work with you both. I would also like to acknowledge my partner

Andreas Vatiliotou, and family, Sheri, Wayne, and Azure-Lee, whose unwavering support and encouragement sustained me throughout this project.

Last but certainly not least, thank you to the amazing staff at Between the Lines, especially Amanda Crocker and Devin Clancy. Your expertise, enthusiasm, and commitment to publishing socially relevant and engaging books are a true inspiration. I feel honoured to be part of the BTL family, and I look forward to many more collaborations in the future.

Notes

Prologue

1 "An Ordinary Heroine," *Man Alive*, CBC, 24 January 1989.

1. Liverpool

1 Gene G. Hunder and Eric L. Matteson, "Rheumatology Practice at Mayo Clinic: The First 40 years–1920 to 1960," *Mayo Clinic Proceedings* 85, no. 4 (April 2010): e17–e30; C. C. Muñiz, T. E. Cuadra Zelaya, G. R. Esquivel, and F. J. Fernández, "Penicillin and Cephalosporin Production: A Historical Perspective," *Revista Latinoamericana de Microbiología* 49, no. 3–4 (2007): 88–98; Margery Williams, *The Velveteen Rabbit* (London: Egmont Books, 2004), first published in 1922; Hunder and Matteson, 2010.

2 Niall Johnson, *Britain and the 1918-19 Influenza Pandemic: A Dark Epilogue* (New York: Routledge, 2006).

3 All archival records, such as registries, census, and passenger lists, have been accessed through ancestry.com unless otherwise noted. England & Wales, Civil Registration Birth Index, 1916–2007, General Register Office: 1924, vol. 8b, page 542.

4 "Liverpool Maritime Mercantile City World Heritage Site Management Plan 2017-2024," Liverpool City Council, 2017; Andrew Lees, *The Hurricane Port: A Social History of Liverpool* (Edinburgh: Mainstream Publishing, 2011).

5 England Census, 1881, Lancashire, Wavertree, District 5a.

6 Railway Employment Records, 1833–1956, National Archives of the UK, Collection, London and North Western Railway Company, Records, Class: RAIL410, Piece: 1802.

7 Anthony Dawson, *The Liverpool and Manchester Railway: An Operating History* (Barnsley, South Yorkshire: Pen and Sword Transport, 2020).

8 James Allanson Picton, *Memorials of Liverpool, Historical and Topographical: Topographical*, vol. 2 (London: Longmans, Green & Company, 1873): 516; England & Wales, National Probate Calendar, Index of Wills and Administrations, 1858–1995: imaged page for 1890.

9 England Census, 1901 and 1891, Lancashire, West Derby, Western, District 09, and West Derby, District 36.

10 England & Wales, Civil Registration Marriage, Birth, and Death Indexes, 1837–1915, General Register Office: 1896, Q3, page 247; 1910, Q4, page 172; 1914, Q2, page 306; 1915, Q4, page 249; 1917, Q4, page 191; and 1920, vol. 8b, page 1210; England Census, 1901, Lancashire, West Derby, Western, District 09, Class:

RG13, Piece: 3488, Folio 32, page 17; Liverpool, England, Church of England Marriages and Banns, 1754–1932, Liverpool Record Office, ref. no. 283-WAV-3-3; Electoral Registers, 1832–1970, Register of Parliamentary and Municipal Voters, Wavertree, 1914–1915.

11 "In the Dark," *Manchester Guardian Bulletin*, 5 May 1926.

12 D. Graham, "History of Helicobacter pylori, Duodenal Ulcer, Gastric Ulcer and Gastric Cancer," *World Journal of Gastroenterology* 20, no. 18 (2014): 5191; England & Wales, Civil Registration Death Index, 1926, Q2, page 156; Certified Copy of an Entry of Death, certificate D 011436-66, Abercromby, Liverpool, 10 May 1926.

13 England & Wales, National Probate Calendar, Index of Wills and Administrations, 1858–1995: 1926.

2. Moonlight Flit

1   Liverpool, England, Church of England Marriages and Banns, 6 November 1926, Liverpool Record Office, ref. no. 283 BBS/3/3; England & Wales, Civil Registration Birth Index, 1927, 1929, 1931, and 1932, General Register Office: vol. 8b, pages 466, 335, 351, and 392.

2   Beryl Potter, letter to Norman Potter, undated, Beryl Potter personal collection.

3   England and Wales Register, National Archives, 1939 Register, ref. RG 101/4434H; Amanda McQueen, "Flammable Workhorse: A History of Nitrate Film from the Screen to the Vault," in *Routledge Companion to Media Technology and Obsolescence*, ed. Mark J. P. Wolf (New York: Routledge, 2019), 103–117; Beryl Potter to Norman Potter, undated.

4   England and Wales Register, National Archives, 1939 Register, ref. RG 101/4434H.

5   Beryl Potter to Norman Potter, undated; John Stevenson and Chris Cook, *The Slump: Britain in the Great Depression 3rd ed.,* (London: Routledge, 2009); Nigel Gray, *The Worst of Times: An Oral History of the Great Depression* (New York: Routledge, 2017).

6   "An Ordinary Heroine."

7   Beryl Potter to Norman Potter, undated.

8   England and Wales Register, National Archives, 1939 Register, ref. RG 101/4434H.

9   Geoff Green, "Reginald Radcliffe," 2021, 1859.org.uk; "The Russian Streets, Stoneycroft," *YO! Liverpool* (forum), 2008, yoliverpool.com.

10 Rino Rappuoli and Enrico Malito, "History of Diphtheria Vaccine Development," in *Corynebacterium diphtheriae and Related Toxigenic Species*, ed. Andreas Burkovski (Dordrecht: Springer, 2014): 225–38.

3. War, Marriage, and Motherhood

1   Carl Chinn, "Zeppelin Raids," Voices of War and Peace, voicesofwarandpeace. org; WW2 People's War (archive), BBC, bbc.co; "Liverpool—Maritime

Mercantile City," World Heritage Committee, 2004; Mike Fletcher, *The Making of Liverpool* (Casemate Publishers, 2004); Malcolm Gladwell, *David and Goliath: Underdogs, Misfits, and the Art of Battling Giants* (Little, Brown, 2013): 132.

2   Josh Parry, "World War II Bombs in Liverpool: Where Was Hit during The Blitz?," Liverpool Echo, liverpoolecho.co; Diane Juda, personal communications, 16 September 2019 and 27 May 2021; Holly Howe, "An Historical Review of Women, Smoking and Advertising," *Health Education* 15, no. 3 (1984): 3–9; Penny Tinkler, "'Red Tips for Hot Lips': Advertising Cigarettes for Young Women in Britain, 1920–70," *Women's History Review* 10, no. 2 (2001): 249–72; Justin Juda, personal communication, 9 December 2019.

3   Carol Harris, *Women at War 1939–1945: The Home Front* (Stroud, Gloucestershire: History Press, 2010); "Women's Voluntary Services—In Pictures," *The Guardian*, 21 May 2016, theguardian.com; "R.O.F. Kirkby 1940–1946: A Photographic History," Imperial War Museums, iwm.org.uk; "Kirkby Royal Ordnance Factory Station," Disused Stations, disused-stations.org; "Munitions Factories in WW2—'Canary Girls,'" My Learning, mylearning.org; "George Cross Following Munitions Factory Explosion," *World War II Today*, 2018, ww2today.com; "Liverpool," National Museums Liverpool, liverpoolmuseums.org; "The Cost of Battle," National Museums Liverpool, liverpoolmuseums.org.

4   Diane and Michelle Juda, personal communication, 28 October 2019; Diane Juda, 16 September 2019.

5   "New Orleans, Passenger Lists, 1813–1963," passenger manifest, *SS Yarmouth*, 1942; "Ships Hit by German U-Boats during WWII: Gypsum Empress (British Steam Merchant)," uboat.net; "World War II Aircraft," Smithsonian Institution, si.edu; "Ships Hit by German U-Boats during WWII: Crewlist from Gypsum Empress (British Steam Merchant)," uboat.net; "U-160 3rd War Patrol," U-Boat Archive, uboatarchive.net.

6   Certified Copy of an Entry of Marriage, General Register Office Liverpool North, 31 October 1945, Beryl Potter personal collection.

7   "Pigeon Racing—A History," Pigeon Racing UK & Ireland, pigeonracinguk.co.

8   Certified Copy of an Entry of Marriage, Liverpool North, 31 October 1945; "West Derby Union Offices," Towner Images, 19 August 2016, flickr.com.

4. To Canada

1   Murray Watson, "The Last Great Exodus from Britain?," Migration Museum, 11 January 2016, migrationmuseum.org; Hayley Elizabeth Wilson, *Childhood Memories of Post-War Merseyside: Exploring the Impact of Memory Sharing Through an Oral History and Reminiscence Work Approach* (Liverpool John Moores University, 2017); Pat Ayers, "Work, Culture and Gender: The Making of Masculinities in Post-War Liverpool," *Labour History Review* 69, no. 2 (2004): 153–68.

2   England & Wales, Civil Registration Birth Index, 1946, vol. 8b, page 919, and vol. 10d, pages 573 and 631; Advert for stockings by Bear Brand 1934, Historia/Shuttershock, shutterstock.com; Stanley Chapman, "Mergers and Takeovers

in the Post-War Textile Industry: The Experience of Hosiery and Knitwear," *Business History* 30, no. 2 (1988): 219–39; Diane Juda, personal communications, 16 September 2019 and 27 May 2021; Beryl Potter letter to Norman Potter, 22 October 1996, Beryl Potter personal collection.

3 Harold Troper, "Immigration to Canada," *Canadian Encyclopedia*, 22 April 2013, thecanadianencyclopedia.ca; Kathleen Paul, *Whitewashing Britain: Race and Citizenship in the Postwar Era* (Ithaca, NY: Cornell University Press, 1997): 34; Freda Hawkins, *Canada and Immigration* (Montreal: McGill-Queens University Press, 1988); Watson, "Last Great Exodus"; Patrick A. Dunae and George Woodcock, "English Canadians," *Canadian Encyclopedia*, 10 February 2010, thecanadianencyclopedia.ca; Marilyn Barber and Murray Watson, *Invisible Immigrants: The English in Canada since 1945* (Winnipeg: University of Manitoba Press, 2015); James Maurice Stockford Careless, "Toronto," *Canadian Encyclopedia*, 17 March 2013, thecanadianencyclopedia.ca; Chris Bateman, "A Million Canadian Post-War Homes," *Spacing*, 21 October 2017, spacing.ca; "Birth of the Suburbs," CBC, cbc.ca; Rosemary Sullivan, *Shadow Maker: The Life of Gwendolyn MacEwen* (HarperCollins, 1995): 96.

4 UK, Outward Passenger Lists, 1890–1960, 16 January 1954, Franconia, Cunard Steam Ship Company Ltd., #147216; Michael von Grace, "Cruise Line History—Cunard's Franconia—Around the World in 133 Days," *The Past and Now*, 12 May 2008, cruiselinehistory.com; UK, Outward Passenger Lists, 1890–1960, 5 November 1954, Empress of Australia, Canadian Pacific, #185887; Reuben Goossens, "MS Seven Seas," ssMaritime, ssmaritime.com; UK, Incoming Passenger Lists, 1878–1960, 17 June 1955, National Archives of the UK, Board of Trade, Commercial and Statistical Department and successors, Inwards Passenger Lists, Class BT26, Piece: 1334.

5 Diane Juda, 16 September 2019 and 27 May 2021.

5. Joining the (Paid) Workforce

1 Beryl Potter, "God's Wonderful Gift to Me," speech notes, ca. 1980s, Beryl Potter personal collection; Nick Moreau, "Kresge Came to Brampton with Its Canadian Head Office in 1979," *Brampton Guardian*, 28 February 2019, bramptonguardian.com; "S.S. Kresge Co.—Gone but Not Forgotten," *My Belleville*, 24 November 2018, mybelleville.net; "S.S. Kresge Company," Encyclopedia of Detroit, Detroit Historical Society, detroithistorical.org; "S.S. Kresge Company, Background Music No. 123," Oddio Overplay, oddiooverplay.com; K. O'Connor, "Auditory Processing in Autism Spectrum Disorder: A Review," *Neuroscience & Biobehavioral Reviews* 36, no. 2 (2012): 836–54; Piers Dawes and Dorothy Bishop, "Auditory Processing Disorder in Relation to Developmental Disorders of Language, Communication and Attention: A Review and Critique," *International Journal of Language & Communication Disorders* 44, no. 4 (2009): 440–65; Diane Juda, 16 September 2019 and 27 May 2021.

2 Dustin Galer, "Family Advocacy and the Struggle for Economic Integration," in *Working Towards Equity* (Toronto: University of Toronto Press, 2018): 35–55.

3   Tom Movold, personal communication, 26 May 2021; Deborah Belle, *The After-
     School Lives of Children: Alone and with Others while Parents Work* (Psychology
     Press, 1999); Jeff Keshen, "Revisiting Canada's Civilian Women during World
     War II," *Histoire sociale/Social History* 30, no. 60 (1997): 239–66; Nancy Denis,
     "Creating 'Perfect' Post-War Families: Advice Literature of the 1940s and 1950s"
     (master's thesis, Laurentian University of Sudbury, 2000); Seymour Solomon,
     "American Headache Through the Decades: 1950 to 2008," *Headache: The
     Journal of Head and Face Pain* 48, no. 5 (2008): 671–77; Kelli Tornstrom, "Does
     Caffeine Treat or Trigger Headaches?," *Mayo Clinic Health System*, 2020; Diane
     Juda, 16 September 2019 and 27 May 2021.
4   "Your Children's Corner," *Liverpool Evening Express*, 14 March 1944, 2.
5   "He's Top Newsboy in Toronto," *The Liverpool Echo and Evening Express,* 15
     February 1962, 2.
6   Potter, "God's Wonderful Gift to Me."

6. An Ordinary Slip and Fall

1   Potter, "God's Wonderful Gift to Me"; Louise Brown, "High Profile: Beryl
     Potter," *Toronto Star,* 27 April 1982, 1; Lawrence K. Altman, "Nixon's Lung
     Damaged by Blood Clot," *New York Times*, 26 September 1974, nytimes.com;
     "Thrombophlebitis," Mayo Clinic, 29 December 2021,; "Health and Medical
     History of President Richard Nixon," Doctor Zebra, doctorzebra.com.
2   A centralized number for emergency services (999 or 911) was not adopted in
     Canada until 1972, and the first call was placed in 1974 in London, Ontario.
3   Additional sources for this chapter: Diane Juda, 16 September 2019; "An
     Ordinary Heroine"; Khamin Chinsakchai et al., "Trends in Management of
     Phlegmasia cerulea dolens," *Vascular and Endovascular Surgery* 45, no. 1 (2011):
     5–14; Shweta Bhatt et al., "Phlegmasia cerulea dolens," *Journal of Clinical
     Ultrasound* 35, no. 7 (2007): 401–404; Mitchell Myers and Brad J. Chauvin,
     "Above-the-Knee Amputations," National Library of Medicine, National Center
     for Biotechnological Information, 2022, ncbi.nlm.nih.gov; G. C. de Oliveira
     Chini and Magali R. Boemer, "Amputation in the Perception of Those Who
     Experience It: A Study Under the Phenomenological," *Revista latino-americana
     de enfermagem* 15, no. 2 (2007): 330–36; Dana S. Dunn, "Well-Being Following
     Amputation: Salutary Effects of Positive Meaning, Optimism, and Control,"
     Rehabilitation Psychology 41, no. 4 (1996): 285; Leen Naji, personal communica-
     tion, 8 February 2021; Brown, "High Profile: Beryl Potter."

7. Six Years of Pain

1   Dustin Galer, "Work Disability in Canada: Portraits of a System," Centre for
     Research on Work Disability Policy, 2018.
2   Thomas J. Abernathy Jr. and Margaret E. Arcus, "The Law and Divorce in
     Canada," *Family Coordinator* 29, no. 4 (1977): 409–413; Douglas W. Allen,
     "No-Fault Divorce in Canada: Its Cause and Effect," *Journal of Economic*

Behavior & Organization 37, no. 2 (1998): 129–49; F. J. E. Jordan, "The Federal Divorce Act (1968) and the Constitution," *McGill LJ* 14 (1968): 209.

3   "Beryl Potter," *Focus On* (magazine), Ontario March of Dimes, 1981/2.

4   Unless otherwise noted, the references for this chapter are personal communication with the following: Richard Hudon, 4 November 2019; Steve Mantis, 4 October 2019; Diane Juda, 16 September 2019 and 27 May 2021; Diane and Michelle Juda, 16 September 2019; and Michelle Juda, 16 February 2021.

8. Addicted

1   Leen Naji, 8 February 2021; "Demerol Oral: Uses, Side Effects, Interactions, Pictures, Warnings & Dosing," WebMD, webmd.com.

2   "Beryl Potter," Ontario March of Dimes.

3   "An Ordinary Heroine." Once believed to be purely a psychological problem of new amputees, phantom pain is the body's way of remember the loss of an extremity through sensations imprinted on the brain. See Richard A. Sherman, *Phantom Pain* (Springer Science & Business Media, 1996); A. D. Houghton et al., "Phantom Pain: Natural History and Association with Rehabilitation," *Annals of the Royal College of Surgeons of England* 76, no. 1 (1994): 22.

4   Potter, "God's Wonderful Gift to Me."

5   Diane Juda, 27 May 2021.

6   Leen Naji, 8 February 2021; Elizabeth Maloney et al., "Suicidal Behaviour and Associated Risk Factors among Opioid-Dependent Individuals: A Case–Control Study," *Addiction* 102, no. 12 (2007): 1933–41; Lishman Ashrafioun et al., "Frequency of Prescription Opioid Misuse and Suicidal Ideation, Planning, and Attempts," *Journal of Psychiatric Research* 92 (2017): 1–7.

7   Potter, "God's Wonderful Gift to Me."

9. Taxi

1   *Life Another Way*, directed by Alex Hamilton-Brown, 1981.

2   "Beryl Potter," Ontario March of Dimes.

3   Diane Juda, 16 September 2019.

4   Robert E. Tooms and Frederick L. Hampton, "Hip Disarticulation and Transpelvic Amputation: Surgical Procedures," in *Atlas of Limb Prosthetics*, 2nd ed., ed. John H. Bowker and John W. Michael (American Academy of Orthopedic Surgeons, 1992): 535–38; Charalampos G. Zalavras et al., "Hip Disarticulation for Severe Lower Extremity Infections," *Clinical Orthopaedics and Related Research* 467, no. 7 (2009): 1721–26.

5   Z. Denes and A. Till, "Rehabilitation of Patients after Hip Disarticulation," *Archives of Orthopaedic and Trauma Surgery* 116, no. 8 (1997): 498–99.

6   Paula Adamick, "Amputee Visits Schools with Message of Hope," *Toronto Star*, 1987.

7   Faysal Naji, in discussion with the author, 11 January 2021.

8   Sabiha Güngör Kobat et al., "Iodine-Induced Retinopathy: A Case Report," *Turkish Journal of Ophthalmology* 50, no. 4 (2020): 255.
9   "An Ordinary Heroine"; *Life Another Way.*

10. Life After

1   Adamick, "Amputee Visits Schools."
2   Potter, "God's Wonderful Gift to Me."
3   "An Ordinary Heroine"
4   Personal communications referenced throughout this chapter: Diane Juda, 29 October 2019 and 27 May 2021, and Michelle Juda, 29 July 2019.
5   "An Ordinary Heroine."
6   Shane Mills, "Don't Offer Pity, Amputee Teaches," *Times Colonist*, 1988.
7   "Beryl Potter," Ontario March of Dimes, is referenced throughout this chapter.
8   *Life Another Way.*

11. Nostalgia

1   Certified Copy of an Entry of Death, certificate EA 7363, entry 38, Liverpool, Amy Catrina Wallace, 3 April 1971, Pauline Barnes personal collection.
2   Potter, "God's Wonderful Gift to Me."
3   "An Ordinary Heroine."
4   "A Brave Woman Wins Her Bet," *Liverpool Echo*, 3 July 1971, 8.
5   "Pre-1990 Benefits," WSIB Ontario, wsib.ca.
6   Robert Storey, "Social Assistance or a Worker's Right: Workmen's Compensation and the Struggle of Injured Workers in Ontario, 1970–1985," *Studies in Political Economy* 78, no. 1 (2006): 67–91.
7   Gregory P. Marchildon, ed., *Making Medicare: New Perspectives on the History of Medicare in Canada* (Toronto: University of Toronto Press, 2012); Marilyn E. Dunlop, "Health Policy," *Canadian Encyclopedia*, 7 February 2006, thecanadianencyclopedia.ca; "History of Canada's Public Health Care," Canadian Health Coalition, healthcoalition.ca
8   Susan Reid, "Struggling against Disabling Attitudes," *Toronto Star*, 4 June 1989, A1.
9   M. Parkinson, *Liverpool Beyond the Brink: The Remaking of a Post Imperial City* (Liverpool University Press, 2019).
10   "Toxteth Riots 1981 Background—and How It All Began," *Liverpool Echo*, 4 July 2011, liverpoolecho.co.
11   "Workers' Compensation Law: A Documentary History in Ontario," Ontario Workplace Tribunals Library, Queen's Printer for Ontario, 2009, owtlibrary.on.ca; "Injured Workers in Ontario Timeline," Injured Workers Online, injuredworkersonline.org.
12   Throughout chapter, personal communications with Diane Juda, 16 September 2019 and 28 October 2019.

12. A New Life

1 Nancy Hansen et al., eds., *Untold Stories: A Canadian Disability History Reader* (Toronto: Canadian Scholars, 2018).
2 Geoffrey Reaume, *Remembrance of Patients Past* (Toronto: University of Toronto Press, 2009).
3 Dustin Galer, *Working Towards Equity* (Toronto: University of Toronto Press, 2018).
4 Geoffrey Reaume, "Eugenics Incarceration and Expulsion: Daniel G. and Andrew T.'s Deportation from 1928 Toronto, Canada," in *Disability Incarcerated: Imprisonment and Disability in the United States and Canada*, eds. Liat Ben-Moshe, Chris Chapman, and Allison C. Carey (New York: Palgrave Macmillan, 2014): 63–80.
5 Galer, *Working Towards Equity*.
6 Geoffrey Reaume, *Lyndhurst: Canada's First Rehabilitation Centre for People with Spinal Cord Injuries, 1945–1998* (Montreal: McGill-Queens University Press 2007).
7 Galer, *Working Towards Equity*.
8 Jon Caulfield, *The Tiny Perfect Mayor: David Crombie and Toronto's Reform Aldermen* (Toronto: James Lorimer, 1974).
9 Archives of Ontario, RG 7-149, Box B363026, file publications, "Mayor's Task Force on the Disabled and Elderly, Access," 1 May 1977.
10 Michael Coxon, letter to Dennis Potter, 10 September 1994, Beryl Potter personal collection.
11 Mary Dartis, "Finding the Courage to Go On" (unpublished term paper, Ryerson University, 1996, Beryl Potter personal collection).
12 "Beryl Potter," Ontario March of Dimes; Brown, "High Profile: Beryl Potter."
13 *Life Another Way* is referenced throughout this chapter.
14 Edith Rason, letter to Dennis Potter, 11 August 1994, Beryl Potter personal collection.
15 "An Ordinary Heroine" is referenced throughout this chapter.
16 Personal communications referenced in this chapter: Diane Juda, 29 October 2019 and 27 May 2021; Anne Abbott, 4 November 2019; Sam Savona, 3 May 2019; and Derek Rumball, 15 January 2020.

13. Ability Forum

1 Galer, *Working Towards Equity*.
2 "Broadcasting Regulatory Policy CRTC 2010-622," Canadian Radio-Television and Telecommunications Commission, 26 August 2010, crtc.gc.ca.
3 "Geoffrey Conway: Cable Pioneer Sought Channel for Children," *Globe and Mail*, 31 March 1988, C7; John Partridge, "Struggle Under Way to Control CUC Broadcasting, Sources Say," *Globe and Mail*, 2 March 1989, B16.
4 *Life Another Way*.
5 Later A&P, now Metro.

6   Brown, "High Profile: Beryl Potter."
7   Pamphlet, 22nd Scarborough Recreation Night, Beryl Potter personal collection.
8   *Life Another Way*.

14. Aware Bear

1   "Terry's Story: A Dream as Big as Our Country," Terry Fox Foundation, terryfox. org.
2   Terry Fox, recorded speech at Scarborough Civic Centre, 11 July 1980.
3   Diane Juda, 16 September 2019.
4   "Declaration on the Rights of Disabled Persons," Office of the High Commissioner for Human Rights, United Nations, 9 December 1975, ohchr.org.
5   "The International Year of Disabled Persons 1981," Department of Economic and Social Affairs, United Nations, un.org.
6   Ontario Legislative Assembly, "An Act to Provide for the Rights of Handicapped Persons," 31st session, 3rd session, Toronto, 1979.
7   David Lepofsky, "The Long, Arduous Road to a Barrier-Free Ontario for People with Disabilities: The *Ontarians with Disabilities Act*—The First Chapter," *National Journal of Constitutional Law* 15 (2004): 125–333.
8   Sandy Naiman, "Potter on the Ramparts: Longtime Activist Girds for Battle," *Toronto Sun*, 29 September 1995.
9   Mark Bromfield, "She Hopes Help Will Come with Her Civic Honor," *Toronto Star*, 19 May 1981, 4.
10 Michelle Juda, 29 July 2019.
11 Ontario Action Awareness Association, Work Plan, 1991, Beryl Potter personal collection.
12 "An Ordinary Heroine" is referenced throughout this chapter.
13 Ontario Action Awareness Association, Work Plan, 1991.
14 *Life Another Way*.
15 Rita Daly, "Scarborough Prepares for Year of Disabled," *Toronto Star*, 7 January 1981.

15. Leaning In

1   Gus Harris, letter to Beryl Potter, 25 June 1981, and Pierre Trudeau, letter to Beryl Potter, 1980, Beryl Potter personal collection.
2   Archives of Ontario, RG 74-30 Office for Disability Issues policy, program and liaison record, B503780, File Rights-1983, written submission to Special Parliamentary Committee on the Disabled and Handicapped, 13 September 1980, Beryl Potter.
3   *Obstacles: Report of the Special Committee on the Disabled and the Handicapped* (Ottawa: Queen's Printer, 1981).
4   Margaret Birch, letter to Beryl Potter, 25 June 1980, and Eric Cunningham, letter to Beryl Potter, 27 June 1980, Beryl Potter personal collection.
5   James Charlton, *Nothing About Us Without Us* (Berkeley, CA: University of California Press, 1998).

6   "History: Brief History about Independent Living at a Glance," Centre for Independent Living in Toronto, cilt.ca.

7   "Programs for the Handicapped," Issue 1, Department of Health, Education, and Welfare, Office of the Assistant Secretary for Human Development Services, Office for Handicapped Individuals, 1980: 3.

8   Niagara Falls, NY Weather History, for 8 February 1981, Weather Underground, wunderground.com.

9   Bromfield, "She Hopes Help Will Come."

10   Referenced in this chapter: Bromfield, "She Hopes Help Will Come"; "Disabled Welcome Committee's Report," *Toronto Star*, 17 February 1981; M. Strauss, "Thousands Ring the Falls for Disabled," *Globe and Mail*, 9 February 1981, 10; Daly, "Scarborough Prepares for Year of Disabled."

11   AO, RG 7-148, Box B100558, File "Publications Posters," Letter, Handicapped Employment Program to Minister of Labour, 11 May 1981.

12   "New Poster on Disabled Called 'In Poor Taste,'" *Toronto Star*, 24 April 1981, A3.

13   Jonathan Milne, interview with author, 31 January 2013.

14   AO, RG 7-148, Box B100558, File "Publications Posters," Brief, Handicapped Employment Program, "HEP Posters," 1 June 1981.

15   Christopher Bell, "Introducing White Disability Studies: A Modest Proposal," in *The Disability Studies Reader,* 2nd ed., ed. Lennard Davis (New York: Routledge, 2006): 275–82; Ulysses Patola, "'Get the Disabled Out of Their Closets': Disability Activism in the City of Thunder Bay and Northwestern Ontario, 1972–1990s," (PhD diss., University of Manitoba, 2019), 439–42, 445–47.

16   Brian Marren, "The Toxteth Riots, 1981: Unemployed Youth Take to the Streets," in *We Shall Not Be Moved: How Liverpool's Working Class Fought Redundancies, Closures and Cuts in the Age of Thatcher* (Manchester University Press, 2016).

16. Transit Activism

1   "Annual Report 1981," Toronto Transit Commission, ttc.ca.

2   Brown, "High Profile: Beryl Potter."

3   Referenced in this chapter: *Life Another Way*; Mark Bromfield, "Group Forms for Year of Disabled," *Toronto Star*, 1981; Kathleen Kenna, "Students Won't Have to Crawl onto Vans," *Toronto Star*, 1981; Mark Bromfield, "Civic Honor for Beryl Potter," *Toronto Star*, June 1981; Brown, "High Profile: Beryl Potter"; "Disabled Demand Better Transit," *Globe and Mail*, 27 June 1981; Diane Juda, 27 May 2021; Potter, "God's Wonderful Gift to Me"; "An Ordinary Heroine"; Dartis, "Finding the Courage to Go On."

4   Beryl Potter, letter to Norman Potter, 22 October 1996, Beryl Potter personal collection.

17. Life Another Way

1 Pat McKee, "Look Beyond," Greenview Publishing Co., 1981; "Look Beyond" was written and recorded by Pat McKee and arranged by John Hudson. Song can be heard at youtube.com.

2 Referenced in chapter: Alex Hamilton-Brown, personal communication, 22 May 2019; "Disabled Benefit from Fashion Show," *Scarborough Mirror*, 20 May 1981; *Life Another Way*.

3 "Whose Life Is It Anyway?," IMDb, imdb.com; "Whose Life Is It Anyway?," Rotten Tomatoes, rottentomatoes.com.

4 Frank Lennon, "Wheelchair Protest, Beryl Potter and Pat Israel . . .," Toronto Star, 4 December 1981, Toronto Star Photograph Archive, Toronto Public Library, torontopubliclibrary.ca.

5 Barbara Amiel, "Movies as a Human Right?," *Toronto Sun*, 8 December 1981.

6 Barbara Amiel, "The New Enforcers for the Disabled," *Maclean's Magazine*, 5 September 1994.

7 Tabitha de Bruin, "Terry Fox," *Canadian Encyclopedia*, 26 May 2008, thecanadianencyclopedia.ca.

18. Rights

1 Yvonne Peters, "Twenty Years of Litigating for Disability Equality Rights: Has It Made a Difference?," Council of Canadians with Disabilities, 26 January 2004, ccdonline.ca.

2 Peters, "Twenty Years of Litigating."

3 Ontario Action Awareness, Work Plan, April–December 1991, Beryl Potter personal collection.

4 Michelle Valiquet, "Activist for Disabled Talks to Students," *Advertiser* (Toronto newspaper), ca. 1982.

5 Scarborough Action Awareness, Information Sheet, ca. 1982, Beryl Potter personal collection.

6 David Baker, personal communication, 16 August 2019.

7 Steve Paikin, *Bill Davis: Nation Builder, and Not So Bland After All* (Toronto: Dundurn, 2016).

8 Mark Bromfield, "Potter's Fighting Back: Queen's Park Protest Set for Thursday," *Toronto Star*, October 1983.

9 Archives of Ontario, RG 74-30, Office for Disability Issues policy, program, and liaison records, B216017, file correspondence—Council members 1982: Beryl Potter, letter to Jack Longman, 28 October 1982; Jack Longman, letter to Beryl Potter, 2 November 1982; Jim Gerrond, letter to Jack Longman, 18 November 1982; Beryl Potter, letter to Bruce McCaffrey, 16 September 1983, B503780, File Rights-1983.

10 "Hon. John Black Aird was a Great Friend of Muskoka," *Herald-Gazette*, 10 May 1995.

11 "New $196 Million Transit Line Opens but Disabled Protest They're Excluded," *Toronto Star*, 24 Mar 1984.
12 Michelle Juda, 29 July 2019.
13 Archives of Ontario, RG 74-30, Office for Disability Issues policy, program, and liaison record, B391297, file Beryl Potter: Gerry Clarke, letter to Shirley Teasdale, Potter Project, 8 August 1985; Muskoka Lakes Secondary School, letter to Beryl Potter, 16 September 1985; Lo-Ellen Park Secondary School, letter to Beryl Potter, 1985; "Northern Ontario High School Students Learn about Disability during Youth Year Tour," Ontario March of Dimes newsletter, 1985.

19. Equity

1   Cameron Crawford and Mary Bunch, *Factors Affecting the Employment and Labour-Force Transitions of Persons with Disabilities: A Literature Review*, Applied Research Branch, Strategic Policy, Human Resources Development Canada (Hull: Human Resources Development Canada, 1998); Derek Hum and Wayne Simpson, "Canadians with Disabilities and the Labour Market," *Canadian Public Policy* 22, no. 3 (1996); Emile Tompa et al., "Precarious Employment and People with Disabilities," in *Precarious Employment: Understanding Labour Market Insecurity in Canada*, ed. Leah Vosko (Montreal: McGill-Queen's University Press, 2006): 113; Cameron Crawford, "Looking into Poverty: Income Sources of Poor People with Disabilities in Canada," Institute for Research on Inclusion and Society, 2013.
2   "PM the Handicap?," *Toronto Sun*, 15 April 1986, 36.
3   Paula Todd, "New Job Bill 'Toothless' Disabled Say in Protest," *Toronto Star*, 15 April 1986.
4   "An Ordinary Heroine."
5   Paula Todd, "150 Disabled Travel to Ottawa to Protest Job Bill with 'No Teeth,'" *Toronto Star*, 15 April 1986, 1, is referenced in this chapter.
6   Personal communication referenced in this chapter: Judy Rebick, 17 August 2021.
7   Paula Todd, "Job Equity Bill 'Has No Teeth' Disabled Say in Ottawa Protest *Toronto Star*," *Toronto Star*, 15 April 1986, A4.
8   Canada, Parliament, House of Commons Debates, 2nd sess., 33th Parliament, vol. 8 (14 April 1986).
9   "PM the Handicap?," *Toronto Sun*.

20. Access

1   Jann Lounder, "Handicapped Still Stranded after No Vote," *Toronto Sun*, 21 April 1986.
2   Legislative Assembly of Ontario, Hansard Transcripts, "Ontario Advisory Council on Multiculturalism and Citizenship," comments of T. Ruprecht, 2nd sess., 33rd Parliament, 25 April 1986.

3   Walter Stefaniuk, "Disabled Woman in Tears as Bus Drivers Reject Pact," *Toronto Star*, 21 April 1986; Mary Gooderham, "Disabled Urge Quick End to Strike at Wheel Trans," *Globe and Mail*, 24 April 1986, C9; Rosie DiManno, "Disabled Stage City Hall Protest to Support Drivers," *Toronto Star*, 24 April 1986; Sandro Contenta, "NDP Blasts Bill to End Strike at Wheel-Trans," *Toronto Star*, 25 April 1986; Derek Ferguson, "Handicapped Take Aim at TTC," *Toronto Star*, 13 May 1986, E6; Laurie Monsebraaten, "TTC to Boost Service for Disabled," *Toronto Star*, 1986, A1; "Wheel Trans Called a 'Mess' since the TTC Took Over," *Toronto Star*, 16 January 1989.

4   "Accessible Transportation for Disabled Persons," GO (newsletter), vol. 1, no. 2, Ontario March of Dimes, 1 September 1987.

5   John Smee, "Premier Becomes Aware," *Scarborough Mirror*, 1987.

21. Order of Ontario

1   Brown, "High Profile: Beryl Potter."

2   Remo Mancini, personal communication, 12 December 2019.

3   *Dini Petty's CityLine*, CityTV, ca. 1988.

4   Diane Juda, 27 May 2021.

5   Archives of Ontario, RG 74-30, Office for Disability Issues policy, program and liaison record, B857948, file Beryl Potter, Scarborough, 1988: Association of Jewish Seniors to Ontario Honours and Awards Secretariat; David Baker to Ontario Honours and Awards Secretariat.

6   "Activists Donald Moore, Beryl Potter among 17 Receiving Order of Ontario," *Toronto Star*, 10 May 1988, A22.

22. Outside Looking In

1   Richard Dechter, personal communication, 2 June 2019.

23. Off the Record

1   "An Ordinary Heroine."

2   Brown, "High Profile: Beryl Potter."

3   Personal communication referenced in this chapter: Michelle Juda, 16 September and 29 July 2019; Diane Juda, 16 September 2019; Justin Juda, 2 December 2019.

4   Brown, "High Profile: Beryl Potter."

24. Dennis

1   "An Ordinary Heroine" referenced in this chapter.

2   Personal communications referenced in this chapter: Diane Juda, 16 September 2019 and 27 May 2021.

3   *Life Another Way* referenced in this chapter.

25. Power of the Story

1   Ontario Action Awareness Association, *No More Whispers* (Avcomm Productions, ca. 1988), video.
2   "An Ordinary Heroine."
3   Susan Peters, "From Charity to Equality: Canadians with Disabilities Take Their Rightful Place in Canada's Constitution," in *Making Equality: History of Advocacy and Persons with Disabilities in Canada*, ed. Deborah Stienstra et al. (Concord, ON: Captus Press, 2003): 24; Paul Longmore, *Telethons: Spectacle, Disability, and the Business of Charity* (New York: Oxford University Press, 2016).
4   Barbara Turnbull, *Looking in the Mirror* (Toronto Star, 1997).
5   Personal communications referenced in this chapter: Tracy Odell, 1 May 2019; Pat Israel, 12 June 2019; Steve Mantis, 4 October 2019.
6   *Dini Petty's CityLine*, CityTV, ca. 1988.

26. An Ordinary Hero

1   "An Ordinary Heroine."
2   Ontario Action Awareness, Work Plan, April–December 1991.

27. Politics

1   Jamie Bradburn, "Orange Shockwave: How Ontario Got Its First-Ever NDP Government," TVO Today, 31 May 2018.
2   "Disabled Activist Seeks Post as MPP," *Toronto Star*, 10 May 1990, A6.
3   Liberal campaign pamphlet, 1990, Beryl Potter personal collection.
4   Beryl Potter, letter to Liberal campaign supporters, 27 June 1990, Beryl Potter personal collection.
5   Camille Bains, "Liberals in Beaches Riding Choose Activist for Disabled," *Toronto Star*, 28 June 1990, E7.
6   Letter from Gregory Peterson, chair of Beryl Potter Liberal Campaign Beaches-Woodbine Finance Committee, to Dr. Hamilton Hall, 6 August 1990, Beryl Potter personal collection.
7   William Walker, "Peterson Is Doing Too Little, Disabled Voters Complain," *Toronto Star*, 13 August 1990, A9.
8   Susan Reid, "Top Advocate for the Disabled Quits Post," *Toronto Star*, 12 May 1989, A6; Susan Reid, "Resignation Upsets Coalition Fighting for Disabled Rights," *Toronto Star*, 13 May 1989, A8; Susan Pigg, "Red Tape Threatens to Bar Disabled from TTC," *Toronto Star*, 11 May 1990, A27; Nancy Wood, "Disabled Vow Fight for Access to Subway," *Toronto Star*, 9 May 1990, A1; "Responses from the Leaders," *Toronto Star*, 25 August 1990, D4.
9   Personal communications referenced in this chapter: Patrick Johnston, 30 August 2019; Michelle Juda, 29 July 2019; Pat Israel, 12 June 2019.

10 "1990 Ontario Election," Canadian Elections Database, accessed 2021, canadianelectionsdatabase.ca.

11 Paul Moloney, "Rookie Lankin Beats Potter to Keep Riding for the NDP," *Toronto Star*, 7 September 1990, A13.

28. Common Sense

1 Archives of Ontario, RG 74-49, Correspondence of the Office for Disability Issues, B317823, file Ontario Action Awareness Association (Beryl Potter): Ron Ross, letter to Ed Philip, 28 February 1991; Ed Philip, letter to Trans-Action Coalition, 23 April 1991.

2 Helen Macpherson, "Amazing Beryl: Disabled Woman Brings Message of Understanding," *North Renfrew Times*, 17 October 1990, 1.

3 Beryl Potter, speech delivered at University of Waterloo, 1992, Beryl Potter personal collection.

4 Archives of Ontario, RG 74-67, Office of Disability Issues, B719475, file Potter, Application for Advocacy Commission documents.

5 Mona Winberg, "They're Appalled," *Toronto Sun*, 18 September 1994.

6 Amiel, "New Enforcers for the Disabled."

7 "Wheel-Trans," W-Five, CTV Television, 21 November 1995.

8 Naiman, "Potter on the Ramparts."

29. Order of Canada

1 Letters to Honours Directorate of Ottawa, Beryl Potter personal collection: Edith Rason, 11 August 1994; Vim Kochhar, 9 August 1994; David Onley, 3 August 1994.

2 "Mrs. Beryl Potter: Order of Canada," Governor General of Canada, gg.ca.

3 Jane Stevenson, "Tom Is Still Stompin' for Canada," *Toronto Sun*, 30 June 1998.

4 Dartis, "Finding the Courage to Go On."

30. Final Stop

1 Mona Winberg, "Let's Maintain Dignity," *Toronto Sun*, 6 March 1994.

2 Beryl Potter, list of accomplishments, Beryl Potter personal collection.

3 Beryl Potter, letter to Norman Potter, 22 October 1996, Beryl Potter personal collection.

4 Personal communications referenced: Diane Juda, 28 October 2019, 16 September 2019, and 1 August 2021.

31. Remembrance

1 "Dynamic Disability Defender Dies," *CP24*, CityNews, 1 May 1998.

2 Victor Carter, "Eulogy for Our Mother," 4 May 1998, Beryl Potter personal collection.

32. Aftermath

1 Mona Winberg, letter to Dennis Potter, 6 May 1998, Beryl Potter personal collection.
2 Personal communications referenced: Diane and Michelle Juda, 16 September 2019; Diane Juda, 16 September 2019 and 28 October 2019; Leen Naji, 8 February 2021.

Epilogue

1 Friedrich Nietzsche, *The Twilight of the Idols*, trans. Anthony Ludovici (Jovian Press, 2018).
2 Romeo LeBlanc, letter to Dennis Potter, 29 May 1998, Beryl Potter personal collection.
3 Toronto City Council, letter to Potter family, 15 May 1998, Beryl Potter personal collection.
4 Legislative Assembly of Ontario, Hansard Transcripts, "Member's Statements: Beryl Potter," comments of A. Curling, 2nd sess., 36th Parliament, 14 May 1998, ola.org.
5 Nicolaas Van Rijn, "Beryl Potter Battled to Get Help for Disabled," *Toronto Star*, 2 May 1998.
6 Marjorie Hampson (née Potter), letter to Dennis Potter, May 1998, Beryl Potter personal collection.
7 Personal communications referenced: David Baker, 16 August 2019; David Peterson, 26 August 2019; Remo Mancini, 12 December 2019; Vim Kochhar, 21 January 2020; David Onley, 22 May 2019; Wendy Murphy, 23 October 2019; Dini Petty, 22 August 2019; Anne Abbot, 28 June 2019; Sam Savona, 3 May 2019; Pauline Barnes, 31 January 2020; Michelle Juda, 29 July 2019; Elvira Muffolini, 16 September 2019.

Index

Page numbers in italics represent
photos.

Abbott, Anne, 104–5, 146–7, 265
Abella, Rosie, x, 169, 170
Ability Forum (TV show), 109–11
accessibility: basic rights list, 124–5; and
    building owners, 187; parking spots,
    256; in Queen's Park, 166; vs. reality,
    186; in Scarborough Town Centre,
    98; Sheppard Ave. E. apartment, 203;
    sidewalk/intersection ramps, 100, 151.
    See also barriers
Action Awareness, 157–8, 181, 183, 187–8,
    209, 233, 234
activism. *See* disability advocacy/
    activism
Adams, Jeff, 145
addiction, 45, 69–70, 71, 257, 258–9, 260.
    See also Carter, Victor Bratton
Advisory Council of Disabled Persons,
    160–1, 184, 187
Advocacy Act 1992, 235, 238
Advocacy Commission 1992, 235–7
Advocacy Council for Disabled
    Persons, 238
Advocacy Resource Centre for the
    Handicapped (ARCH), 158–9
Aigburth Assembly Picturedrome, 7
air raids, 17–18
Aird, John B., 148, 162–3
alcohol, 39–40, 41
Alexander, Lincoln, 189, 242
All-Way Transportation, 106–7, 135–9,
    177–81
Amalgamated Transit Union, 34, 177–80
Amiel, Barbara, 149–52, 237

amputations: to left hip, 74–5; left
    leg, 73–4; and meat chart, 92; and
    mobility, 74–5; and phantom pain,
    70, 75; prosthetic leg, 73; right arm,
    76; right leg, 57–9; and society's
    reactions, 85, 93, 118. *See also*
    Downsview rehabilitation
anger, 102, 185, 200, 201
arrhythmia, 76–7
Arsenault, Francine, 228, 233–4
Aspirin, 3–4
Awareness Day, 123–4
Awareness Month, 130
Awareness Week, 130, 182

Baker, David, 158–9, 181, 233–4, 263
bankruptcy, 93, 95, 238
Barrier Free Design Centre, 187
barriers: and accessibility signs,
    186; cinemas, 149–50, *151*; *Dini
    Petty's CityLine* discussion, 185–7;
    doctors' offices, 247; history of, 98;
    in House of Commons, 172–3; in
    Liverpool, 88, 89; as new to Beryl,
    85; *Obstacles* report acknowledging,
    125; at Operation Horseshoe, 129; and
    Order of Canada reception, 243–4;
    in Shoppers Drug Mart, 255–6;
    and speaking tours, 188; traveling
    long distance, 171–2; washrooms, 1,
    171–2, 200–1. *See also* accessibility;
    discrimination/prejudice; Toronto
    Transit Commission; transportation;
    Wheel-Trans
basic rights list, 124–5
Batty, Jonathan, 227–8
bauxite, 22
Bazelon Center, 158

Bear Brand, 30
Bell, Ivy, 26
Bendale Secondary School, 103–4
Berney, Lloyd, 138
Bill C-62, x, 169–76
Birch, Margaret, 103, 126, 160, 161
birth control, 30
Blind people, 163
blindness, 76, 77, 247–8
Blitz, 17–18
blood clots, 53, 77, 101–2, 252. *See also*
   deep vein thrombosis
Boldt, Arnold, *249*
Bonisteel, Roy, 219, 236
Broadbent, Ed, 176
Buell, Margarita, 164–5
bullying, 42

Cameron, Eva, 64, 86, 93, 257
Cameron, Peggy, *249*
Canada Action Fund, 170
Canada Games for Disabled, 130
Canada Pension Plan, 162
Canadian Back Institute, 188
Canadian Broadcasting Corporation
   (CBC). See *Man Alive*
Canadian Cancer Society, 115
Canadian Human Rights Act, 181–2
Canadian immigration, 31–2
Canadian National Institute for the
   Blind (CNIB), 65, 171
Canadian Rehabilitation Council for
   the Disabled (CRCD), 109
canary girls, 20
cancer, 115, 152
car accident, 73
Carpenter, Sandra, 128
Carter, Dennis Gordon (son). *See*
   Potter, Dennis Gordon
Carter, Diane Margaret (daughter). *See*
   Juda, Diane Margaret (née Carter)
Carter, Victor Bratton (husband): in
   1980s, *86*; about, 21, 23–4; affairs, 58;
   as alcoholic, 39–40, 41, 48, 51, 56,
   70, 257–8; Beryl's going away party,

93; and Cameron, 64, 86, 93, 257;
death of, 258; employment, 30, 34, 51;
Second World War experiences, 21–3;
Toronto arrival, 33. *See also* Potter, B.,
and Carter, V.
Carter, Victor, Jr. (son): in 1950s, *36*;
in 1980s, *86*; and Beryl leaving
Victor, 63; and Beryl's death, 252–3,
255–6; birth of, 28; death of, 257;
employment, 46–7; marriages, 48;
in Navy, 48; and Victor's drinking,
40, 48
CBI Health, 188
Centre for Independent Living Toronto
   (CILT), 128
charity vs. rights model, 214–16
Charter of Rights and Freedoms, 155–6,
   181, 183, 191
children, 118–21, 136, 164–5, 209, 234–5,
   268, 271–2. *See also* International
   Youth Year
Chrétien, Jean, 156
Christmas, 197–8
Churchill, Winston, 32
cinemas, 7, 11, 149–52, *150*
Citizen of the Year award, 126
citizenship, 87
Civic Award of Merit, 126
class, 43
clothes making, 81–2, 83, *146*
Coalition of Provincial Organizations
   of the Handicapped, 156
Coalition on Employment Equity for
   Persons with Disabilities (CEEPD),
   169–76
coffee, 44
Common Sense Revolution, 238–9
Community-access programming,
   109–11
community-run programs, 99, 100. *See
   also individual organizations*
Companion of the Order of Canada, 152
Comsa, Nick, Sr., 136
Connors, Stompin' Tom, 242–3
Constitution, 125, 155, 191–2

Copps, Sheila, 176
Cotret, Robert de, 175
Council of Canadians with Disabilities, 99, 109, 156
Cowie, Jill, 136
Coxon, Michael, 100
Crawford, Fern, 145
Crombie, David, 100
Curling, Alvin, 263

Dailey, Mark, 255
Dave (Diane's boyfriend), 65
David and Goliath (Gladwell), 18
Davis, Bill, *127*, 129–30, 160, 183
de Corneille, Roland, 175
Deaf people, 79, 107, 151
Decade of Disabled Persons, 155, 157, 192
Dechter, Richard, 192
Declaration on the Rights of Disabled Persons, 116
deep vein thrombosis, 53–4, 73, 75, 76, 101–2
deinstitutionalization, 215–16
Demerol, 69–70, 71
demonstrations/protests: cinema inaccessibility, 149–52, *150*; Mulroney's office 1986, 170–1; over Handicapped Persons' Rights Act, 117; Parliament Hill 1986, 1–2, 171–6; Parliament Hill 1987, 192; Queen's Park 1981, 183; social welfare 1983, 161–2; TTC, 136–9, 163–4. *See also* disability advocacy/activism
department stores, 37–8
depression, 60, 65, 69–71, 76, 77–9
developmental disabilities, 42–3
Diefenbaker, John, 92
Dini Petty's CityLine (TV show), 184–7
Dinsdale, Walter, 124
diphtheria, 15–16
disability advocacy/activism: overview, 105–6, 268; assistive equipment, 111; basic rights list, 124–5; Beryl and larger movement, 209–10, 211–18 (*see also* electoral politics);

body as exploitation, 211; body as tool, 210–11, 213; and Charter of Rights and Freedoms, 155–6, 181, 183, 191; children as priority, 209; church inaccessibility, 81; Decade of Disabled Persons, 155, 157, 192; on *Dini Petty's CityLine*, 184–7; and discrimination, 111–12; employment, 130–1; and Harris' cutbacks, 238–9; history of, 99–100, 109; international relationships, 162–3; International Year of Disabled Persons, 116–17, 123, 129–30, 148 (*see also* Scarborough Action Committee); in Liverpool, 88; Operation Horseshoe, 128–9; parking spots, 256; and political cycle, 117; and race, 132; representation, 187; rights vs. charity model, 214–16; and Rumball, 79–80, 107, 160; style of, 107; television, 109–11, 184–7. *See also* demonstrations/protests; electoral politics; fundraising/funding; tours/public presentations; transportation; *individual organizations*
disabled people. *See* people with disabilities overview
Disabled People for Employment Equity, ix
Disabled Persons for Employment Equity. *See* Coalition on Employment Equity for Persons with Disabilities
discrimination/prejudice: airlines, 93; assumptions, 201; challenging, 121, 122; disabled as "special interest," 149–52; and fear, 93, 118; racial discrimination, 32, 33, 131–3; and systems that separate, 111–13; "them and us" paradigm, 167–8; and transportation, 181–2 (*see also* Toronto Transit Commission; Wheel-Trans)
divorce, 63–4, 86
Doctor of Laws, 235
documentaries, 145–8, 213, 219–21
dogs, 97–8, 166
domestic violence, 39–40, 41

domestic work, 29, 40–1, 54, 142
Dominion supermarkets, 111
Douglas, Tommy, 92
Downsview Rehabilitation Hospital,
    61–3, 64
Drew, George, 32
Dreyfuss, Richard, 148
Dunlop, Edward, 160

Eggleton, Art, 130
electoral politics, 222–32, 230–1
elevators, 228
Elgie, Robert, 131–2
Elizabeth II (Queen), 156, 163
employment, x, 130–1, 138, 179–80.
    See also Coalition on Employment
    Equity for Persons with Disabilities
employment equity as term, 169
employment equity bills, x, 169–76
eugenics, 98–9
eye stroke, 76

Famous Players Cinemas, 149–52, 150
fear, 118, 248
Feld, John, 192
Fields, Harry, 233–4
finances, 55, 91–3, 94–5, 141, 142, 259
First World War, 17
flags, 129–30
Flynn, Dennis, 179
forced sterilization, 98–9
Fox, Terry, 115–16, 152, 165
Freda (landlady), 35, 38
fundraising/funding: Action Awareness,
    157; Action Awareness tours, 236;
    Awareness Week, 130; CEEPD,
    170; with Dominion receipts, 111;
    Independent Living Centre, 127; Jerry
    Lewis Muscular Dystrophy Labor
    Day Telethon, 211–12; OUCOT fold-
    ing, 236; OUCOT vs. Trans-Action,
    233; Scarborough Action Committee,
    126; Scarborough Club for Disabled,
    146; Year of Disabled Persons, 130

Galer, Dustin, 271–3
Gardiner, Frederick, 32
gender roles, 43–4. See also domestic
    work
General Crerar Public School, 121
Gerrond, Jim, 161
Gladwell, Malcolm, 18
God, 80, 139
Great Depression, 13
Great Valentine Gala, 242
Greatest Generation, 14
Guaranteed Annual Income
    Supplement, 162
Gypsum Empress (ship), 22, 23

Hall, Hamilton, 188
hallucinations, 45
Hamilton-Brown, Alex, 145–6, 146, 147
Handicapped Employment Program,
    131, 151
Handicapped Persons' Rights Act, 117
Harris, Gus, 123–4, 126
Harris, Mike, 223, 238–9
healthcare system, 91–2
hierarchy of disability, 217–18
hip disarticulation, 74–5
homing pigeons, 25
honours, 111, 126, 127, 189, 190, 235,
    241–4, 245, 249
Hould, Ray, 178
House of Commons, 172–3
houses of industry, 98
Hunt's Bakery, 47, 51–3, 55

I'll Meet You Halfway forum, 118
immigration, 30–3, 99
Immigration Act (1952), 32
independence, 81–4, 99, 142
Independent Living Centre, 127–8
indignity, 243, 247
infantilization, 211
infections, 73–4
International Year of Disabled Persons,
    116–17, 123, 129–30, 148. See also
    Scarborough Action Committee

International Youth Year, 164, 166–8
intersectionality, xi
invisibility/visibility, 200
iodine allergy, 77
Iron Butterfly Parents' Association, 136
irregular heartbeat, 76–7
Israel, Pat, 149, *150*, 213, 216–17, 229

Jerry Lewis Muscular Dystrophy Labor
    Day Telethon, 211–12
Jerry's Kids, 211
Johnston, Patrick, 224–5, 228, 229–30,
    231
Juda, Diane Margaret (née Carter)
    (daughter): in 1950s, *36*; and Beryl
    as mother, 266–7; and Beryl leaving
    Victor, 63; on Beryl liking people,
    39; Beryl visiting, 97–8; on Beryl
    working, 44; on Beryl's activism,
    106; and Beryl's ashes, 256; and
    Beryl's attempted suicide, 59–60;
    and Beryl's back surgery, 188; on
    Beryl's blindness, 247; on Beryl's
    change in personality, 102, 105, 139,
    205, 220–1; and Beryl's deteriorating
    health, 251–2; and Beryl's infection,
    74; on Beryl's makeup, 82; on Beryl's
    migraines, 45; on Beryl's personal
    time, 196–7, 220; on Beryl's smoking,
    199; and Beryl's swollen leg, 54; on
    Beryl's washroom checks, 200–1;
    birth of, 28; birth of Michelle, 67; and
    Dennis, 42, 205, 259–60; domestic
    work, 54; and Downsview patient
    parties, 65–6; employment, 54, 55, 65;
    on Eva and Norman, 38; and George
    wedding, 66–7, *67*; helping Beryl at
    Hunts, 47; Moscow Drive chores, 29;
    on Moscow Drive house, 29–30; start
    of menstruation, 46; Toronto arrival,
    33, 34; on typical suburban life,
    40–1; on Victor and Victor Jr., 40;
    and Victor's affairs, 58; and Victor's
    drinking, 39–40, 257

Juda, George (Diane's husband), 66–7,
    86, 97, 251–2, 257–8
Juda, Justin (Diane's son), 122, 195, *196*,
    197, 199–200
Juda, Michelle (Diane's daughter): in
    1980s, *86*; Beryl as life changing, 267;
    on Beryl's creativity, 82; and Beryl's
    death, 253; and Beryl's electoral cam-
    paign, 226, 232; at Beryl's send-off
    party, 93; and Beryl's stump, 119; on
    Beryl's washroom checks, 201; birth
    of, 67; on Christmas mornings, 197;
    on Dennis, 166, 198–9; on family time
    with Beryl, 198–9

Kavanaugh, George, 201
Kellermen, John, 129
Kirkby, 20
Kochhar, Vim, 189, 241–2, 264
Kresge's, 37–8, 39

Lankin, Frances, 225, 232
Lassen, Georg, 22–3
LeBlanc, Romeo, 243–4, *245*, 263
Leda (tanker), 23
Lepofsky, David, 263
Lewis, Jerry, 211–12
Liberal Party. *See* electoral politics;
    individual politicians
Life Another Way (documentary),
    145–8, 213
Lightfoot, Gordon, *190*
Liverpool, 5–6, 17–21, 26–7, 87–8, 94, 132
Liverpool Echo Evening Express (news-
    paper), 46–7
Liverpool Transport Board, 24
London, Midland and Scottish Railway
    (LMS), 12
Longman, Jack, 160–1
"Look Beyond" (song), 147
Looking in the Mirror (Turnbull), 212
loss, 261
Lucas, Jerry, 180

MacDonald, Flora, 170, 174, 176

Malkowski, Gary, ix, x, 170–1
Man Alive (TV show), 219–21
Mancini, Remo, 183–7, 264
Mantis, Steve, 61, 65, 214
Marathon of Hope charity run, 115–16, 152
March of Dimes, 42–3, 99, 100–1, 164, 216–17
Martha (stepgrandmother), 13–14
May Blitz, 17–18
McCaffrey, Bruce, 161–2
McDonald, John W., 128
McGibbon, Pauline, *127*
McKee, Pat, 147
meat chart, 92
media, 89–90, 167, 210, 255. *See also* television
Meech Lake Accord, 191–2
Mental Health Law Project, 158
Metro Toronto Coordinator for the Disabled and Elderly, 131
migraines, 44–6, 102
Milne, Jonathan, 131
mobility, 74–5
moonlight flits, 12–13
Morgentaler, Henry, 170
Morin, Belinda, 131
Morrice, Denis, ix
Moscow Drive house, 15, 18, 26, 27–30, 88–9
"Movies as a Human Right?" (Amiel), 149–52
Mr. Grizzly the Aware Bear, 119, 120, *234*, 272
Mr. Stumpy, 118–19, 121, 271
MS Seven Seas, 34
Muffolini, Elvira, 267–8
Mulroney, Brian, x, 170, 176, 191, 223
munitions factory, 19–20
Murphy, Wendy, 265
Musgrave, Anne, 233–4
Muskoka Lakes Secondary School, 167

neoliberalism, 238
Niagara Falls, 128–9

Nietzsche, Friedrich, 261–2
Nikias, Angelo, ix, x
northern Ontario tour 1988, 188
Nystrom, Lorne, x, 171, 172–5

Obstacles Committee, 156
Obstacles report, 125
Odell, Tracy, 212–13, 218
Office for Disability Issues, 119, 164, 234, 238
Office of Disabled Persons, 187
Onley, David, 242, 264
Ontario Action Awareness Association. *See* Action Awareness
Ontario Advisory Council on the Physically Handicapped, 160–1
Ontario Advocacy Commission, 152
Ontario Building Code, 187
Ontario Human Rights Code, 117
Ontario Human Rights Commission, 131–2, 187
Ontario March of Dimes, 42–3, 99, 100–1, 164, 216–17
Ontario Medal for Good Citizenship, 126, *127*
Ontario Minister Responsible for Disabled Persons, 183
Ontario tour 1991/92, 234–5, *234*
Ontario Users Council on Transportation (OUCOT), 227, 233, 236
Ontario Works, 238
Open Doors (Action Awareness), 157–8
Operation Horseshoe, 128–9
Operation Pied Piper, 17
opioids, 45, 69, 71, 79, 248
Order of Canada, 241–4
Order of Ontario, 189–91, *191*
"An Ordinary Heroine" (*Man Alive* episode), 219–21

pain as universal, 261
painful blue inflammation, 56
painful white swelling, 56–7
parking spots, 256

Parliamentary Special Committee on the Disabled and the Handicapped, 156

paternalism, 99

Pearson, Lester B., 92

pension, 92

People United for Self Help (PUSH), 192, 227–8

people with disabilities overview, 98–9, 111–12, 167–8, 217–18. *See also* accessibility; barriers; *individual organizations*

Perks, Gord, 223

Peters, Susan, 211

Peterson, David, 158–9, 164, 182, 183, *190*, 193, 222–4, 226, 230, *230*, 263–4

Petty, Dini, 184–7, 265

Philip, Ed, 233–4

phlegmasia alba dolens, 56–7

phlegmasia cerulea dolens, 56

Phoney War, 17

pigeons, 25

pleural effusion, 252

police, 63–4, 192

pools, 198

post-traumatic stress (PTSD), 21

Potter, Agnes (half sister), 6–7

Potter, Amy Catrina (née Braun) (mother), 6; about, 7; and Beryl's illness, 3–4; death of, 85–6, 90–1; and death of Charles, 8–9; home economics education, 19, 29; meeting Charles, 7; meeting William, 11; moving in early years, 12–13; quiet strength of, 14

Potter, B., and Carter, V.: and Beryl's blame of self, 70–1, 87, 258; and Beryl's migraines, 45; and Beryl's swollen leg, 55–6; birth of sons, 28; debt, 55; divorce, 63–4, 86–7; employment, 27–8; forgiveness, 86–7; marriage of, 25–6; Moscow Drive house, 26, 27–30; Norman adopting Dennis, 30, 31; premarital conception, 25; Victor's affairs, 58;

and Victor's drinking, 40, 41, 45, 56, 70; Wychwood homes, 35, *36*

Potter, B. early years: birth of, 4; birth of Diane, 28; death of father, 8–9; deaths of Margaret and Constance, 16; Eric's marriage, 19; helping family, 19; moving, 12–13; munitions factory work, 19–20; at nine years old, *14*; railway work, 24–5, *25*; rheumatic fever, 3–4, 53, 76–7; scarlet fever, 3; Second World War, 17–21; smoking, 19; train ride with Norman, 14–15; at twenty years old, *24*

Potter, B. health: allergy to iodine, 77; amputations (*see* amputations); arrhythmia, 76–7; blaming self, 70–1, 87, 258; blindness, 76, 77, 247–8; blood clots, 53, 77, 101–2, 252; car accident, 73; cardiovascular system, 76; and coffee, 44; deep vein thrombosis, 53–4, 73, 75, 76, 101–2; depression, 60, 65, 69–71, 76, 77–9; as deteriorating in 1990s, 248–53; diabetes, 247; Downsview rehabilitation, 62–3; eye stroke, 76; hallucinations, 45; hospitalized in 1962, 45–6; and humour, 77–8, 105; independence, 81–4, 99, 142; issues from sitting, 247; migraines, 44–6, 102; nightmares, 70; and opioids, 45, 69–70; phantom pain, 70, 75; *phlegmasia alba dolens*, 56–7; *phlegmasia cerulea dolens*, 56; physical therapy, 82, 83 (*see also* independence); recovering second left leg amputation, 75; rheumatic fever, 3–4, 53, 76–7; scarlet fever, 3; slip and fall, 52–3; staphylococcus infection, 73–4; suicide attempts, 59–60, 71, 78, 101; vertebra crack, 188; and Victor losing job, 51

Potter, B. personal life: as activist, ix–x; after *Life Another Way* release, 148; anger and hope, 102; Canadian citizenship, 87; change in personality, 102, 105, 137, 139, 205, 220–1;

and Christmas/presents, 197–8; at the cottage, 195, *251*; and crutches, 55; death of, 253, 255, 263, 266; and Dennis, 42–3, 141–2, 204–6, 249; and Diane's wedding, 66, *67*; and dogs, 97–8; domestic work as compulsion, 40–1; and Downsview patient parties, 64–6; employment after Liverpool move, 94; employment in Toronto, 37, 38, 39, 47, 51–3; finances, 55, 91–3, 94–5, 141, 142; and Fox, 115–16, 153, 165; funeral of, 255–6; home from leg amputation, 58; humour, 77–8, 105; independence, 81–4, 99, 142; lack of family/personal time, 196–7, 220–1, 256; leaving Toronto, 33–4; Liverpool move 1972, 93–4; Liverpool visit 1971, 88–91, *90*; as militant, 137, 162; and Milne poster, 132–3; and mother's death, 85–6; name change, 95; new peer group, 80, 81, 98; and Norman, 30–1, 249–50; personal and activist life intertwined, 200–1; quiet strength of, 14; remembrances of, 263–8; and Rumball, 79–80; as self-conscious/introverted, 13, 16, 45, 51, 102; Sheppard Ave. E. apartment, 203; subsidized Scarborough apartment, 97; Toronto arrival, 33, 34–5; trips with Joan, 207–8; writing in *Liverpool Echo Evening Express*, 46–7

Potter, B. photographs of: in 1950s, *36*; in 1970s, *90*, *207*; in 1980s, *86*, *127*, *140*, *143*, *146*, *150*, *190*, *269*; in 1990s, *196*, *230–1*, *234*, *245*, *249*, *251*

Potter, Bertram (half brother), 6–7

Potter, Catherine (Kit) (sister-in-law), 19

Potter, Charles Ferdinand (father), 4, 5–6, 7–9

Potter, Charles, Jr. (brother), 8, 11, 93, 94

Potter, Dennis Gordon (son): in 1950s, *36*; in 1970s, *90*; in 1980s, *86*, *165*; in 1990s, *196*; as assistant/driver, 140–1, 165–6, *166*, 204–6; and Beryl leaving Victor, 63; and Beryl's aging, 249–50; on Beryl's anger, 201; as Beryl's cheerleader, 81, 83; and Beryl's death, 253, 255, 258; birth of, 28; on Christmas mornings, 197; death of, 260; and dogs, 97; as driver and assistant, 140–1; employment, 55, 94; health of, 206, 251, 258–60; helping Beryl at Hunts, 47; Liverpool visit 1971, 88–91; Michelle on, 199; and Mona, 258; and Mr. Grizzly, 119; name change, 95; nominating Beryl for Order of Canada, 241; and Norman, 249–50, 259; and Norman adopting, 30, 31, 249–50; as over-spender, 91, 95, 142, 259; pressure on, 141–2, 250; in special education, 42–3; stomach surgery, 251

Potter, Eric Riby (brother), 7, 12, 19, 266

Potter, Eva (sister-in-law), 30, 34–5, 38

Potter, Gwen (sister-in-law), 93

Potter, Harriette (grandmother), 5

Potter, Henry (grandfather), 5–6, *6*

Potter, Marjorie (sister), 8, 266

Potter, Norman (brother): about, 30–1; adopting Dennis, 30, 31, 249–50; on Beryl's change in personality, 137; birth of, 8; Diane on, 38; on early family life, 11; relationship with Dennis, 249–50, 259; Toronto arrival, 34–5; train ride with Beryl, 14–15

Potter, Teresa (half sister), 7

poverty, 169

prejudice. *See* discrimination/prejudice

presents, 197–8

prosthetics, 73

protests. *See* demonstrations/protests

public presentations. *See* tours/public presentations

Pyke, Lynne, 136

Québec, 155, 191, 192

Queen Street Mental Health Centre, 158

Queen's Park Legislature, 126, 147–8, 166, 189–90

racial discrimination, 32, 33, 131–3
Radcliffe, Reginald, 15
Rae, Bob, 224, 232
Rae Days, 237–8
railways, 5, 8, 12, 24–5
ramps, 100, 151
Rason, Edith, 180, 241
Rebick, Judy, ix–xi, 170–2
rehabilitation hospitals, 99
religion, 80, 139
representation, 187
residential hospitals, 98
Reville, David, 235
rheumatic fever, 3–4, 76–7
Riby, Annie, 7
Riby, Charles Morrison (stepgrand-
    father), 7, 13–14
rights vs. charity model, 214–16
RMS Empress of Australia, 33
RMS Franconia, 33
RMS Queen Elizabeth, 34
Rose (friend), 41
Rose Cottage, 7–8, 9, 12, 15, 90, *90*
Ross, Ron, 233
Rotary Toronto, 126
Rouveroy, Rob, *146*
Royal Alexandra Theatre, 242–3
Royal Navy, 21
Rumball, Bob, 79–80, 107, 153, 160, *249*
Rumball, Derek, 107
Ruprecht, Tony, 178

S. S. Kresge Company, 37–8, 39
salicylate tablets, 3–4
Savona, Sam, xi, 104, 105, 172, 174, 265
Scarborough, 97, 98, 109–10
Scarborough Action Committee, 123,
    124, 126, 157
Scarborough Advocacy Centre for
    Disabled Persons and Their Families
    (Action Awareness). *See* Action
    Awareness
Scarborough Civic Centre, 115–16, 118
Scarborough Rapid Transit (RT), 163–4

Scarborough Recreation Club for
    Disabled Adults, 102–6, 111, 146
Scarborough Recreation Night, 111
Scarborough Town Centre, 98, 103, 182
scarlet fever, 3
Second World War, 17–23
sensationalization, 212
separatism, 155
Shadow Maker (Sullivan), 3
slavery, 5
Smith, David, 155
smoking, 19, 199, 226
social assistance, 238
social housing, 97
Spanish Flu, 4
Special Parliamentary Committee on
    the Disabled and Handicapped, 124
St. Brougham's, 26
St. Clair and Oakwood intersection, *48*
station mistresses, 24–5
Stein, Shari, 171
stereotypes, 131, 211–12
sterilization, 98–9
storytelling, 210–11, 212
Strawberry Field Girls' Orphanage, 30
streetcars, 43, *48*. *See also* Toronto
    Transit Commission
strikes, 8, 177–80
substance abuse, 45, 69, 71, 257, 258–9,
    260. *See also* Carter, Victor Bratton
suicidal ideation, 59–60, 71, 78, 101,
    148–9, 257
Sullivan, Rosemary, 3, 32
Sunnybrook Hospital, 73
surveillance, 63
Sutton Place Hotel, 55, 93
Sweeney, John, 228
Symington, David, 162

TAG-18 convoy, 22
taxes, 151, 161
taxis, 106, 135
television, 69–70, 109–11, 167, 184–7,
    219–20

Temporarily Able-Bodied (TAB) person, 185, 218
Terry Fox Hall of Fame, 153, *249*, 264
Tipping, Mary, 6–7
Toronto overview, 32–3
Toronto Transit Commission (TTC), 34, 51, 163–4, 177–81, 227–8. *See also* streetcars; Wheel-Trans
tours/public presentations: in 1980s, *166*, *269*; in 1990s, *234*; overview, 117–21, 271–2; GTA tour 1988, 187; International Youth Year tour, 164–5, 166–8; northern Ontario tour 1988, 188; Ontario tour 1991, 234–5; southern Ontario tour 1987, 182
Toxteth riots, 132
track walkers, 24
Trans-Action Coalition, 106–7, 177–81, 227–8, 233–4
transportation, 106–7, 135–9, 163–4, 227–8. *See also* Toronto Transit Commission; Trans-Action Coalition; Wheel-Trans
transportation tour 1987, 182
Trillium Cable, 109–10
Trimmer, Joyce, 138, 236
Trudeau, Pierre Elliot, 115, 124, 125, 152–3, 155, 191
Turnbull, Barbara, 212
Turner, John, 176

U-160, 22–3
unemployment statistics, 169. *See also* employment
United Nations, 116–17, 155

universal health care, 91–2
University of Waterloo, 235
US State Department, 128–9

VE (Victory in Europe) Day, 23
vertebra crack, 188
visibility/invisibility, 200

Wallace, Constance (Connie) (half sister), 11, 15–16
Wallace, Joan (half sister), 11, 26, 88, 91, 207
Wallace, Leslie (half brother), 11, 90
Wallace, Margaret (Peggie) (half sister), 11, 15–16
Wallace, William Ralston (stepfather), 11, 12, *12*, 15, 26, 88
War Amps, 272
washrooms, 1, 171–2, 186, 200–1
West Derby Union Offices, 26
West Rouge Public School, 122
wheelchair basketball, 145
wheelchairs: demonstrations of use, 182; at House of Commons, 172–3, 220; in Shoppers Drug Mart, 255–6; in washrooms, 1, 171–2, 186, 200–1
Wheel-Trans, 100, 106–7, 135–9, *140*, 163–4, 177–81
Whose Life Is It Anyway (film), 148–9
Winberg, Mona, 236, 237, 244, 258, 266
withdrawal, 69, 79
Workers' Compensation Board, 55, 91–2, 94–5, 97, 203
Wosley, John, 174
Wrye, Bill, 179–80

Dustin Galer is a professional historian with a PhD in history from the University of Toronto. He wrote the first book-length history of the Canadian disability rights movement, *Working Towards Equity*, and has published widely on the topic of disability history and labour. He works as a personal historian producing family and corporate history projects and is currently working on his next book about the tragic death of a developmentally disabled man and the complicated quest for justice. He lives in Hamilton, Ontario where he can often be found toiling away in his garden.